ARCHITECTURAL DESIGN

GUEST-EDITED BY
MARIANA LEGUÍA

LATIN AMERICA AT THE CROSSROADS

03|2011

ARCHITECTURAL DESIGN
VOL 81, NO 3
MAY/JUNE 2011
ISSN 0003-8504

PROFILE NO 211
ISBN 978-0470-664926

wiley.com

IN THIS ISSUE

ARCHITECTURAL DESIGN

GUEST-EDITED BY
MARIANA LEGUÍA

LATIN AMERICA AT THE CROSSROADS

5 EDITORIAL
Helen Castle

6 ABOUT THE GUEST-EDITOR
Mariana Leguía

8 INTRODUCTION
Latin America at the Crossroads
Mariana Leguía

16 Simultaneous Territories: Unveiling the Geographies of Latin American Cities
Patricio del Real

EDITORIAL BOARD
Will Alsop
Denise Bratton
Paul Brislin
Mark Burry
André Chaszar
Nigel Coates
Peter Cook
Teddy Cruz
Max Fordham
Massimiliano Fuksas
Edwin Heathcote
Michael Hensel
Anthony Hunt
Charles Jencks
Bob Maxwell
Jayne Merkel
Peter Murray
Mark Robbins
Deborah Saunt
Leon van Schaik
Patrik Schumacher
Neil Spiller
Michael Weinstock
Ken Yeang
Alejandro Zaera-Polo

22 PREVI-Lima's Time: Positioning Proyecto Experimental de Vivienda in Peru's Modern Project
Sharif S Kahatt

PREVI-Lima led the way in the 1960s as the seminal informal housing project – low-rise and high-density – with flexibility integral to the design.

26 The Experimental Housing Project (PREVI), Lima: The Making of a Neighbourhood
Fernando García-Huidobro, Diego Torres Torriti and Nicolás Tugas

32 Elemental: A Do Tank
Alejandro Aravena

38 Tlacolula Social Housing, Oaxaca, Mexico
Dellekamp Arquitectos

42 Governing Change: The Metropolitan Revolution in Latin America
Ricky Burdett and Adam Kaasa

52 The Olympic Games and the Production of the Public Realm: Mexico City 1968 and Rio de Janeiro 2016
Fernanda Canales

58 Articulating the Broken City and Society
Jorge Mario Jáuregui

64 Formalisation: An Interview with Hernando de Soto
Angus Laurie

68 Playgrounds: Radical Failure in the Amazon
Gary Leggett

76 Urban Responses to Climate Change in Latin America: Reasons, Challenges and Opportunities
Patricia Romero-Lankao

As the main emitters of greenhouse gases in Latin America, cities will determine climate change in the region.

80 Filling the Voids with Popular Imaginaries
Fernando de Mello Franco

86 Civic Building: Forte, Gimenes & Marcondes Ferraz Arquitetos (FGMF), São Paulo
FGMF

90 A City Talks: Learning from Bogotá's Revitalisation
Enrique Peñalosa

96 Bogotá and Medellín: Architecture and Politics
Lorenzo Castro and Alejandro Echeverri

104 From Product to Process: Building on Urban-Think Tank's Approach to the Informal City
Interview with Alfredo Brillembourg by Adriana Navarro-Sertich

110 Latin American Meander: In Search of a New Civic Imagination
Teddy Cruz

118 Supersudaca's Asia Stories (AKA at Home in the First, Second, Third, Fourth and Fifth Worlds)
Supersudaca

124 When Cities Become Strategic
Saskia Sassen

128 Organising Communities for Interdependent Growth
Enrique Martin-Moreno

134 Universities as Mediators: The Cases of Buenos Aires, Lima, Mexico and São Paulo
Mariana Leguía

144 COUNTERPOINT
Looking Beyond Informality
Daniela Fabricius

ARCHITECTURAL DESIGN
MAY/JUNE 2011
PROFILE NO 211

Editorial Offices
John Wiley & Sons
25 John Street
London
WC1 N2BS

T: +44 (0)20 8326 3800

Editor
Helen Castle

Managing Editor (Freelance)
Caroline Ellerby

Production Editor
Elizabeth Gongde

Design and Prepress
Artmedia, London

Art Direction and Design
CHK Design:
Christian Küsters
Hannah Dumphy

Printed in Italy by Conti Tipocolor

Sponsorship/advertising
Faith Pidduck/Wayne Frost
T: +44 (0)1243 770254
E: fpidduck@wiley.co.uk

All Rights Reserved. No part of this publication may be reproduced, stored in a retrieval system or transmitted in any form or by any means, electronic, mechanical, photocopying, recording, scanning or otherwise, except under the terms of the Copyright, Designs and Patents Act 1988 or under the terms of a licence issued by the Copyright Licensing Agency Ltd, 90 Tottenham Court Road, London W1T 4LP, UK, without the permission in writing of the Publisher.

Subscribe to △

△ is published bimonthly and is available to purchase on both a subscription basis and as individual volumes at the following prices.

Prices
Individual copies: £22.99 / US$45
Mailing fees may apply

Annual Subscription Rates
Student: £75 / US$117 print only
Individual: £120 / US$189 print only
Institutional: £200 / US$375 print or online
Institutional: £230 / US$431 combined print and online

Subscription Offices UK
John Wiley & Sons Ltd
Journals Administration Department
1 Oldlands Way, Bognor Regis
West Sussex, PO22 9SA
T: +44 (0)1243 843272
F: +44 (0)1243 843232
E: cs-journals@wiley.co.uk

[ISSN: 0003-8504]

Prices are for six issues and include postage and handling charges. Individual rate subscriptions must be paid by personal cheque or credit card. Individual rate subscriptions may not be resold or used as library copies.

All prices are subject to change without notice.

Rights and Permissions
Requests to the Publisher should be addressed to:
Permissions Department
John Wiley & Sons Ltd
The Atrium
Southern Gate
Chichester
West Sussex PO19 8SQ
England

F: +44 (0)1243 770620
E: permreq@wiley.co.uk

Front cover: Ricardo La Rotta Caballero, La Quintana, 'Tomas Carrasquilla' Park Library, Medellín, Colombia, 2007. © Sergio Gomez
Inside front cover: Gary Leggett, P.A.I.D. (Project in Assistance of International Disasters), Jan Van Eyck Academie and Yale University, 2010. © Gary Leggett. Concept CHK Design

EDITORIAL
Helen Castle

Since the 1950s, Latin America has had a particular fascination for architects. While Europe was still war-torn, a bright new Modernist urban future was being realised on the South American continent. This was epitomised by Lúcio Costa's and Oscar Niemeyer's vision for Brasília. In the early 1960s a new kind of debate started to open up around the question of housing in response to the massive and often unofficial expansion of South American cities in the form of informal settlements. *D* was instrumental in bringing this to international attention with its seminal August 1963 issue on dwelling resources in South America co-edited by John FC Turner.[1] Turner, a graduate from the Architectural Association (AA) in London, was appointed in 1957 by Eduardo Neira, a Peruvian architect educated at the University of Liverpool, to work as an assistant to the Director of the Office for Technical Assistance to Popular Urbanisations of Arequipa (OATA). In the late 1950s, Arequipa, a city in southern Peru, already had Urbanizaciones Populares, or informal settlements, covering a thousand hectares, an area far greater than that of the official urban area. By the time a major earthquake hit the region in January 1958, Turner had taken over as Director of OATA. With funds available from earthquake reconstruction, it became apparent that far more housing units could be built through a self-build programme in the Urbanizaciones Populares than in the traditional city. In 1962, Turner was stirred to produce a publication on urbanisation in South America by an article by James Morris' (now Jan Morris) for *The Sunday Times* colour supplement: 'an appallingly misleading, bleeding heart view of the *barriadas*'; it also came to the attention of the British Ambassador in Peru, who called Turner and suggested he do something about it.[2] This just happened to coincide with a trip by Monica Pidgeon, the longstanding Editor of *D*, who toured the *barriadas* with Turner. The resulting *D* was one of the first illustrated publications to positively investigate the possibilities of urban housing and self-build in Latin America.

This title of *D*, so adeptly guest-edited by Peruvian-British architect Mariana Leguía, also confidently portrays Latin America. This time as a continent that is on the cusp of change. The most obvious manifestation of this is perhaps Brazil's burgeoning economy and Rio de Janeiro's successful bid to host the 2016 Olympic and Paralympic Games. It is, however, the advocacy of design solutions that engage with informal settlements and directly address social and economic problems that provide the most compelling thread to this issue, picking up where Turner left off. Teddy Cruz also argues potently for the lead that Latin American municipalities have taken, politically reconnecting public policy, social justice and civic imagination and addressing inequality through new models of urban development (see pp 110–7). With the intensification of urbanisation in Asia and elsewhere in the world, the engagement with the informal provides an international paradigm for working towards pragmatic solutions to housing. It is an approach that has far-reaching implications both for architects' future mediations in the city and also for occupiers of settlements. In her Counterpoint to the issue, Daniela Fabricius very bravely raises her head above the parapet and questions whether in settling for informality, we might just be failing in our aspirations for a large portion of the population and accepting that they must continue to live precariously on sites of scarcity and deprivation.

Add your own opinion to the debate at: www.architectural-design-magazine.com. *D*

D, Vol 33, August 1963
Born in Chile, Monica Pidgeon, *D*'s longstanding editor, had a personal interest in Latin America. In Lima in 1962, she met the British architect John Turner. The result was the pioneering 1963 issue on housing.

Notes
1. For an insight into this period see 'Interview of John F C Turner, World Bank, Washington DC, 11 September 2000' available at http://siteresources.worldbank.org/INTUSU/Resources/turner-tacit.pdf, an edited transcript by Roberto Chavez with Julie Viloria and Melanie Zipperer, audited by Rufolf V van Puyembroeck, Legal Department and Assistant. A further edited version is also published in 'La Collective', 1 March 2010, Supersudaca Reports 1.
2. Ibid.

Text © 2011 John Wiley & Sons Ltd. Image © Steve Gorton

LLAMA urban design (Mariana Leguía and Angus Laurie), Housing development and retail unit, Lima, 2010
top: This is one of the few new buildings in Lima that does not have a 3-metre (9.98-foot) security wall. Along with the retail unit on the ground floor, this will help activate the public realm.

Yncluye (Mariana Leguía, Nelson Munares and Maya Ballén), Proposal for the Plaza de la Democracia, Lima, 2009
above: Through creating a protected but permeable facade facing the busy surrounding roads and at the same time activating the inactive walls of the third facade, the proposal aims to generate a public square for the city of Lima that acts as an anchor of activity and a cultural centre.

LLAMA urban design, Small is More, 2007
opposite: This strategic approach for zoning, taking into consideration diversity of use through pedestrian distances, will give different results in the way the public realm is activated and used throughout the day.

ABOUT THE GUEST-EDITOR
MARIANA LEGUÍA

Mariana Leguía is a Peruvian-British architect and urban designer currently based between Lima and Toronto. In 2007, along with her partner Angus Laurie, she co-founded LLAMA Urban Design (www.llamaurbandesign.com). The practice focuses on giving the city back to pedestrians. To achieve this goal, it has developed urban strategies that encourage encounter between a diversity of users within the public realm through enhancing the small scale and diversity of land use and tenure in both regeneration and urban expansion projects. Within her own research, 'Small is More', at the London School of Economics (LSE) in 2006–7, Mariana found that integration and activity in the public realm depends not solely on density or the traditional concept of land use, but is related to the diversity and pixelation of programme mainly along the ground floor of buildings, where small-scale units with a mix of uses can create a balance of activity, achieving a level of integration among different socioeconomic groups. As part of LLAMA urban design, she is currently working to develop this research into a book.

In 2002, she co-founded the Lima-based practice (Y)ncluye. Ciudad (www.yncluye.com), through which she has developed new participatory design processes, which have been put into practice for projects in Chincha and in Pisco, 200 kilometres (124.2 miles) south of Lima. The practice is concerned mainly with the design of public, civic or community buildings as anchors of activity for the configuration of public spaces.

Between 2006 and 2009, Mariana worked extensively on different urban projects for a large architectural office in London, including a masterplan for the historic Covent Garden in central London and a number of other major international urban projects in Russia, Europe and the Middle East. Between 2002 and 2003 she worked as a collaborator at Estudio Teddy Cruz in San Diego, California, a practice based on the US–Mexican border zone.

Her experience has led to a blending of the global and the local, from bottom-up methodologies applied in remote villages in the Peruvian Andes to her large-scale strategic work for entirely new cities in Europe and the Middle East.

Mariana is currently a professor in the Faculty of Architecture and Urbanism of the Catholic University of Peru. She holds an MSc in City Design from the Cities Programme of the LSE, and a degree in architecture and urbanism from Ricardo Palma University in Peru. She has lectured in universities in both Peru and the UK.

Text © 2011 John Wiley & Sons Ltd. Images: pp 6(t), 7(b) © LLAMA urban design, Mariana Leguía, Angus Laurie; p 6(t) © Mariana Leguía; p 6(b) © (Y)NCLUYE. arquitectura. ciudad. Mariana Leguia, Maya Ballen, Nelson Munares

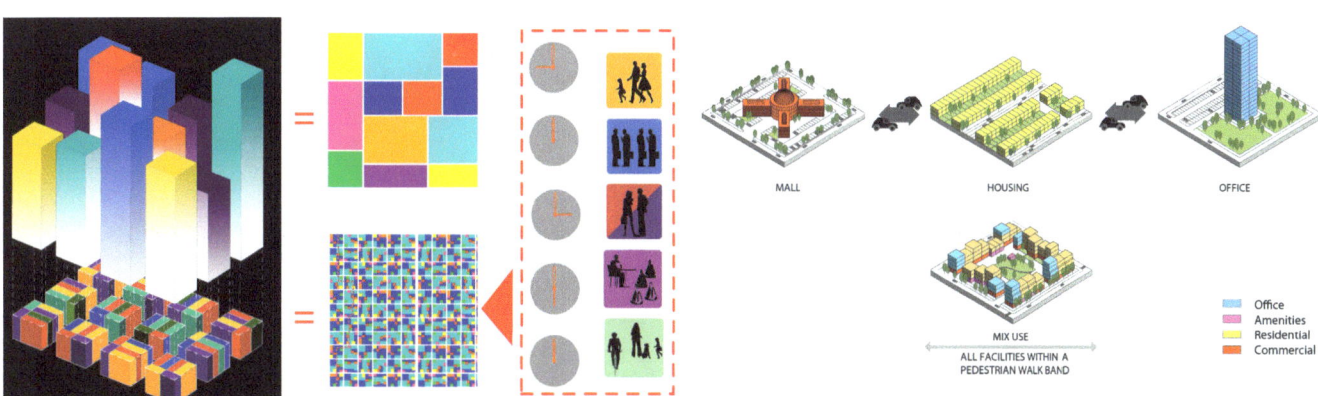

INTRODUCTION
By Mariana Leguía

LATIN AMERICA AT THE CROSSROADS

Lúcio Costa and Oscar Niemeyer with Roberto Burle Marx, City of Brasília, Brazil, 1956–1960
previous spread right (top and bottom) and opposite left: A landmark in the history of town planning, the utopic 'city of the future' was built over an uninhabited desert with scarce water and few animals and plants. The Brazilian Congress and the Presidential Palace are major iconic features not only of the city, but of modern architecture across Latin American.

Invasions on Lima's coast, 1969–89
previous spread top left and opposite right: Vacant land was taken overnight by squatters. Today these areas form part of the consolidated and sprawling city of Lima.

Alfredo Dammert, Mercado Central, Lima, 1963–4
previous spread bottom left: Informal street traders surround the modern structure of the city's Central Market in 1989. As part of a recent local improvement programme, the informal vendors have been forced to leave.

Differences encroaching on Peru
below: Urban grid between a planned area and an informal area of Lima, divided in some sectors by a wall. There is a notable difference in the levels of vegetation and landscaping together with the scale of the plots.

Latin American citizens are constantly reminded of the social polarities in our cities through the urban form where 3-metre (9-foot) tall security walls and bars on windows are the norm within island-like enclaves of wealth. Within this context, architects currently work to produce well-designed interior spaces that deliberately turn their back on the public realm – streets and public spaces – resulting in large sections of cities where the street is overlooked only by inactive walls. Until the last 20 to 30 years, with obvious exceptions such as Curitiba,[1] there has been little consideration among Latin America's architects and urbanists as to how practitioners might mitigate strong social and spatial polarities and challenge the prevailing architectural language of segregation and fear.

Even today, many Latin American architecture students are taught to look to Europe and the US to learn from the latest trends of the northern hemisphere. On the rare occasions when Latin America-based projects are studied, these generally are the grand projects from the mid-20th century that were an imposition of occidental thought in anticipation of progress and modernity, but within a different social and political reality where older residents can still remember life within a feudal system. This transposition of modernity is exemplified in projects like Brasília, perhaps the largest-scale 'realization of Le Corbusier's theories and ideas built anywhere in the world',[2] and in the Modernist university projects that took root in Rio de Janeiro and Bogotá in the 1930s, in Caracas in 1944, and in Mexico in 1954.[3]

The development of these grand projects was extolled in a number of exhibitions and publications of the time, including MoMA's 'Brazil Builds' (1943)[4] and 'Modern Architecture in Latin American Since 1945' (1955).[5] At the time, none of the cities had the industrial capacity to produce the prefabricated materials required, as predicated by the modern discourse, in order for the projects to be realised.[6] They were only feasible through the availability of mass cheap labour. Since then, the centralised, utopian model has broken down.

The socioeconomic climate behind these modern projects triggered an increasing informality and mass migrations from the countryside leaving cities socially and spatially divided. All in all, over the last 70 years, Latin America has undergone an urban revolution comparable to the mass migrations resulting from the industrial revolution in Europe, which took place over a period of 200 years.

In response to urban expansion, mainly during the 1960s and 1970s many governments initially sought to house migrants in large superstructures or tower blocks, mimicking postwar housing projects in Europe. Despite their grand intentions, such projects represented a vision that clashed with the social and cultural reality of the time, as the dwellers for which these units were built were 'mostly rural migrants, and were still very dependent on a traditional subsistence type of economy'.[7] Many failed, as single-use Modernist apartment blocks did not work well within an informal economy where the dwelling is envisioned not only as a home, but as a site of production;[8] where the built form is capable of offering multiple opportunities for the user and for its use.

Subsequent exhibitions and international publications, including 'Architecture Without Architects' (1964),[9] tackled a new set of concerns relating to Latin America's rapid urban expansion. During this time, Peter Land, on behalf of the Peruvian government and the United Nations, conceived the Experimental Housing Project (PREVI) (1968) (see article on pp 22–5), an ambitious social housing project that drew in international figures including, among others, James Stirling, Aldo van Eyck and Christopher Alexander. The aim of the project was to develop methodologies for producing 'low-rise high-density housing'[10] with limited funds.

This issue of 𝐷 does not stand alone, but revisits an older story, following on from John Turner's often-quoted article from 1963 entitled 'Dwelling Resources in South America',[11] which marked a moment in time in the representation of the region, leaving us in suspense – until now.

Since then, much has changed. Hernando de Soto, who published *The Other Path* in 1986, made a case supporting informality, showing that people living in informal areas were in fact entrepreneurs who contributed to the economy and who wanted to integrate, but were excluded by innumerable barriers.[12] In 1996, Alan Gilbert, the first to coin the term 'mega-city', published T*he Mega-City in Latin America*,[13] seeing informal settlements as a potential solution to the rapid growth in Latin America's cities, and making a clear argument for their consolidation.

Once a blind spot in cities' representation, informality is now considered an asset to be understood and incorporated. This paradigm shift towards viewing informality as a positive generator for the city rather than as a blight has created the opportunity for architects to develop new methods of research and responses to work within this challenging context. Additionally, as sustainability becomes an increasingly important issue, informal settlements offer a number of innovative sustainable solutions embedded in a culture in which resourcefulness and recycling are necessities rather than trends.[14]

I learned about these processes and the richness of the informal parts of Tijuana in comparison with the sterile planned areas of San Diego while working in collaboration with Teddy Cruz and experiencing the border region between Mexico and the US in 2002–3. It became clear that the same phenomenon was repeated in my home city, Lima, and in many other Latin American cities. The wall that divides San Diego from Tijuana is similar to the countless walls in Latin American cities that separate wealthy planned neighbourhoods from informal, no-go areas, or the 3-metre (9.98-foot) security walls that separate middle- and upper-class homes from the street.

Malecón 2000 Foundation with local architects (Douglas Dreher and Luis Zuluaga) and architects from Oxford Brooks University (Alberto Fernandez Davila, Raul Florez, Mariano Jakobs and Noe Carbajal), Malecón 2000, Guayaquil, Ecuador, 2000
opposite top and centre: Malecón 2000 is an urban regeneration project of the former Malecón Simón Bolívar. With a 2.5-kilometre (1.5-mile) extension of the riverfront promenade next to the River Guayas, it is adding value in the city's central neighbourhoods which had been suffering a long decline due to flight to the suburbs. Over 300,000 people use the Malecón daily, for recreation or to engage in commercial activities. Following this project the municipality also regenerated the adjacent area of Cerro Santa Ana, once a no go-area.

Paraisopolis, Morumbi, São Paulo
opposite bottom: Tuca Vieira's now famous image of the Paraisopolis favela clearly synthesises the strong spatial and social divide between the informal areas of Latin American cities which often stand next to planned and segregated areas of great affluence.

Reinventing new methodologies of communication: participatory workshops in Peru
below, from top to bottom: Architecture & Participation course run by architects Maya Ballén, Mariana Leguía and Claudia Amico in Chincha, Peru (2007), workshop run by Espacio Expresión in Pisco (2009), and (Yncluye (Mariana Leguía and Maya Ballén) in Pisco (2005).

After this experience, and within my own practice in Peru, it became clear that it is necessary to develop participatory methodologies, to challenge the ways in which we represent ideas in projects, and to understand that when designing for communities, architects need to work with their desires and not only with finished forms. Desires relate to programme; how people will use and interact in a space rather than the form of the space itself. Furthermore, in trying to achieve a successful public realm, the development of a design needs a holistic approach, looking at economics, policy and managerial strategies that can help projects make visions into reality. On the other hand, social, political and economic strategies, such as those of Hernando de Soto, are generally not spatial, and for this reason their success can vary drastically based on their interpretation and physical manifestation on site.

Through these new processes of change in the understanding and application of theory, universities and faculty members have become important in developing alternative methodologies to encourage new modes of architecture that, within multidisciplinary approaches, can integrate students, communities, government agents and professionals.

At the same time, new urban strategies by municipal governments have drastically improved some cities including Curitiba, Medellin and Bogotá, and the latter received the Venice Architecture Biennale's Golden Lion Award for Architecture in 2006 for being at the forefront of urbanism. Another notable example is Guayaquil in Ecuador, where the Malecón 2000 project, together with a reconfiguration of the city's public transport, succeeded in drawing people back into the centre and in consolidating the once no-go informal settlement of Cerro Santa Ana into a tourist destination.[15]

Sebastian Irarrazaval, Escuela Manuel Montt, Retiro, Chile, 2010
below left: This modular system was developed from containers in just one week, in a rapid response to the collapse of a school during the 2010 earthquake.

Gualano + Gualona Arquitectos, Civic Centre, Pueblo Bolivar, Uruguay, 2007
below right: Sponsored by Venezuela's President Chavez after a visit to Uruguay, the new civic centre includes a multi-purpose room, a health centre, public toilets, rooms for community meetings and a children's playground.

al bordE arquitectos (David Barragán and Pascual Gangotena), Escuela de Buena Esperanza, El Cabuyal, Manabí, Ecuador, 2009
opposite: The majority of the local population of Manabí was illiterate due to the lack of a primary school. The new school not only responded to this urgent need, but also introduced an alternative construction technique using the methodologies and local materials of the region.

Evidenced by the adoption of the bus rapid transit (BRT) model (first developed in Curitiba in 1974) in a number of cities across North America, Europe and Asia, the world now looks to Latin America for inspiration. These progressive policies by city mayors have provided fertile ground for new methodologies developed by Latin American architects, which are showing great potential to alleviate social segregation and spatial injustice, widening the discourse in so many ways. These alternative practices are increasingly gaining attention in international publications and exhibitions. Comparing these exhibitions to the historic ones of the 1940s and 1950s demonstrates a profound re-evaluation of the role of architects in Latin American society – as agents of social change.[16]

This issue on Latin America comes at a critical moment in time, when the image of the region's nation-states is in flux as stable governments, economic growth and globalisation are reshaping its cities and societies. The issue illustrates the current processes of urban expansion in Latin America and the corresponding alternative home-grown methodologies. As Rio prepares to host the 2016 Olympics,[17] Latin America will likely receive more international attention than at any time in history. Both the World Cup (2014) and Olympics (2016) in Rio de Janeiro have started to produce positive urban results due to new initiatives for the regeneration of formerly paralysed, no-go areas of th city. The Morar Carioca project will deal with this complex task over the coming years and will be undertaken by 40 architects recently selected in a competition organised by the Institute of Architects of Brazil (IAB).[18]

In parallel, its wealth and diversity of resources has drawn increased foreign investment into new territories; the Amazon region, at the heart of the continent, is considered the lungs of Earth, but also a site of conflict between those who wish to preserve it, and others who hope to exploit its vast resources.

Latin America at the Crossroads exposes these new strategies and social roles, informed by the informal and the solutions practitioners have developed to stitch together polarised areas of the region's cities. Such solutions to urban problems represent the vanguard in mitigating strong social and spatial divisions in cities across the globe. Rather than constructing major projects in search of an El Dorado, like Voltaire's protagonist Candide, Latin America is learning from the benefits of tending its own garden. ⌁

Notes
1. Curitiba's urban regeneration took place mainly through the 1970s.
2. Valerie Fraser, *Building the New World: Studies in the Modern Architecture of Latin America 1930–1960*, Verso (London), 2000, p 1.
3. Ibid, p 62.
4. Philip Goodwin, *Brazil Builds: Architecture New and Old 1652–1942*, MoMA (New York), 1943.
5. Henry-Russell Hitchcock, *Latin American Architecture Since 1945*, MoMA (New York), 1955.
6. Fraser, op cit, p 7.
7. Ibid, pp 120–1. In the 1969 ⌁ editorial on Caracas, Walter Bor praised the 'make-shift accommodation' of the poor and criticised high-rise flats for being 'restricted in floor space and social amenities'. See Walter Bor, 'Venezuela', ⌁, August 1969, p 425.
8. Teddy Cruz, 'Small Scale, Massive Change: New Architectures of Social Engagements', curated by Andres Lepik, MoMA, Autumn 2010.
9. Bernard Rudofsky, *Architecture Without Architects*, MoMA (New York), 1964.
10. A concept widely explained in the article on PREVI–Lima by Fernando García-Huidobro, Diego Torres Torriti and Nicolás Tugas Faúndez, pp 26–31 of this issue.
11. John Turner, 'Dwelling Resources in South America', ⌁, Vol 33, August 1963.
12. Hernando de Soto, *The Other Path*, Basic Books (New York), 1989, p 12.
13. Alan Gilbert (ed), *The Mega-City in Latin America*, United Nations University Press (New York), 1996.
14. This was well represented in the last Holcim awards, an initiative of the Holcim Foundation for Sustainable Construction based in Switzerland, which took place in Mexico in 2010.
15. Alberto Fernández-Dávila: http://titofd.blogspot.com/2008/04/regeneracin-urbana-del-cerro-santa-ana.html.
16. In the 2006 Venice Architecture Biennale, entitled 'Cities Architecture and Society' and curated by Richard Burdett, Bogotá received the Golden Lion Award for Architecture for being at the forefront of urbanism. In 2009, the 4th International Architecture Biennale in Rotterdam, 'Open City: Designing Coexistence', curated by Tim Rieniets, Jennifer Sigler and Kees Christiaans, developed many of these themes. Later on, 'Small Scale, Massive Change: New Architectures of Social Engagement', curated by Andres Lepik (MoMA, Autumn 2010), demonstrated new methods of social engagement by alternative practices from all over the world, including four representatives (Teddy Cruz, Alejandro Aravena, Jorge Jáuregui and Urban-Think Tank) from Latin America (see pp 110–114, 30–7, 58–63 and 104–9 of this issue).
17. The second time in history for a Latin American country and the first for a South American country.
18. Juan Arias, '40 arquitectos cambiarán la cara de 215 favelas de Río de Janeiro' (40 architects will change the face of 215 favelas in Rio de Janeiro), 9 December 2010; see www.elpais.com/articulo/internacional/arquitectos/cambiaran/cara/215/favelas/Rio/Janeiro/elpepuint/20101209elpepuint_2/Tes.

Text © 2011 John Wiley & Sons Ltd. Images: pp 8, 11(r), 13 © Archivo El Comercio; pp 9, 11(l) © Nelson Munares; pp 10, 12(t&c) © Mariana Leguía; p 12(b) © Tuca Vieira; p 13 © (y)ncluye and Espacio Expresión; P 14(l) © Sebastian Irarrazaval; p 14(r) © Gualano+Gualano arquitectos; p 15 © al bordE arquitectos, David Barragán & Pascual Gangotena

Patricio del Real

SIMULTANEOUS TERRITORIES
UNVEILING THE GEOGRAPHIES OF LATIN AMERICAN CITIES

The harmonious, utopian image that housing in Latin America exuded across the world in the postwar years is very much at odds with the current view of the region, in which unbridled shantytowns dominate. **Patricio del Real** sets out to understand how such a rupture might have been possible: What was the process of exclusion at play in these Modernist projects? How does Modernism represent simultaneous territories in which emerging challenges to the social and political status quo were merely muffled by the architectural seduction of the 1950s?

Carlos Raúl Villanueva and Taller de Arquitectura del Banco Obrero,
Urbanización 23 de Enero, Caracas, Venezuela, 1955–8
The use of primary colours on the facades of the superblocks attempts to minimise the oppression of the exposed structural grid and mask the extreme economy of the construction. At the same time, pictorial and geometric abstraction undergirded the universalism that drove the Venezuelan integration of the arts.

In its October 1950 issue, *Architectural Review* claimed that the Pedregulho housing development 'may be about to make an outstanding contribution to another phase of the modern movement'; *L'Architecture d'Aujourdhui*, in its 1955 issue dedicated to Mexico, exalted the Presidente Juárez neighbourhood unit in Mexico City as the clearest example of how the deep consciousness of tradition could exercise a positive influence in a modern world; and a year earlier, *Domus* had called on Caracas, with its extraordinary superblock housing developments, to become the world capital of modern architecture.[1] By the end of the 1940s, Latin America had become a cynosure of Western modern architecture. Riding the spectacular economic growth as well as the technological and industrial expansion of the war years, and honing the development of modern architecture and design that had started two decades before, the entire region burst with building after building, which created ripples throughout every major architectural magazine.

In their pages, the stylish balance between tradition and innovation – the sensuality of the landscape in 'glamorous' Rio de Janeiro or in 'silent' Mexico, the pleasures of life in 'loose' Havana or 'elegant' Buenos Aires, picturesque societies in 'charming' Bogotá or 'serene' Montevideo, or the dynamic economies in 'booming' Caracas and 'industrious' São Paulo – presented to European and North American readers an appealing quasi-likeness, exotic, yet familiar. But above all, Latin American architecture of this period was seen as, in one word, harmonious. These were images of a Western world lacking the contradictions and conflicts that had torn Europe apart; in a place still untouched by unbridled US commercialism. These hopeful images were, however, simplistic accounts. Early on, many critics saw through the dreamy pictures reproduced in every article, aware of the incompleteness of the utopia, the unevenness of the societies, the remnants of a dark tradition, and the small enclaves of progressive Modernism that announced the conflicts that, from the 1960s onward, would engulf the entire region into the imaginary of a Third World.

The predominant images today of *favelas-ranchos-villas miseria-barriadas-barbacoas* – the slums that characterise the contemporary Latin American city for outside observers – force us to return to Modernist housing projects to understand the mechanisms of exclusion that these structures enacted and the dual, if not multiple, geographies they constructed. A project such as Mario Pani's 1948 Presidente Alemán housing complex in Mexico City was created for the 'modern' citizen: the burgeoning middle and professional classes associated with governmental corporatism that crafted a singular modern nation through an activist state. Yet, these projects took many built forms, including Wladimiro Acosta's Hogar Obrero (1941–51), with its elegant insertion into the urban grid of Buenos Aires, and the Unidad Vecinal Portales (1954–66), by Bresciani, Valdés, Castillo and Huidobro in Santiago, which followed International Congresses of Modern Architecture (CIAM) planning strategies. These, like many others, manifested formal and technological experiments that underscored the conflicts between architectural production and the logics of mass housing, and they ultimately revealed a partial industrialisation identified early on by developmental economists such as Raúl Prebisch.

The growth of industrialisation confronted a labour-intensive and craft-oriented architectural production organised in small studios and managing a developing standardisation as the act of building negotiated infrastructural hindrances such as a limited transportation network.[2] But partial technological industrialisation in architecture was not the only barrier to an inclusive modern world. Housing policies and organisations such as the Fundaçao da Casa Popular in Brazil, or the Banco Central Hipotecario in Colombia, deployed a bureaucracy of exclusion through screening and selection processes that prevented many of the working poor from gaining access to any citizens' utopia. In all, these programmes were created by corporatist enclaves tied to a working-class public sector and were based on notions of liberal ownership and bourgeois family values that emerged as early as 1906 in Chile with the Law on Worker's Housing.[3] These values were also discussed within the Pan-American Congress of Architects, such as the 1927 Buenos Aires meeting which engaged the problem of 'Casas Baratas – Low Cost Houses'.[4] The early postwar housing projects carry the aura of a progressive state unfolding a landscape of shared social values. These projects also reveal a weak state that could act only through symbolic gestures in the realm of social housing.[5] The general lack of urban planning across the region exposed the inability of the state to coordinate and control a disarticulated urban landscape dominated by rampant speculation.[6] The seductive black-and-white photographs promoted locally and circulated across the world completed the exclusion of the urban poor by creating a distinct geographic imaginary and an actual restricted defensible space as the accelerated process of urbanisation accentuated the fragmentation of cities through growing peripheral slums and deteriorating colonial cores.

The geographic imaginary of Modernism created yet another territory as housing policies were reorganised under persuasive national planning programmes, and new state institutions – including the Corporación de la Vivienda in Chile or the Comisión Nacional de Viviendas in Cuba – sought to produce modern citizens through technocratic efficiency. These levelled techno-legal territories, however, had to contend with charged political urban landscapes administered through populist quid pro quo 'contracts' that legalised land appropriations and effectively made visible a marginal and now-vocal countergeography. The active demands of the urban poor, not to mention those of the rural poor, signalled the hinging of Modernist geographies and countered the imagined distance between them. Nowhere is this more evident than in the Peróns' Argentina, where every possible imaginary was mobilised to build and secure not only a 'popular' political base but also the modern activist nation.[7]

Affonso E Reidy, Conjunto Habitacional Pedregulho, São Cristóvão, Rio de Janeiro, 1948–54
The unfinished main serpentine residential block can here be seen in the background. To ensure the construction of the social infrastructure, including the swimming pool also seen here, Reidy scheduled them first to avoid the budgetary shortfalls typical in this kind of project that might have prevented their completion.

The geographic multiplicity that Modernism produced allowed for a technological colonisation from the ground up as the Division of Housing and Planning of the Organization of American States (OAS) deployed programmes of assisted self-help – which echoed the Puerto Rican experience – throughout the region.

The geographic multiplicity that Modernism produced allowed for a technological colonisation from the ground up as the Division of Housing and Planning of the Organization of American States (OAS) deployed programmes of assisted self-help – which echoed the Puerto Rican experience – throughout the region.[8] The OAS colonisation of the everyday became prevalent with the creation in 1952 of the Inter-American Housing Center (CINVA) in Bogotá. Although CINVA emphasised regional coordination of technical and socioeconomic research, it also served to deepen the influence of the US, fastening low-income housing to foreign aid programmes and to a technological development that, under the banner of the Alliance for Progress in the 1960s, showed its true plastic nature by retooling old corporatist modernisation to fit military regimes. A devastated landscape of Modernism, unhinged yet again, was now concealed under the bruised and swelling geography of dependency.

Amid these rich worlds of expanding ideas, needs and desires, and simultaneous geographies, the work of the Banco Obrero in Caracas (1952–6) rises to the foreground since it was able to cohere the centrifugal forces of modernity. Specifically aimed at slum clearance, the massive 85 superblocks of the 2 de Diciembre complex (today 23 de Enero) and its companion projects of Cerro Grande, El Paraiso and Cerro Piloto, all located in Caracas, fused master Modernist aesthetics with mass production and experimentation, clearly locating itself in the dreamy orb of the Western world. This clean geography, however, was performed through exclusionary practices that symptomatically erased the ever-growing and invading slums, which were carefully eliminated in every photo opportunity.[9]

It should also be noted that this Modernist utopia, celebrated by *Domus* as the 'land of liberty', was possible only under a dictator enabled by the oil wealth of Venezuela.[10] In this respect, less ambitious programmes under democratic governments aimed at developing a national consensus fared better within a diversifying political urban landscape and a restless countryside demanding land reform, which reached boiling points in Bolivia (1952) and Guatemala (1954).

The advent of the Cuban Revolution, and a decade later Salvador Allende's democratic socialism, proved that the dreams of development channelled through Modernism and its unfolding territories were not enough, and that the geography of contestation unleashed by modernisation could not be suppressed. One must return to the iconic images of Modernism in the region to rescue the simultaneous territories caught in them to listen to the emerging challenge that is being muffled by the architectural seduction of the 1950s. It is in these images we can witness the dynamics of presence played out in architecture precisely at the moment of the region's greatest international visibility.

As the current architecture of Latin America regains currency in contemporary architectural magazines, it is worth asking how this visibility will be replayed; to what geography do these images belong? What territories, if any, do these images unleash? We live in a time in which there is an acceleration of images that are sustained by the return of an imagined geography embodied by the mobile elite. But if the Modernist geographic unfolding was once performed through static visual seductions, today these unhingings of the built landscape are performed through the rapid consumption of images.

Bresciani, Valdés, Castillo and Huidobro, Unidad Vecinal Portales, Santiago de Chile, 1954–66
Built on former university agricultural research lands, the slender five-storey housing blocks were designed to minimise their impact on the site. Open bridges and ramps develop a network of public pedestrian circulation enhanced by a street within the blocks through which cars can circulate. This street allowed the architects to circumvent height restrictions.

The fascination exerted by slums anchors us. In fact, it creates a suture: the slow-moving landscape of anti-modern, romantic dreams and actual human hardship articulates our relationship to Modernist visual seduction and to our contemporary too-fast architecture. The architect's quest remains how to build upon this raw joint.

If, as the French philosopher Jacques Rancière has articulated, utopia is not a dreamy and unrealisable future, to paraphrase his words, but an intellectual construction that brings together a space of thought with an actual perceptible space, it is then worth asking whether these latest images of contemporary architecture of Latin America are merely staged visions of a failed Modernist seduction or attempts at a speedy escape into the world of Western privilege? Instead, contemporary Latin American architecture may fulfil a promise to reveal the geography of the city as a site of productive conflict. ⌂

Notes
1. *Architectural Review*, Vol 108, No 646, October 1950; *L'Architecture d'Aujourdhui*, Vol 26, No 59, April 1955; *Domus*, No 295, June 1954.
2. On the profession in Brazil see: Henrique Mindlin, *Modern Architecture in Brazil*, Reinhold (New York), 1956. The Argentinian context offers a counter example with larger team-based architectural production. See Jorge Francisco Liernur, *La Arquitectura en la Argentina del siglo XX: La construccion de la modernidad*, Fondo Nacional de las Artes (Buenos Aires), 2001. For Chile, see Fernando Pérez Oyarzún, Rodrigo Pérez de Arce, Horacio Torrent and Malcolm Quantrill, *Chilean Modern Architecture Since 1950*, Texas A & M University Press (College Station), 2010.
3. Law 1838 of 1906 on Worker Housing established the Consejo de Habitaciones Obreras, an organisation that promoted the construction of low-cost units and rationalisation along hygiene principles. See Rodrigo Hidalgo Dattwyler, 'La Reestructuración de la Administración Pública y Las Innovaciones en la Política de Vivienda en Chile en la Década de 1950', *Scripta Nova: Revista Electrónica de Geografía y Ciencias Sociales*, No 69–76, 2000.
4. For a general outlook, see Manuel Ruiz Blanco, *Vivienda Colectiva Estatal en Latinoamérica: Periodo 1930–1960*, Instituto de Investigación, Facultad de Arquitectura, Urbanismo y Artes, Universidad Nacional de Ingenieria (Lima), 2003. For Brazil, see Nabil Bonduki, 'Otra mirada sobre la arquitectura brasileña: La producción de vivienda social (1930–1954)', *Block*, No 4, 1999, pp 110–21.
5. For Pani, see Mario Pani, *Mario Pani: Arquitecto*, Universidad Autónoma Metropolitana/Noriega Editores (Mexico), 1999. For Acosta, see Juan M Otxotorena, *Wladimiro Acosta: 1900–1967*, Escuela Técnica Superior de Arquitectura (Pamplona), 2008.
6. The economic boom years for the region saw their dawn with the lack of capital that sent Chile and Brazil into crisis in the mid-1950s. The need to increase capital investments in Latin America was a primary concern in US economic circles. Washington, however, refused any form of aid and was instead keen on the promotion of private investment in the region.
7. See Anahi Ballent, *Las huellas de la política: vivienda, ciudad, peronismo en Buenos Aires, 1943–1955*, Universidad Nacional de Quilmes/Prometeo (Buenos Aires), 2005. Also Rosa Aboy, 'The Right to a Home: Public Housing in Post-War II Buenos Aires.' *Journal of Urban History* 33, No 3, 2007, pp 493–518.
8. Puerto Rican housing programmes were modelled on New Deal policies that managed federal subsidies through national, regional and city agencies. Highly dependent on technical expertise, these programmes were aimed at slum clearance and the development of a house-owning middle class. Puerto Rico was included within the activities of CINVA from the outset. See *Inter-American Housing and Planning Center. Cursillo de introducción institucional. El intercambio científico y documentación del CINVA, por Luis Florén*, Centro interamericano de vivienda y planeamiento, Servicio de intercambio científico y documentación (Bogotá), 1958.
9. I would like to thank Helen Gyger for bringing this to my attention, and for her comments on an early draft of this essay. See also Viviana d' Auria, 'Caracas' Cultural [Be]longings: The Troubled Trajectories of the TABO *Superbloque*', in *Latin American Modern Architectures: Ambiguous Territories*, Routledge, forthcoming.
10. See Gio Ponti, 'Venezuela, patria della libertà', *Domus*, No 317, April 1956, p 2.

Text © 2011 John Wiley & Sons Ltd. Images: p 16 © Fundación Villanueva; p 18 Marcel Gautherot © Instituto Moreira Salles; p 19 © Archivo de Originales. Centro de Información y Documentación Sergio Larraín García-Moreno. Facultad de Arquitectura, Diseño y Estudios Urbanos. Pontificia Universidad Católica de Chile

A TIMELINE OF COLLECTIVE HOUSING IN LATIN AMERICA
By Supersudaca

As captured here by Supersudaca, the history of social housing is one of rising and falling densities and a wide range of approaches from formal Modernism to the informal. Commencing in the 1930s with 'New Deal' low-rise neighbourhood units, it was characterised in the postwar period by huge housing ensembles, which preceded even their European counterparts. By the 1970s, large-scale urban development had given way to the unplanned and the ad hoc with the unchecked growth of low-rise squatter settlements as the efficient gave way to the flexible, and big boxes were replaced by small units.

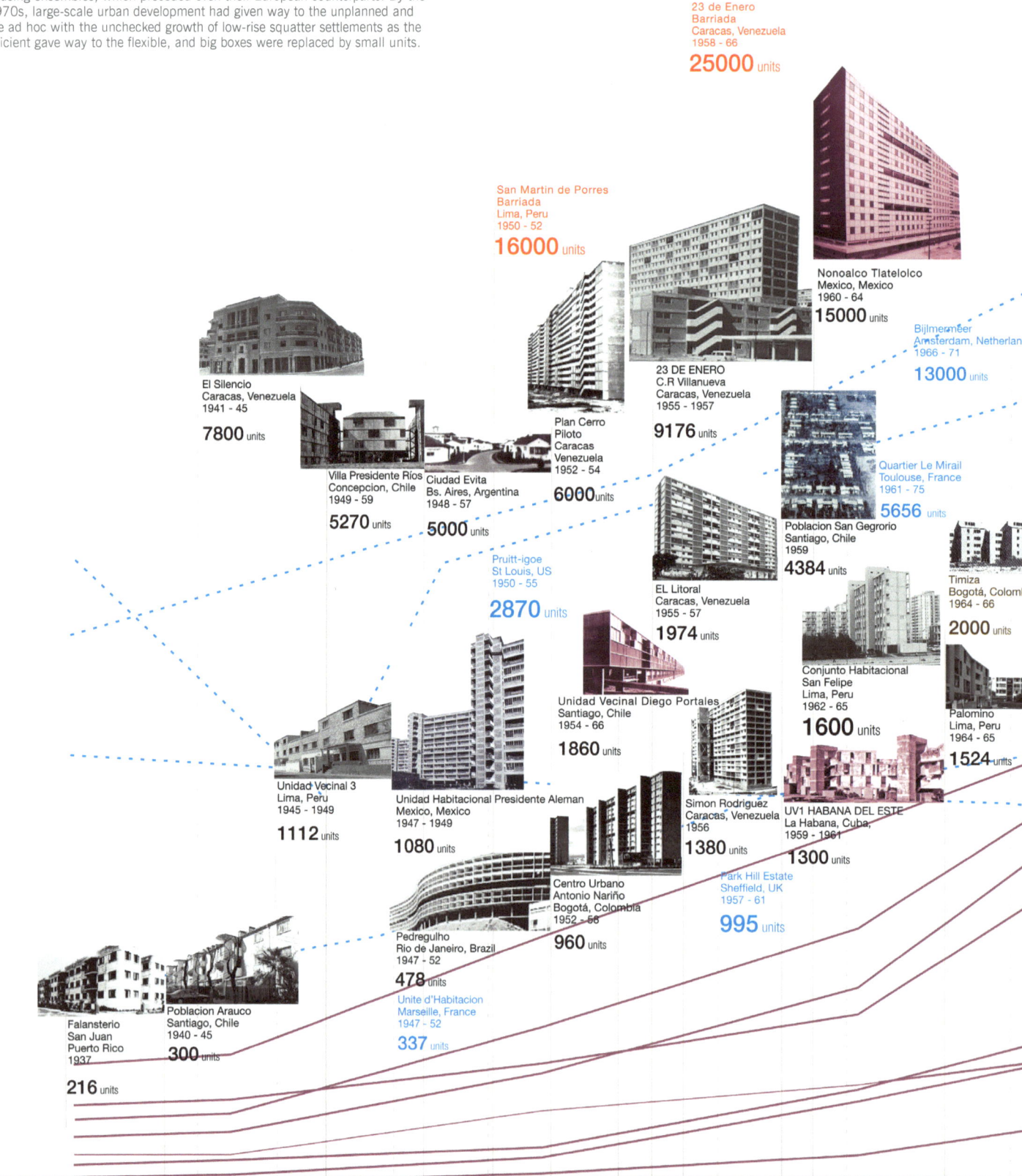

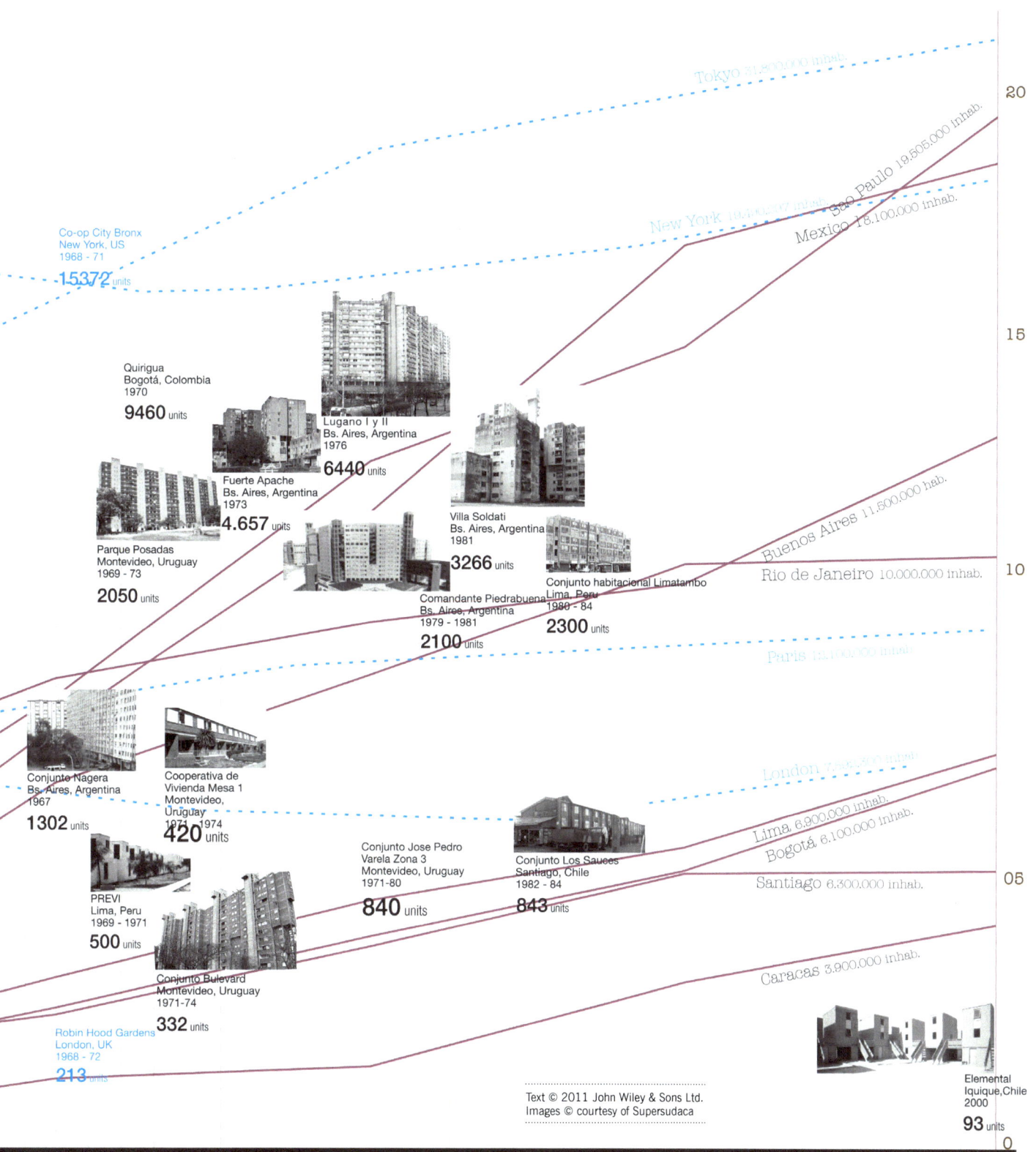

Sharif S Kahatt

PREVI-LIMA'S TIME
POSITIONING PROYECTO EXPERIMENTAL DE VIVIENDA IN PERU'S MODERN PROJECT

Launched in 1968, the PREVI-Lima housing competition brought informal urbanisation to the attention of architects worldwide. The competition brief required the design of low-rise, high-density expandable homes, grouped in neighbourhoods. Here **Sharif S Kahatt** puts PREVI´s experimental project within the social, political and theoretical context of the time.

PREVI Office, Urban project site plan for 2,000 units, Lima, Peru, 1968–75
opposite: Designed by the PREVI Office team directed by Peter Land, the final project combines the competition entry clusters with urban infrastructure and service buildings.

below: Aerial view of the project's first phase in 1975 showing the different clusters of the PREVI competition entries. This first phase was the only one built. The subsequent phases were planned to be connected through the pedestrian spine and a central community service building.

The aim of the PREVI-Lima was to produce a new generation of *unidades vecinales* (neighbourhood units) with spatial and formal qualities able to ultimately achieve social meaning and to create a sense of community through the dwellers' appropriation of the houses and public spaces. *Unidades vecinales* were the most significant product of the Peruvian Modern Project, a political and cultural modernisation movement that gained momentum in the 1940s. This overlapping of Anglo-Saxon modernisation and traditional patterns endured for several decades, reaching its climax in the 1960s. Proyecto Experimental de Vivienda (PREVI) (1968–75) was a Peruvian government initiative and United Nations-sponsored project. It was the most significant effort to overcome the housing and urbanisation crisis in a third world country in those years, and its strategies are still relevant today.

Lima's *barriadas*, or shantytowns, emerged in the 1950s and were one of the fastest growing forms of urban settlement for the poor. Between 1940 and 1972, the city grew from nearly 650,000 to 3.5 million inhabitants, an increase of approximately 500 per cent, and the number of squatters grew from 1 per cent to 25 per cent of the total population. In response to this, the Peruvian government launched a consulting group to identify the housing crisis problems and the potential solutions. The Comisión de la Reforma Agraria y Vivienda (CRAV) (1956–8) was led by architect Adolfo Cordova, advised by architect Eduardo Neira and anthropologist José Matos Mar. The housing deficit was the result of deep structural social and economic problems, and CRAV therefore proposed the improvement of the *barriadas* as the best way to tackle it.

Accordingly, the team promoted the idea of site-and-service developments (neighbourhoods with a minimum number of units that provided only basic services such as power, water and perimeter walls) and self-help construction to overcome the government's lack of economic resources to provide mass housing. This resulted in the expandable housing unit concept, the *viviendas elemental* (elemental houses), that were to be completed progressively by their owners with technical assistance provided free of charge by the government through the Corporación Nacional de la Vivienda (CNV). CRAV also believed that the self-help process would connect the people with their houses as they built them. Hence from the mid-1950s, ideas of participation in architecture and urbanism began to take shape in Lima's squatter towns. Indeed, even though participation has always been associated with advocacy and participatory planning ideas drawn from the international scene, British architect John Turner took from his involvement in housing in Peru an understanding of the possibilities of pluralistic and inclusive representation of citizens' interests in urban development.

Turner worked in various Peruvian cities for government agencies between 1957 and 1965, dealing with emergency housing and on the improvement of the *barriadas* and self-build projects. This context of uncontrolled urbanisation and informal settlements was surveyed and exposed by him in his article 'Dwelling Resources in South America', in the now legendary 1963 issue of *⌂*.[1] Since then, and in Turner's subsequent writings on the subject, *barriadas* and self-build have represented people's fundamental freedoms: to budget one's own resources, community self-selection, and to shape one's own environment. According to Turner, enabling the individual to have these choices was the best way of realising freedom in the contemporary industrialised society. Similarly, 'open form' and 'open design' – as the 'open work' theory – were already present in urban housing experiments such as Ciudad de Dios (1954–8), the first site-and-service project in Lima by the Corporación Nacional de la Vivienda.

PREVI-Lima competition, 1969
The Peruvian and international proposals developed by the PREVI Office. The proposals show diversity in the design of the clusters and different interpretations of public space and pedestrian networks.

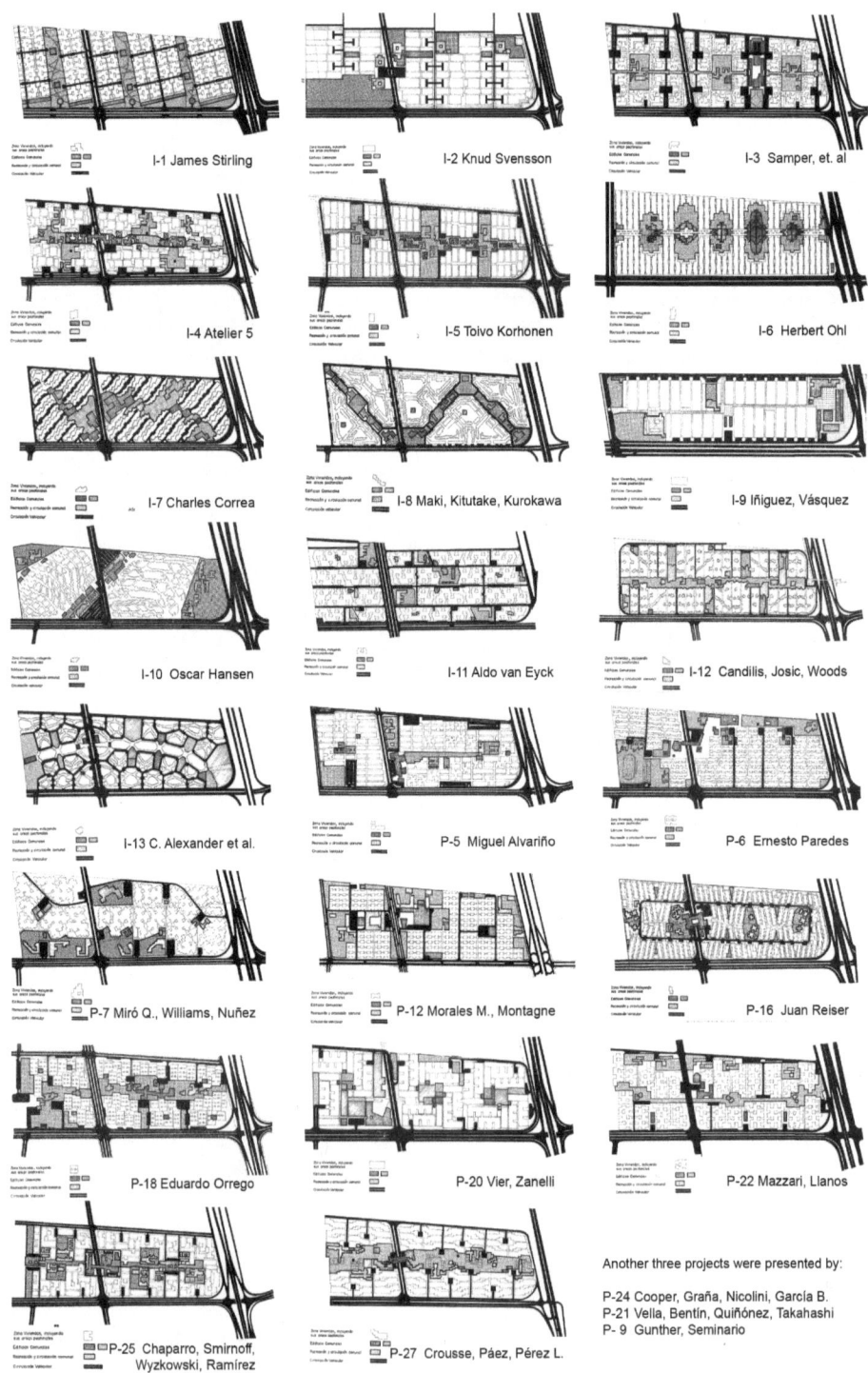

Another three projects were presented by:

P-24 Cooper, Graña, Nicolini, García B.
P-21 Vella, Bentín, Quiñónez, Takahashi
P- 9 Gunther, Seminario

Synthesising all these experiences, the PREVI competition was promoted by Peruvian president and architect Fernando Belaúnde and sponsored by the United Nations Development Program (UNDP) between 1968 and 1975. Its objective was to outline solutions to the overwhelming informal urbanisation in developing countries and to create new models for economic housing. The main aim of PREVI's director, the British architect Peter Land, was to adopt current thinking on prefabrication and mass-housing production and to adapt it to the constraints and sociocultural context of a developing world city such as Lima. Land, who had been teaching urbanism in Lima since 1964, had been working on preliminary studies for low-income housing since 1966, and in 1968 was all ready, along with his project office, to launch the PREVI international competition.

The competition brief was for a proposal for 1,500 housing units on a desert site of 40 hectares (98.8 acres) next to the Pan-American Highway, 8 kilometres (4.9 miles) north of Lima's downtown. Plots were to be no smaller that 80 square metres (861.1 square feet) or larger than 150 square metres (1,614.5 square feet), with a built area between 60 and 120 square metres (645.8 and 1,291.6 square feet). The basic unit was to be the one- or two-storey patio house that could be expanded up to three storeys high, based on a standardised modular design for easy production. PREVI's plan was for an initial settlement of 8,400 inhabitants, growing to a population surpassing 10,000. In order to minimise built space and maximise public space, an innovative approach was required. Sustainable factors such as orientation, ventilation, sun and noise control needed to be considered. The project also needed to serve different family sizes and interpret Lima's traditional public spaces – plazas, church atria, *paseos* and *alamedas* – in order to encourage social interaction.

PREVI thus called for an urban-architecture project based on six main requirements: establishing high-density, low-rise urban housing as an urban principle; organisation of the neighbourhood based on the concept of 'cluster' around a plaza to generate a sense of community; interpretation of the notion of *casa-que-crece* (expandable house), with a garden/patio to allow growth and change; a landscape plan with lighting and street furniture; prefabricated low-cost materials for mass production; and the envisioning of an entirely human-scale pedestrian environment neighbourhood with traffic separation.[2]

The jury met in Lima in September 1969 to elect the six winning proposals, though none was ever fully realised.[3] Conflicts between Peru's new military regime and UNDP officials meant a dead-end for PREVI. Although the PREVI Office produced a new neighbourhood plan for 2,000 units, including 24 of the originally proposed 26 clusters, the project was scaled down in scope and its potential impact greatly reduced, its 500 evolving units becoming just a test of the solution. Nevertheless, PREVI's houses embody the hybridisation of the Peruvian Modern Project and also embrace the physical overlapping and rich negotiation of the complexities of local urban culture.

After PREVI, Peter Land left Lima and the project experienced a number of delays before finally being inhabited in 1977. Since then, only one *unidad vecinal* (Los Proceres) in the early 1980s deliberately followed this strategy in Lima, and the idea slowly vanished. However, though it may have been idle for many years, such a concept now seems to be serving as an important platform for fresh mass and popular housing initiatives around the world. One can see Turner's ideas recaptured and developed in Mike Davis' *Planet of Slums*,[4] or more specifically, the whole idea of PREVI revamped in Chile's Elemental housing competition in 2003 and the various city housing projects by Alejandro Aravena/Elemental office (see pp 32–7). Bold ideas seem to be back. ⌂

Notes
1. Turner's relevant work includes: John FC Turner and William Mangin, 'Dwelling resources in South America', in Monica Pidgeon and Patrick Crooks (eds), ⌂, Vol 33, August 1963; John FC Turner, 'The Squatter Settlement: Architecture That Works', in Monica Pidgeon and Gwen Bell (eds), *The Architecture of Democracy*, ⌂, Vol 8, No 38, 1968; Horacio Caminos, John Turner and John Steffian, *Urban Dwelling Environments*, MIT Press (Cambridge, MA), 1969; John FC Turner and Robert Fichter (eds), *Freedom to Build: Dweller Control of the Housing Process*, Macmillan (New York), 1972; John FC Turner, *Housing by People: Towards Autonomy in Building Environments*, Marion Boyars (London), 1976
2. See 'PREVI-Lima: Low Cost Housing Project', in ⌂, Vol 4, 1970.
3. The organisation of the competition, although effectively carried out by Peter Land and his team at Banco de la Vivienda, was officially run by the Colegio de Arquitectos del Peru and the International Union of Architects (UIA), and the announcement made by the Housing Ministry and the United Nations Organization on 23 September 1969. The members of the jury (Eduardo Barclay, Manuel Valega, Ricardo Malachowski, Darío González, Alfredo Pérez – Peru; José Antonio Coderch – Spain; Halldor Gunnlogson – Denmark; Álvaro Ortega – UN; Carl Koch – USA/UIA; Ernest Weissman – UN; and Peter Land – UN) chose six 'official' winners of the competition. These were Atelier 5 (Switzerland), Maki, Kitutake, Kurokawa (Japan), Ohl (Germany), Mazzari, Llanos (Peru), Chaparro, Smirnoff, Wyzkowski, Ramírez (Peru) and Crousse, Páez, Pérez León (Peru). Although there was an official recognition of the winners, none of the winning proposals was built in its entirety; nor was the project divided between the six winners as suggested.
4. Mike Davis, *Planet of Slums*, Verso (London), 2006.

Text © 2011 John Wiley & Sons Ltd. Images: p 20 © Drawing: Sharif Kahatt; p 21 © PREVI Office; p 24 © Sharif Kahatt

Fernando García-Huidobro
Diego Torres Torriti
Nicolás Tugas

THE EXPERIMENTAL HOUSING PROJECT (PREVI), LIMA THE MAKING OF A NEIGHBOURHOOD

The original vision at PREVI-Lima was only ever partially realised: less than a third of the 1,500 planned housing units were built and the governmental crisis of the late 1960s meant that the occupants were left to their own devices. **Fernando García-Huidobro, Diego Torres Torriti and Nicolás Tugas** look at how, abandoned by the authorities, the families at PREVI turned into incidental architects, completing the project and rendering the neighbourhood an integrated part of the city.

opposite: On-site survey sketch.

below: Isometric schemes of the original project and the current state of the neighbourhood, highlighting selected case studies.

PREVI-Lima, carried out between 1968 and 1975 through an international[1] and a national[2] competition, was an opportunity for an internationally diverse group of renowned architects of the time, such as James Stirling from the UK, Atelier 5 from Switzerland, Charles Correa from India and Christopher Alexander from the US, to test the concept of low-rise high-density housing.

The concept was a statement against the Modernist model of urban design that was heir to the time of the first CIAM,[3] the negative effects of which were already being experienced in certain European and Latin American cities. Its primary goals were flexibility of the housing element combined with different land-use strategies. The commitment of the PREVI initiative to this low-rise high-density housing concept thus produced a proposal for a neighbourhood of different housing typologies to suit diverse family sizes and with various expansion possibilities.

Although the original aim of the competition was to build 1,500 units of the winning project in different phases,[4] in the end the jury[5] instead proposed building a small piece of each of the 26 project entries as a 'collage' neighbourhood of 467 units in the first and, as it was to turn out, only phase of the initiative. The Development Group,[6] an interdisciplinary team led by the British architect Peter Land, was in charge of the design of the masterplan and construction of the neighbourhood that would stitch all the different bits together. However, the governmental crisis of the late 1960s delayed the schedule; it became impossible to provide technical assistance and advice to the end users and, after delivering the houses, the project was discontinued and the experience forgotten.

In 2003, the current state of PREVI was researched as part of our architectural degree thesis at the Pontificia Universidad Catolica de Chile.[7] This focused on verifying how the families, turned into incidental architects, had completed the project and transformed it into a consolidated and integrated piece of the city. The houses have been transformed, dozens of small businesses flourish and special rental systems for subdivisions of the original units make up a dense, active neighbourhood.

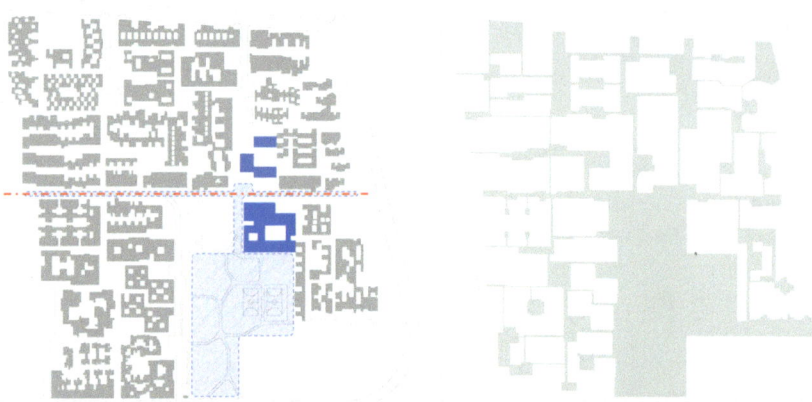

Despite the lack of technical advice, PREVI has become a high-quality urban neighbourhood. So what were the strategies of the original plan? What was the logic behind this transformation, and what are the lessons to be learned from the project?

Dynamic Habitat

The lack of resources typical of social housing projects has several consequences in the overall quality of the houses: for example, their inability to adapt to changing family needs, and their tendency to decrease in value over time. Taking into account the efforts families make to transform their properties is necessary in order to design projects that can accommodate change while preserving the quality of the built environment. But even more important is recognising housing as a dynamic process that has consequences on the efficiency of public spending: increases in property values have a direct impact on the quality of life of their inhabitants, whether in terms of the improved standard of the dwelling itself, or the increase in capital which allows the family to move on to a better house or wealthier neighbourhood.

The PREVI neighbourhood was planned for expansion; its urban layout allows for the interventions of each family yet resists a higher density, increasing the value of both the properties and the neighbourhood. It is an example of how such increases in value have encouraged subsequent generations to remain in the same neighbourhood, preventing the cycle of deterioration that results when family incomes increase and their houses are unable to respond to their new aspirations, forcing them to move away and ultimately limiting the neighbourhood to low-income families.

Open Urban Design: Support for Development

The PREVI project succeeded in delivering what would otherwise have been very difficult to achieve in a low-income neighbourhood: metropolitan-scale infrastructure and services, and a sophisticated network of public spaces offering access to each plot that also articulates the different modes of transportation. It was the foundations of an unfinished city, planned to be self-completed, which in the end was transformed by the community beyond what had been planned into a functional neighbourhood and thriving economy – evidence of the delicate balance between economic planning and free market design.

The urban approach included three main strategies:

1. A pedestrian axis that connects educational and sports facilities and the main park. Running through the centre of the neighbourhood, the pedestrian street activates and defines its core, allowing any public transport to stop to make the whole system more efficient.

2. A network of small plazas and pedestrian passages based on the relationship between the urban unit (the plaza) and the social unit (the self-organising community). This urban/social connection promotes the collective care and maintenance of public space, allowing the plazas to serve as an extension of the domestic space. This plaza-and-passage scheme also articulates the different clusters formed by the original projects.

3. Traffic separation, with perimeter roads, cul-de-sacs and parking areas – a layout that does not interrupt the pedestrian network of public spaces. Avoiding the fragmentation of traditional street layouts in this way means significantly reduced air and noise pollution, and increased safety, improving quality of life.

Multi-Scale Thinking

The PREVI experience demonstrates the importance of having a planning team with a comprehensive urban approach; since only with a complex and collective understanding of the urban phenomenon beyond the residential is it possible to create optimal strategies that enable its eventual users to continue the project's development. PREVI's approach

opposite and below left, from left to right: Main pedestrian and amenities axis; pedestrian structure of community plazas and walkways; traffic structure, vehicle penetration and parking areas.

below right: New uses at PREVI. Commercial uses tend to be located towards the perimeter streets and the main pedestrian street. Educational uses surround the main park.

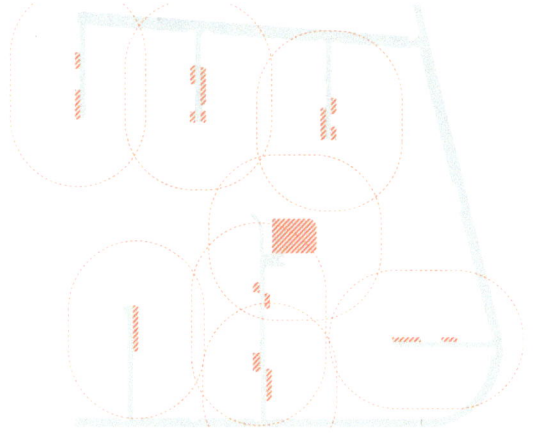

Understanding the location patterns of new uses … makes it possible to design a neighbourhood well prepared for change, without generic or overdetermined zoning, that promotes entrepreneurship (in the form of new family businesses) to strengthen the local economy.

incorporated the metropolitan scale (connectivity), the neighbourhood scale (service provision), the vicinity scale (the network of plazas and pedestrian corridors), and the housing scale (expansion strategies).

Change of Use

The transformation of a house depends to a great extent on the family's needs. However, the location of a house within a diverse urban fabric is also a determining factor for its potential development. The emergence of new uses beyond the residential is directly related to the various aspects of the neighbourhood design. In PREVI, the properties facing the perimeter roads connecting the neighbourhood with the city have been transformed into convenience stores. The main pedestrian street also has a large number of shops, but these are more of the local corner-shop kind. Around the central park, the houses have been transformed into a couple of nurseries and a school that use the park for various activities, intensifying the use of public space. Understanding the location patterns of new uses such as these makes it possible to design a neighbourhood well prepared for change, without generic or overdetermined zoning, that promotes entrepreneurship (in the form of new family businesses) to strengthen the local economy.

Self-Managed Transformation: A Family Pattern

The 'family evolution pattern' is the sequence in which a family satisfies its changing needs, and is key in the design of neighbourhood projects planned to be self-managed or self-completed. The pattern follows the following stages: 1) installation – the family makes minor modifications to secure the property and to establish its own identity; 2) densification – the family grows and incorporates new family nuclei, the stage that demands the greatest building effort; and 3) consolidation and diversification – once completed, the house is divided into different units, in many cases incorporating new uses.

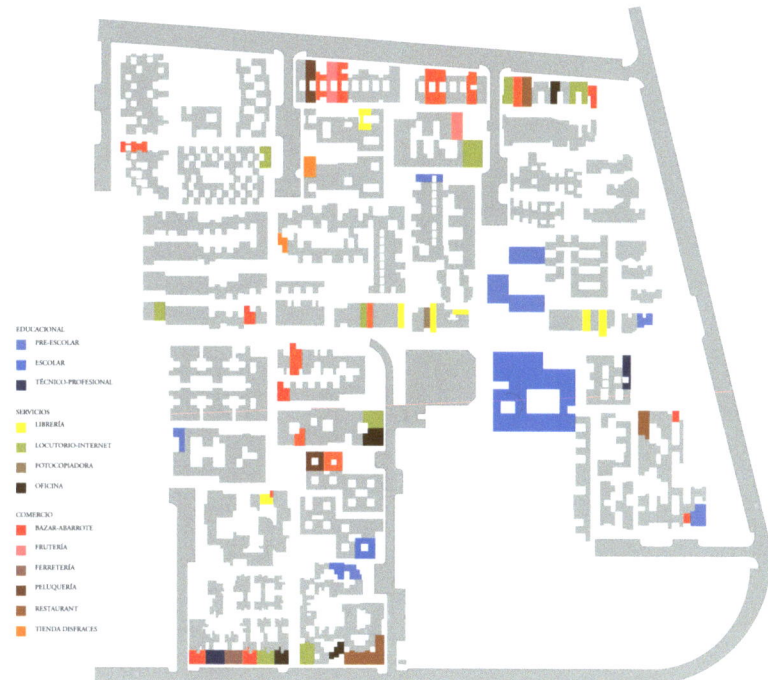

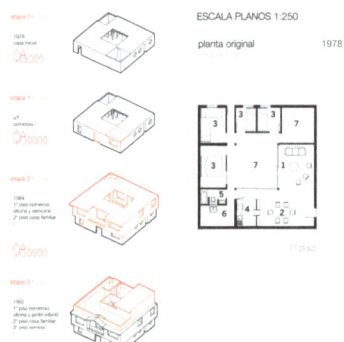

ESCALA PLANOS 1:250

planta original 1978   plantas transformadas 2003

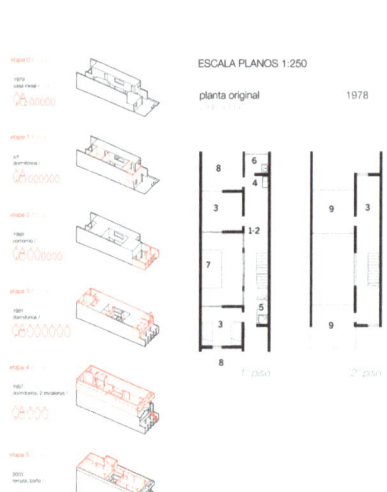
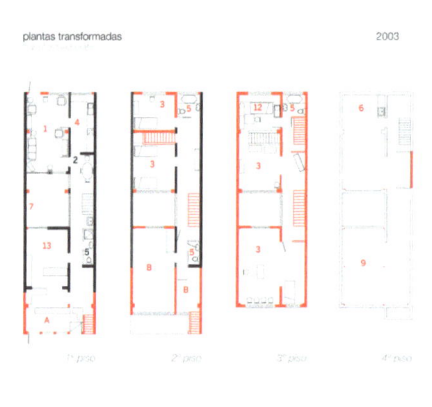

ESCALA PLANOS 1:250

planta original 1978   plantas transformadas 2003

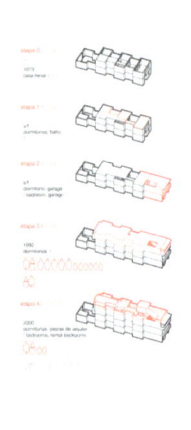

ESCALA PLANOS 1:250

planta original 1978   plantas transformadas 2003

opposite top: Fernandez family house in a Kikutake, Maki, Kurokawa design. The installation of a shop and rental apartment consolidates the house, thanks to the potential of the original project: the double frontage that allows for separate access for the family and the shop, the patio which separates both uses and provides environmental quality, and the stairs that enable the division of the house and provide versatility. The lack of definition of the frontyard space means the houses can expand up to the boundary of the sidewalk.

opposite centre: Zamora family house in a James Stirling design. A rigid perimeter, not easily modified and which delineates the property; the pillars that mark out the corners of the yard and allow a permeable, fluent connection between the living quarters and the yard; and the top slabs for the subsequent extensions, all make this type one of PREVI's successes. The family has taken advantage of the strategic position of this corner house, in front of a community plaza and the main park, to build a shop and a couple of offices.

opposite bottom: Castro family house in a Charles Correa design. This house was designed to accommodate a 12-children family by expanding the original unit by 3.5. After 11 of the children moved abroad, leaving just one daughter in charge, the house was transformed into a boarding house with 10 rooms, communal spaces and an independent apartment for the owner. The double frontage allows for independent access. On a larger scale, all the houses of this type were expanded up to the outermost lines of their facades, transforming the original irregular clusters into regular blocks.

Added Value

The virtue of such projects is in the added value created by such extensions and changes. To achieve this, the initial stage of the project must include guidelines that are flexible enough to allow for future customisation, but also impose certain safety and environmental conditions. This is facilitated by the provision of the correct structural elements and vacant spaces for inhabitants to carry out extensions to their houses later on. The permanent fixtures, such as the central yard or base of the house, a sidewalk or a plaza, must also be clearly identified.

The first stage must also begin a process that promotes the domestic economy, the formation of social networks and the incorporation of 'income units'; that is, independent houses or facilities which families can use to increase their income. Examples of this include the multifamily house and, to a greater extent, the 'hyperhouse'.[8] In the latter case, the value of the house lies not only in its capacity as a home, but also in its potential for generating income and strengthening the family's economy. It thus represents an optimal approach to social investment in housing issues.

A Turning Point

Half a century after the regional urban crisis, the built environment in Latin America shows that its governments were, to a large extent, convinced that the social crisis was a housing crisis. The housing deficit somehow resulted in the mass-production of the isolated housing block, the building of low-density projects on the outskirts of the cities, and the implementation of projects to provide services and facilities such as water, sewerage and electricity only when demand far exceeded supply – all of which have had the negative effect of planning for marginalisation. PREVI-Lima is a repository for the concepts of the functional city and low-rise high-density housing, and a counterpoint in its approach to cooperative urban strategies and in its close relationship with the social unit. The now almost four decades of constant consolidation, increase in families' capital and the transformation of public spending into social investment confirm the PREVI experience as a valid approach to achieving a successful development. ⌁

Notes
1. The following 13 international teams were invited: James Stirling (UK); Esquerra, Samper, Sáenz, Urdaneta (Colombia); Knud Svensson (Denmark); Atelier 5 (Switzerland); Toivo Korhonen (Finland); Charles Correa (India); Herbert Ohl (Germany); Kikutake, Maki, Kurokawa (Japan); Iñiguez de Onzoño, Vásquez de Castro (Spain); Hansen, Hatloy (Poland); Aldo van Eyck (the Netherlands); Candilis, Josic, Woods (France); Christopher Alexander (US).
2. The Peruvian teams selected in an open competition were: Miguel Alvariño; Ernesto Paredes; Miró-Quesada, Williams, Núñez; Gunter, Seminario; Morales, Montagne; Juan Reiser; Eduardo Orrego; Vier, Zanelli; Vella, Bentín, Quiñones, Takahashi; Mazzarri, Llanos; Cooper, García-Bryce, Graña, Nicolini; Chaparro, Ramírez, Smirnoff, Wiskowsky; Crousse, Páez, Pérez-León.
3. The first five versions of the Congrés International d'Architecture Moderne (CIAM), introduced between 1928 and 1937, had housing as the main issue. Gathered around the figure of Le Corbusier, CIAM developed the concept of high-rise housing blocks and strict urban zoning to tackle the urban problems and future challenges at the time.
4. The jury, made up of national and foreign members, defined three prizes at the same level for the teams in each category. The international teams were: Atelier 5; Herbert Ohl; and Kikutake, Maki, Kurokawa. The Peruvian teams were: Mazzarri, Llanos; Chaparro, Ramírez, Smirnoff, Wiskowsky; and Crousse, Páez, Pérez León.
5. The jury members were Peter Land (UN), José Antonio Coderch (Spain), Halldor Gunnlogsson (Denmark), Ernest Weissmann (UN), Carl Koch (USA, UIA), Manuel Valega (Peru), Ricardo Malachowski (Peru), Eduardo Barclay (Peru) and assistants Darío González (Peru) and Álvaro Ortega (UN).
6. The Development Group consisted of international and national specialists during the different stages of the project. In the initial stages, the project was carried out by Peter Land (architect, creator of the PREVI initiative and head consultant) and Álvaro Ortega (architect, interregional consultant for the UN) as supervisor. The national managers included Fernando Correa Miller (architect), Carlos Morales Macchiavello (architect) and Oscar Pacheco (architect) as three of the 10 co-managers of PREVI. Raquel Barrionuevo de Machicao (civil engineer and drains engineer) and Javier Santolalla Silva (civil engineer) were involved in all the phases of the project, including the comprehensive assessment of PREVI.
7. The research has now been published as: Fernando García-Huidobro, Diego Torres Torriti and Nicolás Tugas, Time Builds!: The Experimental Housing Project (PREVI), Lima. *Genesis and Outcome*, Gustavo Gili (Barcelona), 2008.
8. The term refers to the capacity of such houses to have a multidimensional programme or complementary uses that can generate an income through the inclusion of small businesses or rooms for rent.

Text © 2011 John Wiley & Sons Ltd. Images © Fernando García-Huidobro, Diego Torres Torriti and Nicolás Tugas

ELEMENTAL A DO TANK

Alejandro Aravena has gained international honours and awards for his pioneering work at Elemental. An independent practice with a 'social conscience', Elemental seeks to deliver greater equality for urban dwellers and improve the quality of people's lives. It has formed key partnerships with Universidad Catolica de Chile (Chile's Catholic University) and the Chilean oil company, COPEC. Here Aravena describes some of the works that have informed Elemental's strategy: from its first housing project in Iquique in northern Chile to a sustainable masterplan with Arup for the coastal town of Constitución in the wake of the Chilean earthquake.

Elemental is a for-profit company with a social conscience working on projects that capitalise on the city's capacity to create wealth and provide a short cut to equality by improving quality of life without having to wait for income redistribution. Elemental has been operating since 2002, and since 2006 has worked in partnership with Universidad Catolica de Chile (Chile's Catholic University) and the Chilean oil company, COPEC. This unusual combination of academic excellence, corporate vision and entrepreneurship has been instrumental in enabling Elemental to expand its scope in the city. It is currently engaged in upgrading urban infrastructure, transportation networks, services and housing.

Elemental Housing

When Elemental first took off at Harvard University in 2000, social housing was associated with a dearth of economic and professional resources that meant limited options for poor families. Elemental sought to change this negative association, using professional skills to work with social housing providers. The aim was to generate a technical scenario that would guarantee value gain over time without the need to change existing policies or market conditions.

'There have been perhaps two major moments in the history of social housing. The first came in 1927, when, in the Weissenhofsiedlung of Stuttgart, the best architects at the time, made built contributions to try to solve the problem of low-cost housing. The second came in 1970, after the PREVI-Lima project (1968–75), when attempts by avant-garde architects to help overcome a housing deficit came to an end. We are planning to write the third chapter of this story by again bringing the best architects to solve that most difficult of architectural issues: extremely low-cost housing that can be a real means to overcoming poverty.'[1]

Elemental Iquique (2003) was the first project in Chile to apply the company's design criteria and confirm that the methodology worked. Five years after its construction, there was an overall increase in the value of both houses and neighbourhood. The project, in a city in the North Chilean desert, involved settling 93 families on the site – where they had been squatting for the last 30 years in the heart of Iquique´s downtown – instead of displacing them to the periphery. The budget was US$7,500 per family. The opportunity to develop this site allowed Elemental to test its own developed design criteria for ensuring that each unit appreciated in value so that social housing could become a social investment instead of a social expense. Success was achieved by clearly identifying the restrictions and then working with the families themselves in participative workshops, proving feasibility on a local level. The results? People were able to double the area of their original homes (36 square metres/387.5 square feet) at a cost of only $1,000 each. Today, five years later, any house in the Elemental Iquique project is now valued at over $20,000.

When Elemental first took off at Harvard University in 2000, social housing was associated with a dearth of economic and professional resources that meant limited options for poor families. Elemental sought to change this negative association, using professional skills to work with social housing providers.

Elemental_Renca, Santiago, 2008
opposite: Community workshop where both the project's limitations and its benefits were communicated through paper models made by the families.

Elemental_Lo Espejo, Santiago, 2007
top: Elemental housing shown before and after customised expansion. The house grew from 36 square metres (387.5 square feet) to 72 square metres (775 square feet).

Elemental, Quinta Monroy, Iquique, 2005–6
above: First half of the house built at a cost of US$7,500; the second half (self-construction) for $750. The market value of the house after completion was $20,000.

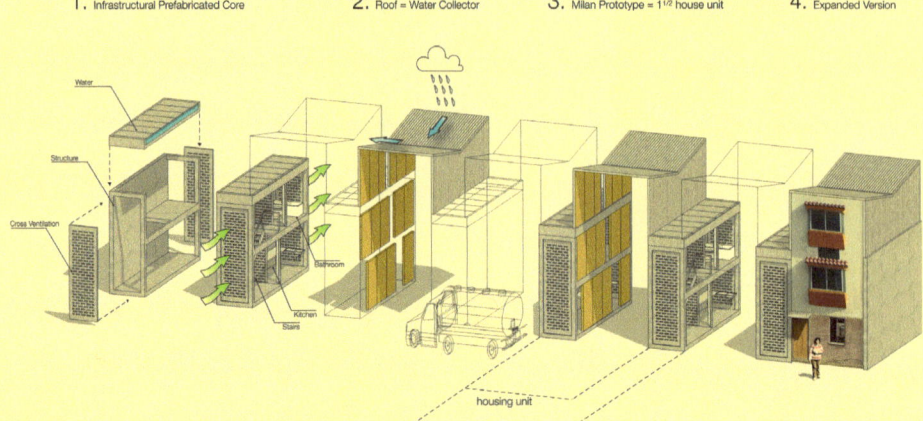

Resolving the housing problem of the world's poor requires action on a massive scale that can only be achieved by worldwide cooperation in the transfer of technology. Elemental is committed to developing projects together with local builders and governments around the world, transmitting its experience through specific projects.

Elemental_E-block, Prefabricated prototype, 2008
top: The new prefabricated prototype, customisable through self-construction by the owners.

Elemental_Monterrey, Mexico, 2010
centre: First Elemental housing project located outside Chile. Winner of the Brit Insurance Prize for Architecture, 2010.

Elemental_Paraisópolis, São Paulo, 2011
above: This high-density housing complex, located in the Paraisópolis favela on the outskirts of São Paulo, is currently under construction.

Scale and Speed

By 2030, the population of the world living in cities will have increased from 3 to 5 billion, with 2 billion of these living below the poverty line. The problem the world needs to solve is to build a 1-million-inhabitant city per week for the next 20 years for $10,000 dollars per family. Elemental is working on a 'scale and speed strategy' to share its experience and quality standards with poor communities around the globe.

Scale

Resolving the housing problem of the world's poor requires action on a massive scale that can only be achieved by worldwide cooperation in the transfer of technology. Elemental is committed to developing projects together with local builders and governments around the world, transmitting its experience through specific projects. For example, the company has worked in partnership with the Make It Right Foundation-New Orleans, the City of São Paulo and the government of Nuevo León, Mexico, to develop projects using Elemental's design principles. In Mexico, the Housing Institute of Nuevo León commissioned a group of 70 homes on a site of 0.6 hectares (1.48 acres) in a middle-class neighbourhood in Monterrey (2010). This project demonstrates the adaptability of the design criteria abroad, empowering local builders by giving them the knowledge that allows them to take these same innovations and apply them themselves.

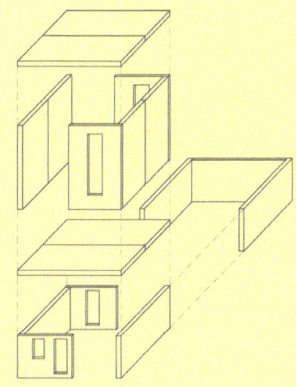

Speed

The key to increasing the speed of construction lies in prefabrication. Historically, prefabricated systems have been criticised for their inability to adapt to varied situations. However, if the goal is to prefabricate only half a house, this problem no longer exists. Each owner, when building the second half of his or her house, is responsible for customising the final solution. Moreover, while the first half becomes more strategic (ie, concentrating on the difficult parts of the house), it achieves a more universal application, justifying and confirming the advantages of prefabrication. These concepts were implemented in the Milan Triennale prototype (2008) that can be assembled in 24 hours, successes which then led to the second phase development of the E-block, a second-generation of prefab prototypes that with speed and flexibility can generate housing for whole neighbourhoods where resources are scarce.

Elemental's Response to the Chilean Earthquake

On 27 February 2010, an earthquake measuring 8.8 on the Richter scale, and resultant tsunami hit Chile, affecting the greater part of the country. Two days after the incident, Elemental began work on three different projects, at varying speeds and scales, to assist the people and cities of Chile.

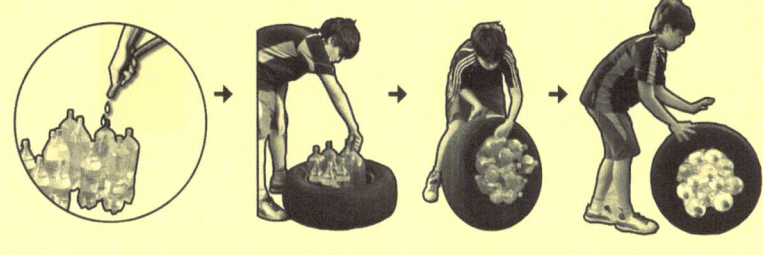

Elemental_Milan, Prefabricated prototype, 2008
top: Isometric showing the prefabricated concrete panels that can be assembled in 24 hours, and the built result.

Elemental_Rolling Water, 1st-day response, Chile, 2010
above: First-day relief response following the 8.8 magnitude earthquake – an innovative strategy for distributing water by rolling it along instead of carrying it.

The municipality and government of Constitución contacted Elemental inviting the company to join a team of Chilean organisations and the international engineering firm ARUP to work on PRES, a masterplan for the sustainable reconstruction of this coastal city.

1st-Day Response

The process of collecting water from a central distribution tank is inefficient for two reasons: water is heavy, making it impossible to carry large quantities at any one time, and containers that can efficiently hold and carry water are not readily available. Under normal circumstances, a family needs between 20 and 25 litres (5.5 gallons) of water daily to meet their basic drinking, cooking and washing needs. Obviously, these simple tasks will require much more time if water has to be collected several times rather than once.

Referencing methods of transporting water in Africa, Elemental proposed rolling water instead of carrying it. Rolling water is a more efficient means of transporting this necessity. The process, which is so easy that even a child can do it, consists of: 1) filling plastic bottles with water; 2) packing the bottles tightly inside a tyre; 3) lifting the tyre into an upright position; and 4) rolling the tyre alongside you.

10th-Day Response

Each 32-square-metre (344.4-square-foot) Elemental emergency housing unit was designed to utilise natural light and cross-ventilation and to be assembled within 48 hours by a team of three people. Made from 14 structurally insulated panels (SIPs) that can later be reused for constructing permanent accommodation, it is possible to build 50 units daily. The goal was to buy time so that the quality of reconstruction was of a higher standard; otherwise the urgency and pressure to provide solutions would compromise the end result.

100th-Day Response

The municipality and government of Constitución contacted Elemental inviting the company to join a team of Chilean organisations and the international engineering firm Arup to work on PRES, a masterplan for the sustainable reconstruction of this coastal city. About 80 per cent of the city was destroyed by the earthquake and resultant tsunami; the team had 90 days to completely redesign the city including its infrastructure, energy distribution systems, waste management, housing, public spaces and facilities.

One part of the masterplan consisted of a 7-kilometre (4.3-mile) long park to be situated along the river and coastal edge of the city. Not only does this provide much-needed green space, but a heavily wooded area serves to mitigate the effects of future tsunamis, with a modeled potential reduction in the force of the water of up to 41 per cent and of its height by up to 28 per cent.

PRES also plans for increased density at the city centre while transforming certain streets into pedestrian walkways. In addition to the reconstruction of keynote public buildings, different housing typologies were designed to take account of variables such as surface area and to allow for the possibility of expansion. And with reconstruction came the opportunity to capture the city's renewable energy potential. Photovoltaic lights were incorporated into the new pedestrian walkways and, rather than electricity, solar

Elemental_Emergency House, 10th-day response, Chile, 2010
top: Relief response for the 10th day following the earthquake – an emergency shelter made of 14 SIP panels which can be assembled within 48 hours.

Elemental_PRES, 100th-day response, Chile, 2010
above: Relief response for the 100th day following the earthquake. A sustainable masterplan for the reconstruction of Constitución, a city left with 80 per cent destruction due to the earthquake and resultant tsunami. The proposal called for construction of a park along the coast of the river and ocean to mitigate future tsunami damage.

panels are used to heat water for homes. Also, the residual heat produced by the cellulose plant near the city centre would be harnessed to heat public buildings and facilities.

Citizen Participation

Implementing PRES involved meshing the know-how and experience of professionals and local authorities with the views and aspirations of the citizens. Utilising the design of Elemental's emergency housing unit, a town hall was built in the city centre that housed various forums and discussion groups on the city's development. During the 90 days within which the redesign of the city had to be completed, the town hall received 6,300 visitors, more than 1,200 ideas were deposited in its mailbox, and 4,230 votes were counted in community polls. It was an unprecedented level of participation that allowed the vision and priorities of the city's citizens to be incorporated within the final proposal.

Chile has a history of destructive earthquakes, but each one has left behind a legacy of improved construction standards. In part due to the latest disaster, Elemental believes it is now necessary to design coastal cities with an inherent ability to withstand tsunamis, and to consider seismic isolation for basic services and utilities serving all cities.

One last point. Under normal circumstances, Chilean (and other Latin American) cities do not grow at the same rate as per capita income. Which is why the process of reconstruction with its emphasis on public space within the city's natural and geographic setting is an opportunity to improve upon the city's potential for growth. ᴅ

top: The mitigation park was designed to reduce the speed and height of tsunami waves by means of trees and landscaping that create friction with the water.

above: The town hall served as a venue for the citizens and designers to meet to discuss and vote on the development of the city.

Note
1. Alejandro Aravena, 'Elemental: Building Innovative Social Housing in Chile', *Harvard Design Magazine* 21, Fall/Winter 2004/5.

Text © 2011 John Wiley & Sons Ltd. Images © Elemental

Dellekamp Arquitectos

TLACOLULA SOCIAL HOUSING, OAXACA, MEXICO

Oaxaca in southern Mexico is one of the most economically marginal states in the country, with a large portion of its population requiring social housing. This has been further exacerbated by the widespread adoption of a suburban American housing model that has led to local communities becoming socially and culturally alienated. At Tlacolula, in Oaxaca, **Dellekamp Arquitectos** describe how they have set out to create a housing development that engenders locality and a sense of community through a traditional barrio neighbourhood design.

Dellekamp Arquitectos, Social Housing, Tlacolula, Oaxaca, Mexico, 2010–
opposite: The system of shifting modules is designed to provide courtyard spaces that offer the benefits of collective shading and cross-ventilation. The variety of units also offers a number of different-sized courtyards.

below: The Tlacolula housing modules can be combined in a variety of ways to create a diverse and unique urban experience. Furthermore, each is painted in bright unique colours inspired by the colourful traditions of local Oaxacan culture.

bottom: Each home in the development is built around a courtyard with open access from the outside, strengthening communication between neighbours and accommodating local customs.

Tlacolula is a housing development project that bets on locality: it interprets ancestral solutions embedded in local traditional architecture, speaks to the local aspirational model by integrating culturally rich uses of public and private space, and aims at creating an urban system that grows and adapts to the community's needs. Currently under construction, the 1,200-unit project by Dellekamp Arquitectos, for local private developer Novaterra Inmobiliaria, is located 26 kilometres (16.1 miles) from the city of Oaxaca, Mexico, most of whose population is in need of social housing due to their low income.

Although the region has exploited its long-standing traditions to attract tourism, social housing development has culturally and socially alienated local communities. Developers across the country have purblindly implemented a distortion of the suburban American housing model that has proven unsuitable to local conditions. When made to fit native constraints, this model has led to isolated, overcrowded neighbourhoods severed from major city services and cultural hubs.[1] By fragmenting informal social networks and stagnating social mobility, the overall effect has been to undermine the communities' identity and wrest long-term surplus value from them and transfer it to property. The standardised model systemically produces 'block dwellers' rather than 'city dwellers'. Moreover, it is environmentally detrimental: it overlooks climate restrictions, public health, service quality, local resources, workplace commutes, education availability and the social fabric.

Tlacolula proposes a viable alternative model that hinges on community engagement to facilitate civic integration and aspirational expression. Houses are designed as an ecosystem that leads to a site-specific, sustainable and self-sufficient eco-social setup that integrates transport hubs and commercial, service and green areas. The project follows four main strategies. First, it actively engages residents, giving them a voice in how their community is developed.

Houses are designed as an ecosystem that leads to a site-specific, sustainable and self-sufficient eco-social setup that integrates transport hubs and commercial, service and green areas.

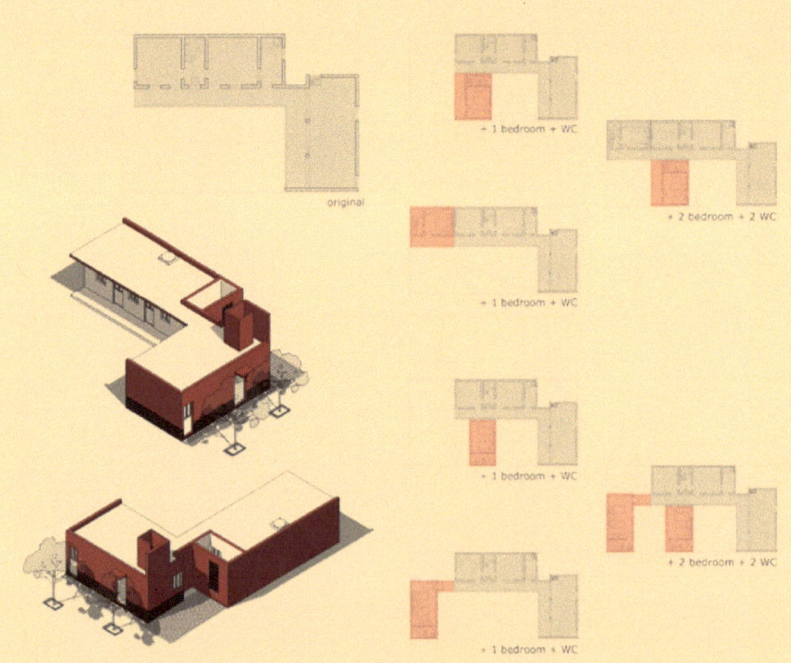

Second, it draws from vernacular building forms and idioms – a sense of place and belonging is key to preserving the spirit of community. Third, it creates a system rather than a grid – plots, walkways and streets facilitate informal social networks while clearly defining the private realm through a framework for individual expression. Finally, it provides a network of open public spaces to establish a well-defined civic realm where public spaces function as an integral part of the community's self-image and identity.

Tlacolula restores community through traditional barrio neighbourhood design. Courtyard exterior circulation, one of the idioms of local barrio design, frees up 50 per cent of each unit's plot. The houses delineate traffic-free roads and are connected through a network of walkways that interweave service and green spaces. Streets and parking areas have been pushed to the periphery to create a pedestrian-friendly environment that reduces car use.

Produced using local materials and to suit different income levels, the units can be articulated into a panoply of patterns. The system of shifting modules yields benefits such as collective shading and cross-ventilation, and the houses also employ other simple energy-reduction practices such as solar heaters and rainwater collection. All vegetation is local and irrigated with rainwater harvested and filtered through permeable pavements. The flexible nature of this system allows it to adapt and shift to accommodate different topographic conditions, climates and family settings. The dwellings are designed to grow, within a predetermined set of construction guidelines, with home-owners' needs, to increase the value of their housing patrimony. The result is affordable, sustainable, opportunity-filled housing within a community that supports its residents and their requirements. 𝕯

Note
1. Jeffrey H Cohen, 'Remittance Outcomes in Rural Oaxaca, Mexico: Challenges, Options and Opportunities for Migrant Households', *Population, Space and Place* 11, 2005, pp 49–63.

Text © 2011 John Wiley & Sons Ltd. Images © Dellekamp Arquitectos

opposite: Located just outside the city of Tlacolula, this project for 1,200 homes employs socially and environmentally sustainable strategies to create a growing and flexible system. As the project continues to be built, the housing units will form a network of pedestrian streets linked to service and green areas.

top and centre: Inspired by the vernacular courtyard house, each unit includes a courtyard that provides a space for conversation, games and leisure.

bottom: In order to support ample amounts of vegetation, the development is designed to be hydrologically sustainable and efficient.

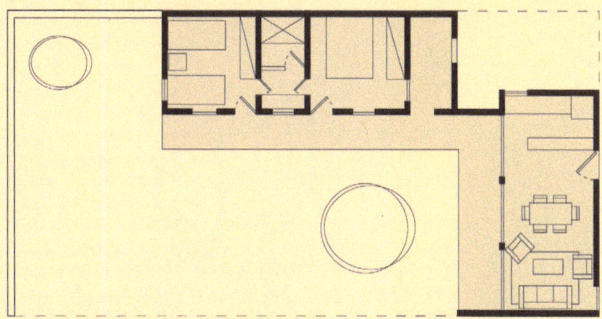

Ricky Burdett
Adam Kaasa

GOVERNING CHANGE

In 21st-century Latin America, cities are taking the lead. With the greatest populations and economic output concentrated in large-scale metropolises, there is a real sense that the largest cities are outgrowing their national contexts. In many cases, power has been devolved at a municipal level. This has enabled mayors to implement infrastructural and transport projects. As **Ricky Burdett and Adam Kaasa** highlight in their discussion of two particular initiatives in São Paulo and Mexico City, it has also opened the way for innovative new community projects.

THE METROPOLITAN REVOLUTION IN LATIN AMERICA

Change makes lucid the relationship between people, architecture and the form of their cities, and the agents that govern them.

For thousands of years Latin America has been a region of cities, but also a region of change. Whenever governments change, or empires come and go, those same cities remain, often taking on different social roles and physical shapes. Change makes lucid the relationship between people, architecture and the form of their cities, and the agents that govern them. In 1535, Lima, then known as La Ciudad de los Reyes, came into existence as one of the most important early port cities of the Spanish Empire, shifting the centre of power in the region from Cuzco, the capital of the Inca Empire deep in the Andes, to the primacy of coastal trade. From 1815 to 1821, Rio de Janeiro became the capital city of the Portuguese Empire when royals fled from Lisbon during the Napoleonic Wars in Europe. And São Paulo, a small and relatively unpopulated outpost at the turn of the last century, transformed as fast as the movement of capital into one of the largest metropolitan regions in the Americas. This is a region of endemic change but constant cities.

Over 200 years ago, revolutionary leaders across Latin America took up arms against their colonial rulers. By 1840 the modern map of Latin America was redrawn. From old-world empires to new-world nations – Colombia and Peru, Argentina and Brazil – the region's nation-states as we know them today were carved out of the viceroyalties of Spain and Portugal. Governance in Latin America seems to have come in waves of scale, moving from empires of conquest to nations of revolution. Perhaps now a third governance revolution is taking place, one that will transform the architecture and urban realms of those cities as drastically as did the move from the lake city of Tenochtitlán at the heart of the Aztec Empire, to Mexico at the centre of the viceroyalty of New Spain, to Mexico City as exemplar of the modern urban condition of the 21st century. This revolution is a metropolitan one.

Complexity and Change: Comparing Latin American Cities

From a distance, a metropolitan revolution in Latin America reveals certain similarities, two of which stand out. First, most of the larger Latin American cities concentrate percentages of population and economic output that far outweigh their national averages.[1] While cities have been magnets for investment and trade throughout the region's history, they now appear to be outgrowing their national contexts. This is not to say that Lima is no longer in need of the national framework afforded by Peru, but it does imply that social and economic policies created at the national level no longer make scalar sense for the complexities of large individual cities. Cities are the drivers of change in the 21st century.

Second, while the wealth and centrality of cities has long been subject to the political use and abuse of empire, or of national governments, recent devolution has increased real governmental authority in leadership at the local scale. Since 1997, for example, citizens of Mexico City have been able to elect their mayor directly for the first time in that city's history, even though he is responsible for the central Federal District (Distrito Federal) that contains about one-third of the 22 million population that spills over on to the state of Mexico. Previously appointed by the national government, the mayor of Mexico City DF remains one of the most important offices in the country, now with the local legitimacy and endorsement of its constituents.

A similar constitutional amendment in Argentina in 1993 created the autonomous city of Buenos Aires with the power to elect its own leadership. In 2007, the city embarked on a new decentralisation scheme, creating new *comunas* managed by seven-member elected committees. These have authority over social and cultural policies at the neighbourhood level as well as the management of green spaces and secondary roads.

In Brazil, the 2001 federal Statute of the City gave more power to local government to use masterplanning to avoid being held ransom by urban land markets. Yet still today the mayor of São Paulo, the country's largest city and its economic engine, governs over only part of the built-up area of this vast urban plateau, while large sections are the responsibility of the governor of the larger state of São Paulo, who often has different priorities to the more localised interests of the city administration.

While the 1990s onwards saw shifts towards greater metropolitan governance, there remained difficulty in regionally integrated decision-making within these metropolitan regions, let alone between the federal, state and metropolitan scales. However, the complexity and richness of the metropolitan introduces more textured analysis of the contemporary urban landscape than is often offered by more macroeconomic or

Complex land use and governance
opposite: View from the Carlos Laso Bridge heading into Santa Fe, Mexico City's largest business district. It boasts Latin America's third-largest mall. The diversity of land use in Mexico City adds to the complexity of planning governance.

Good governance and integrated decision-making
below: The governance charts of São Paulo, Buenos Aires and Bogotá demonstrate that urban change requires integrated decision-making across federal, state, metropolitan and neighbourhood scales.

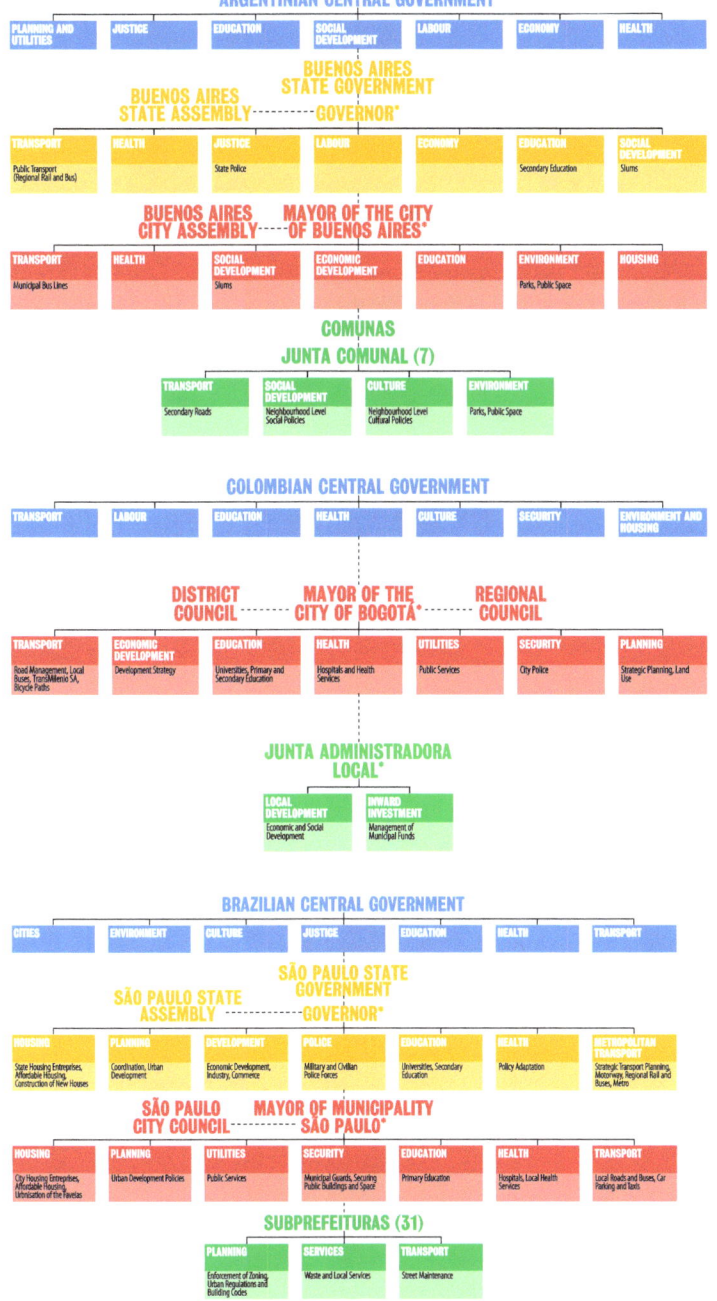

planning analysis. It is true that urban and social change in large cities is never without national political consequence; still, these recent changes mark the important rise of local governance authority in Latin America and the move for national change to start at the local city scale.

A third striking similarity is the high levels of inequality, and the resulting spatial organisation of wealth and poverty. Many large and successful Latin American cities continue to act as funnels, consolidating rural populations into larger and larger conurbations, and yet the region remains one of the most unequal on the planet.

Much of the growth remains on the outer edges of cities, like the Guarapiranga-Billings reservoirs in São Paulo, with little access to services or amenities. Central areas of cities also remain drastically divided, allowing multiple layers of a city to operate simultaneously and in the same spaces but with limited intersection. Gated residential communities and heavily guarded 'public' spaces like shopping centres have become legitimate responses to the reality of urban violence, creating a complex system of hierarchies of space within the city. Exclusive hypermobilities of extensive highway systems and overpasses, coupled with the inaccessibility of public transit and high land values, fracture the lived experience of the rich and the poor, thus affecting the physical layout of the city. Cities become the spatial distillation of gross inequalities. Still, these same cities play host to the saturated space of innovation and civic engagement where those inequalities begin to change.

City Different: Spatial Representation, Density and Transportation

Latin American cities share certain urban conditions, like holding large concentrations of wealth and population, being at the centre of recently devolved governance and being radically unequal. However, if we zoom in to the level of urban neighbourhoods, each is incredibly complex. Compared to São Paulo or Buenos Aires, whose municipal administrative boundaries do not begin to account for their urban populations, the vast majority of Bogotá's citizens live within these boundaries. This is a very important distinction. It means that municipal governments are able to make decisions and implement infrastructural and urban-planning changes

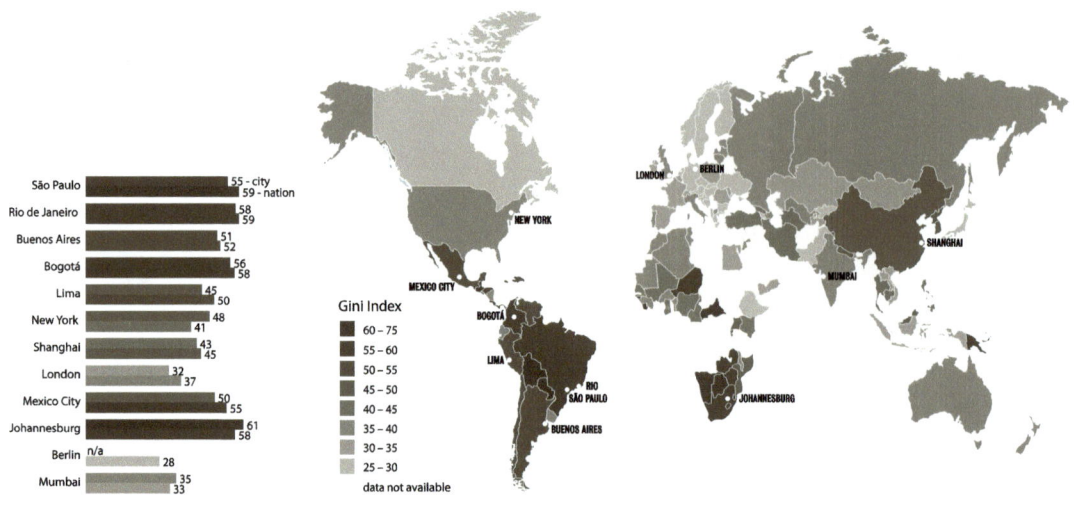

The disjuncture between political administrative boundaries and the actual built-up area of a city offers challenges for devolved governmental decision-making, particularly with respect to quality of design, equity of space, city finances, control over growth, land use and transportation.

Acute inequality
opposite top: Latin America is one of the most unequal regions on the planet, rivalled only by some countries in Africa. Latin American cities, however, consistently prove to be more equal than their respective nations. Here we compare material inequality using the Gini index, The lower the Gini index, the more equal the income and wealth distribution.

Informal housing and urban ecologies
opposite bottom: São Paulo is grappling with the recent informal urbanisation of its Guarapiranga-Billings reservoirs at the south end of the city. An increase of dwellings in the area threatens the water quality of the entire region, while at the same time highlighting the difficulty of housing vulnerable populations.

Real cities and abstract boundaries
left: One of the fundamental issues with city government is the disjoint between political administrative boundaries and where people actually live. The metropolitan footprint therefore acts as a visual representation of the actual lived city, stressing the need for local integrated decision-making. Top to bottom: Buenos Aires, Bogotá, Lima, Mexico City, Rio de Janeiro and São Paulo.

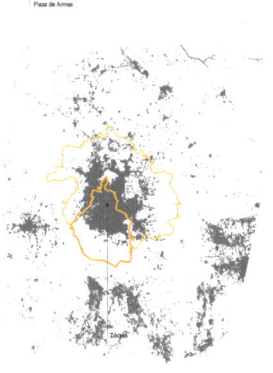
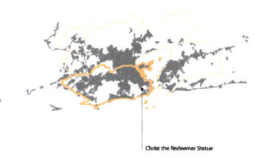
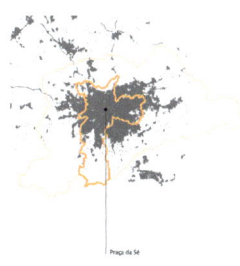

or architectural design standards that will likely affect a very large proportion of their city's larger population. For example, the overwhelming majority of Bogotá's residents are served by the TransMilenio initiative, largely attributed to the mayoral leadership of Enrique Peñalosa who prioritised bus rapid transit over traditional rail-based metro transport and the massive infrastructure requirements of the private car (see pp 90–5).

The disjuncture between political administrative boundaries and the actual built-up area of a city offers challenges for devolved governmental decision-making, particularly with respect to quality of design, equity of space, city finances, control over growth, land use and transportation. At the same time, calls for metropolitan or regional governance bodies to coordinate large infrastructural decisions across these political lines are gaining salience.

While density maps differ more slightly across our cities, when compared with the typology of buildings they reveal an incredible story. Take the two largest cities in Latin America, Mexico City and São Paulo, each with similar populations and average densities. Mexico City, however, has a peak density of over 48,300 people per square kilometre with São Paulo only reaching 29,380 people per square kilometre. Mexico City, we can say, has a building typology capable of accommodating larger concentrations of residents. The comparison becomes striking, however, when we look to the typologies prevalent in these two cities: São Paulo's skyline is dominated by high-rise apartment blocks, while Mexico City's is consistently low-rise. Urban form and density are therefore two important debates routinely juxtaposed, but not necessarily related.

Transportation infrastructures also differ greatly from city to city. Transport is a fundamental character in the life of a city, and the nuances of each system contain unique challenges that demand unique solutions. São Paulo and Buenos Aires have the largest proportions of people using cars for travel. In Mexico City and Lima, the majority of residents use mini-buses, while Rio de Janeiro has the most people who walk as their main form of mobility. In São Paulo and Buenos Aires, integrated planning mechanisms are required so that state and federal infrastructural decisions for the metropolitan regions, often beyond the city limits, support rather than hinder municipal transport goals. On the other hand, large national transport policies and frameworks

Population density and building height
below: Mexico City (top: population 19,890,011) and São Paulo (bottom: population 19,226,426) have similar average densities. Mexico City's is 12,541 people per square kilometre and São Paulo's is 10,299 people per square kilometre. However, their spatial organisation of density differs drastically; São Paulo is consistently high-rise, and Mexico City (right) low-rise.

> Mayors are increasingly called into debates about environmental and social sustainability, urban infrastructure and social inequality.

are unlikely to reflect the subtleties of the terrain of Rocinha, the largest favela in Brazil, located on the hillside of Rio de Janeiro. Driven by auto-construction, basic sanitation and transport, infrastructure is better here than in most favelas across the country due to systematic local community intervention.

The relationship between official and lived city limits, social inequality, territory and urban form, density, urban morphology and transportation speaks to the complexity of urban conditions, and points us to the requirement for new and innovative devolved forms of integrated governance. Mayors are increasingly called into debates about environmental and social sustainability, urban infrastructure and social inequality. However, with built-up areas often crossing traditional administrative political borders of government, informal governance structures begin to exert influence on urban forms. With a growing rift between experts and citizens over what the priorities for city government should be, local civic leaders alongside community groups offer complementary systems of urban implementation.

Equalising City Moves: Community Groups and Urban Change

The first of these initiatives[2] is the Cortiço Rua Solón, a raw, partially completed, concrete-frame multistorey structure. Abandoned after the death of the developer in the 1970s, the building housed a squatter community maintaining a precarious system of electrical and water supply and a very basic form of waste disposal. By the late 1990s, an overcrowded 70 families were living in all available spaces including the incomplete elevator shafts. This is an example of the wrong kind of density: a density of the vulnerable. The building needed improvement if this group of urban poor was going to keep a safe and habitable roof over their heads.

Its location in Bom Retiro, close to São Paulo's central district, added formal developmental pressure, but the community reached out to form a unique partnership with local government, human rights groups and private enterprise, and with students from the University of São Paulo's Faculty of Architecture. The result was a de-densification process rehousing 30 families, and treatment of the collective electricity, water and sewage systems. Finally, with internal spaces cleaned and improved, the building's facade was finished and a new

Auto-construction and community development
left: Development of new concrete and brick houses in Rocinha, the largest favela in Brazil located on the hillside of Rio de Janeiro, is largely driven by auto-construction. Even so, basic sanitation and infrastructure are better here than in most favelas across the country due to systematic community intervention.

Moving in the city
below: Transport infrastructure is a critical driver of urban form, enabling centralisation of economic functions and the accommodation of a growing population along metropolitan rail and bus routes. Clockwise from left: the modal splits of Bogotá, Lima, Buenos Aries, Mexico City, Rio de Janeiro and São Paulo.

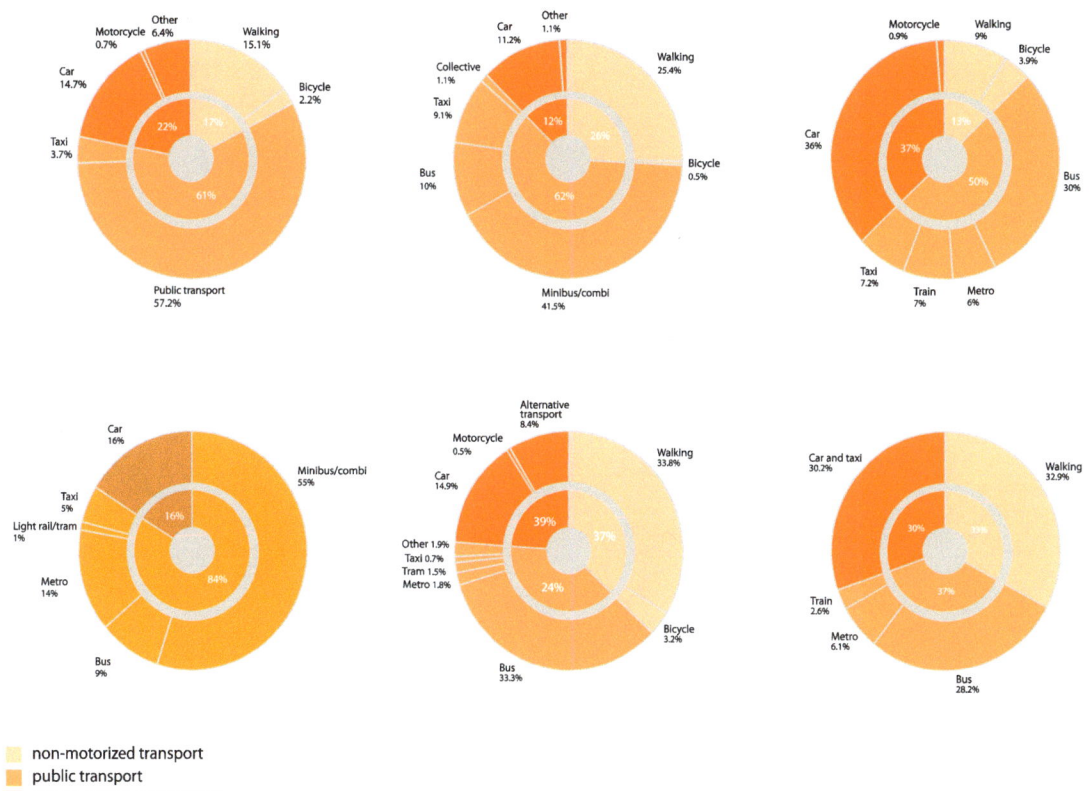

- non-motorized transport
- public transport
- private motorized transport

Public and expert opinions
below: There are marked differences between the public's perception of the city and that of key stakeholders and experts with regard to the main challenges in São Paulo. The public view (left) was gathered by the Urban Age São Paulo poll conducted by Ipsos Mori in June 2008 of 1,000 residents living within the São Paulo Metropolitan Region. The perception of leaders and experts (right) was extracted from meetings in August 2007 with 44 key individuals working in various urban spheres of government and private practice.

Cortiço Rua Solón and innovative regeneration partnerships
bottom: Cortiço Rua Solón is a raw, partially completed, concrete-frame multistorey structure located in the Bom Retiro neibourhood. Constructed in the 1970s, the building remained unfinished due to the death of the developer, and was subsequently squatted. In partnership with the University of São Paulo's Faculty of Architecture, the building was retrofitted for the community with improved electrical, water and sewage facilities.

Community-based complex urbanism
opposite: Asamblea Comunitaria de Miravalle is a community-based project that runs a comprehensive set of cultural, health, environmental, educational and employment programmes within a low-income neighbourhood on the southeastern outskirts of Mexico City. Located in the borough of Iztapalapa and founded by indigenous urban migrants, it runs a community garden, recycling centre, and educational and computer literacy programmes, and reclaimed a landfill site as a public space with an amphitheatre to house most of the community programming.

17% TRAFFIC
17% COST OF LIVING
33% TRANSPORT
7% COST OF HOUSING
3% RANGE OF HOUSING
44% HEALTH SERVICES
43% CRIME

PLANNING 33%
DOWNTOWN REVITALIZATION 27%
TRANSPORT 80%
HOUSING 60%
HEALTH 7%
CRIME 33%
ENVIRONMENT 13%
LABOUR 20%

name – Edifício União – was fixed to the bright-orange exterior. The revived state of the building, and the residents' increased agency in making it happen, triggered a new-found motivation that led many of them to make improvements inside their own apartments. Far from a top-down governmental intervention that would likely have demolished the building and rehoused the residents in far-off public housing, as in Cidade Tiradentes, this kind of devolved governance, to the smallest of urban units, the building, showcases a renewed and revolutionary local civic engagement in São Paulo with great effect on building an inclusive built environment.

A second notable initiative brings us to the heart of the other largest metropole of the Americas, Mexico City; or if not the heart, perhaps more like the fingertips. The Asamblea Comunitaria de Miravalle is a community-based project that runs a comprehensive set of cultural, health, environmental, educational and employment programmes within a low-income neighbourhood on the southeastern outskirts of the city. Located in the borough of Iztapalapa and founded by indigenous people from different ethnic backgrounds who migrated to the city, Miravalle is another example of a partnership bringing together several local and metropolitan organisations.

A project set up to collect and recycle two tonnes of PET plastic per week generates employment for some 30 local young people. A vegetable garden grows much of the food for their low-budget cantine, which provides affordable meals for over 300 members of the community. Art workshops, dance classes, a skateboarding court and educational programmes aimed at developing technological literacy sharpen the social impact of the centre. Spatially transformative, among the partnership's first achievements was the transformation of a former waste dump into a well-used public space, complete with an amphitheatre for community programmes. The precise scale of Miravalle's governance intervention allows it to recover the notion of public space, helping to alleviate urban and social problems in the near future and reinvigorating the combination of urbanity and community.

Both Cortiço Rua Solón and the Asamblea Comunitaria de Miravalle are revolutionary forms of local governance operating in Latin American cities. What is pronounced is the resurgence of collective will to foster democratically run and accountable

locally bound and responsive institutions. Perhaps the idea of a metropolitan revolution does not quite capture their resilience and impact. Still, the devolution of ideas and initiatives in the city towards citizen engagement is having lasting effects on urban and architectural interventions in cities across Latin America.

Deep History and the Metropolitan Impetus

> Next morning, we came to a broad causeway and continued our march towards Iztapalapa. And when we saw all those cities and villages built in the water, and other great towns on dry land, and that straight and level causeway leading to Mexico, we were astounded. These great towns and cues and buildings rising from the water, all made of stone, seemed like an enchanted vision from the tale of Amadis. Indeed, some of our soldiers asked whether it was not all a dream. It is not surprising therefore that I should write in this vein. It was all so wonderful that I do not know how to describe this first glimpse of things never heard of, seen or dreamed of before.[3]

Over 500 years ago, Bernal Díaz del Castillo, marching towards Iztapalapa with the armies of Hernan Cortés, encountered the dream-like, almost magical city of Tenochtitlán (later to become Mexico City) floating in the middle of a large lake. Tenochtitlán surpassed all other cities at the time, including Venice and Constantinople, with the size of its buildings and population, and the sheer incongruity of an entire city rising out of the water. Today, in that same neighbourhood of Iztapalapa, we encounter the Asamblea Comunitaria de Miravalle, a new kind of Latin America, and we are once again privy to 'glimpse[s] of things never heard of, seen or dreamed of before'. It is a locally based dream.

This deep and local history is also a transnational one. Latin American cities are inherently multicultural. They are not just simply hybridities of an indigenous and European culture, the quintessential *mestizo*. Across Latin America, more than 200 indigenous languages are still spoken. These are deeply multicultural places. In Lima we might hear German, Hindi, Arabic and Japanese, not to mention the recently established official languages of Quechua and Aymara. José de Souza Martins writes of the transitive multiculturalism of São Paulo, a multiculturalism that is less about a national immigration policy and more about an urban condition to become someone new and different.[4] Newness and the capacity for difference are precisely the kinds of urban social and spatial sensibilities that are thriving across these cities, and reflected in the shifts in both informal and formal modes of governance.

We are witnessing the third large-scale revolution in governance in Latin America, from empire to nation to city. In terms of urban social change, Mexico City became the only place in Mexico to legalise abortion in 2007, and in 2009 it became the first jurisdiction in all of Latin America to legalise same-sex marriage. While same-sex unions have been recognised in Buenos Aires since 2002, it took eight years before the nation caught up with the city. Cities are beginning to grow impatient with the national norm. In terms of the physical, new forms of urban infrastructures move us into the realm of ordinary, everyday architectural interventions that operate one building or community garden at a time. The metropolitan revolution is upon us, and its impact is only beginning to be felt in the structures that will govern for complexity and change in Latin America's cities. 𝌀

Notes
1. All facts, figures and data, unless otherwise noted, come from two recent Urban Age publications: Ricky Burdett (ed), *South American Cities: Securing an Urban Future*, Urban Age (London), 2008, and Ricky Burdett, Philipp Rode et al, *Cities and Social Equity: Inequality, Territory and Urban Form*, Urban Age (London), 2009. The Urban Age programme is part of LSE Cities, an International Centre of Excellence located at the London School of Economics and in partnership with the Deutsche Bank's Alfred Herrhausen Society. From its beginnings in 2005, it has hosted conferences in New York, Shanghai, London, Mexico City, Johannesburg, Berlin, Mumbai, São Paulo and Istanbul. All Urban Age materials are freely available online at www.urban-age.net.
2. The two initiatives mentioned here were recipients of the Deutsche Bank Urban Age Award (DBUAA). In 2008, Cortiço Rua Salón won the competition in a field representing 133 of the best community-led urban projects in the city. In 2010 the Asamblea Comunitaria de Miravalle was chosen as the recipient from over 193 applications. The DBUAA was established in 2007 to encourage citizens to take initiatives to improve their cities. It is a travelling award organised in parallel with the Urban Age programme. In 2007 it was given in Mumbai, in 2008 in São Paulo, in 2009 in Istanbul, and in 2010 in Mexico City. In 2011 the award will be presented in Hong Kong. For more information on the award, the jury and the application process, visit www.alfred-herrhausen-gesellschaft.de/en/38.html.
3. Bernal Díaz del Castillo [1576], *The Conquest of New Spain*, trans JM Cohen, Penguin Books (London), 1963, p 214.
4. See José de Souza Martins' essay 'The Multicultural City' in Rickey Burdett, *South American Cities*, op cit.

Text © 2011 John Wiley & Sons Ltd. Images: pp 42-3 © Armin Linke; pp 44, 48(t) © Philipp Rode; pp 45, 46(t), 47, 48(b), 49(b), 50(t) © LSE Cities, London School of Economics and Political Science; p 46(b) © Nelson Kon; p 49(t) © Dante Busquets; pp 50(b), 51 © Alfred Herrhausen Society, Deutsche Bank

THE OLYMPIC GAMES AND THE PRODUCTION OF THE PUBLIC REALM
MEXICO CITY 1968 AND RIO DE JANEIRO 2016

For Brazil, which is currently the world's eighth largest economy and is tipped to become the fifth, the Olympic and Paralympic Games in 2016 represent a unique opportunity. **Fernanda Canales** looks at Rio de Janeiro 2016 in light of Mexico City 1968, and considers how the Games should provide an occasion for both urban regeneration and also recasting the city's often previously conflicting image for an international audience.

Rio de Janeiro, 2016
opposite: The new projects, Barra Media Village (by BCMF Arquitetos) and Barra Cluster (by BCMF Arquitetos and LUMO Arquitectura) for Barra de Tijuca, a nouveau-riche neighbourhood at the wealthiest end of the city, where more than half of the new facilities will be located.

Mexico City, 1968
below: Housing and sports facilities built alongside Anillo Periférico on the outskirts of the city, where the idea of a new and modern territory was implemented.

It is almost a cliché to say that the Olympic Games have been a strategic tool for the deployment of urban agendas. However, prior to the 1968 Olympic Games in Mexico City, with the possible exception of Berlin 1936, no other city had embarked on such an ambitious urban revitalisation project that combined infrastructure, culture and communication as a way to reimagine a city. This moment may well represent a turning point between the idea of architectural and cultural modernity and another based on political and social renewal.

In the case of Latin America – Mexico in 1968 and Brazil in 2016 – the Olympic Games not only explain much of the urban and social agenda of these countries, but also account for the idea of modernity itself. In both cases, with an interval of almost 50 years, the main aim has been that of presenting an image of a unified, homogeneous and planned territory. Instead of understanding the Olympic Games merely as an excuse to upgrade transportation systems, improve housing and infrastructure, they have increasingly become a great anti-crime policy, a health policy, a social equaliser: an assertion of modernity and cohesion.

The Olympic Games in Mexico City offered a renewal strategy based primarily on representation. They were the first Olympic Games in the world to be televised in colour and to be 'aired' live via satellite communications, attesting to the profound relevance given to their representation as image.[1] The social crisis characterised by the student rebellions of 1968, came to a head with the Tlatelolco massacre in which hundreds were killed by military forces scarcely 10 days before inauguration. The Games were thus constructed by decisions based on *what* to show and *how* to show it. The exaltation of structures of power, exemplified by the relevance given to the formal power of institutional architecture, set the tone for a city that wanted to be seen from the outside, and was therefore made to be perceived in motion, primarily through television, by car or by plane.

Mexico City, 1968
below: Project by Mathias Goeritz in which a 17-kilometre/10.5-mile (vehicular) route of sculptures made by artists from diverse countries connected the different dispersed Olympic sites, tracing the path and expansion of the Anillo Periférico (peripheral ring) in an interesting mixture of culture, art and infrastructure. Anillo Periférico was in itself a model of urban modernity, as had been the case of Torres de Satélite built by Goeritz and Luis Barragán a decade earlier.

bottom: The construction of the modern city was based on the idea of mobility and the use of cars.

Barcelona, 1992
opposite: Villa Olimpica, a legacy of the Olympics of 1992 which regenerated the city, and especially its relationship with the waterfront.

The Olympics in Mexico were a spectacular communication and design programme, but above all they were the vehicle to present a facade of unity and modernity.

The Olympics in Mexico were a spectacular communication and design programme, but above all they were the vehicle to present a facade of unity and modernity. This emphasis on coordination, or 'Olympic identity', was highlighted by the beginning of the construction of the subway system as a new way of organising the city. Unlike the graphics – which would become a landmark – and the artistic contributions – with the creation of the Cultural Olympics planned to last the entire year – the first Olympic Games in Latin America produced little architecture worth noting. They were particularly characterised by specific interventions scattered around a growing urban footprint. The choice of locations was based on the availability of government-owned property and on adaptations on existing buildings, accentuating the pressing need for a coherent and strong image. The entire city, already brimming over, was imagined as the Olympic stage, unlike past Olympic Games where most construction lay within Olympic villages.[2]

As social contrasts and the demand for national democratisation increased after the student riots, architecture, as well as public space, gradually became more monumental and representative and less a place for interacting. Public congregations began to represent a threat to government authorities, which favoured not the use of open architecture characterised by plazas and patios, but a new city thought out for the use of cars. While the population doubled (from 3 million to 6 million), the urban area increased by more than 100 per cent, from 200 to 320 square kilometres (77.2 to 123.5 square miles), and the number of cars tripled, from 130,000 to 450,000 in a fast-growing area where 60 per cent of the settlements were created illegally.

While in Mexico, after the confrontation in Plaza de las Tres Culturas in Tlatelolco, public space took on negative connotations for the political order, in other examples, Barcelona being the most paradigmatic, the creation of a modern metropolis was based on the idea of a city focused on open spaces. Operation Barcelona '92 consisted of transforming old factories, opening the city towards the sea and giving the outskirts a monumental nature, but above all it was based on the transformation of a city by defining its public space, conceived as a system for guaranteeing citizenship and freedom.[3]

Whereas the Olympic Games in Mexico City signified the end of a period marked by the figure of the architect as a planner or strategist[4] – from Mario Pani to Ramírez Vázquez[5] – the Olympics in Barcelona in 1992, on the other hand, marked the beginning of the city of architects. As a result of the successful 'Barcelona model', architectural euphoria has nurtured many of the Olympic strategies since then (from Beijing to London).[6] However, for London 2012, the sustainable legacy angle is stronger. Bringing the East End closer to the centre, replacing polluted areas with green spaces and thinking long term – 30 years instead of the just weeks that the Olympic Games usually last – are the main ingredients of the upcoming Games, planned for all spectators to arrive by public transport, on foot or by bicycle, and for infrastructure to be downsized, sold and reused.

In a manner similar to that of London's green agenda and that of Beijing's ostentation of modern China on the global stage, Brazil plans to use the Olympics as a way of showing off the country's transformation. The Rio de Janeiro Olympic and Paralympic Games in 2016[7] are based to a great extent on fostering the BRIC (Brazil, Russia, India and China) economies. They are planned to take place in metropolitan Rio, mainly in Barra de Tijuca where more than half of the Olympic facilities will be located, but also in the districts of Maracaná, Copacobana and Deodoro. This choice is intended to focus the Olympic investments on the regions where the greatest amount of development is currently aimed, although a prevailing rhetoric promises to distribute the Games' benefits among the general population.[8]

Rio de Janeiro, boasting on one hand its condition as one of the five most urbanised cities of Southern America[9] and, on the other hand, its 90 kilometres (55.9 miles) of beaches and image of virginal paradise, has always been a city conflicting between two main ideals: that of development understood in terms of building and growth and that of conserving nature. The dichotomies between its exuberant nature and an urban landscape sprawling across its territory have defined its

Rio de Janeiro, 2016
below: Aerial View of Rio de Janeiro, October 2010.

opposite: Street view of Rio de Janeiro, February 2010. Nature and informality clustered in different pockets across Rio form a strong visual contrast to the planned city.

split identity. With the Olympics, Rio regains the capital condition that had been stolen by Brasilia in 1960 and searches for the possibility of reimagining the coexistence of informal growth with planning, as well as reconciling nature with urban development in a territory where dichotomies are accentuated due to an extreme topography which challenges the idea of a planned and socially homogeneous city.

President Lula da Silva has asserted that the word 'favela' – used to describe the shantytowns where more than one million people live in Rio[10] (a third of the population in 2001) – will disappear in time for the Games,[11] and he has also announced an ecological seal backed by the idea of a green city. Hence, the Olympic and Paralympic Games in Rio have become a political and social discourse: an attempt to 'civilise' the city. The favelas praised by Le Corbusier during his travels in the 1930s and considered by Richard Neutra as 'the hopeful reserve of the community',[12] now become a symbol of the desire and promise to rewrite the social and urban history of Rio.

The Games are part of a broader political and touristic campaign intended to sell the idea that landscapes of inequality and uneven development can be transformed into efficient, safe and socially homogeneous territories. Intense worries and complaints have already arisen due to ecological legislations that obstruct the interests of real-estate speculation. The credibility of pacifying favelas is also at stake – with almost half of the 1,000 slums of the city dominated by violence[13] – but Brazil, being the world's eighth-largest economy and heading to become the fifth,[14] overtaking the UK and France, has to integrate the squalid districts within the city, transforming *favelados* into citizens in a project for the city that attempts to build in seven years more infrastructure than in the past 50 years.

The Olympics as a strategy of representation reveals the forces at work behind the urban agendas of cities. Whether large-scale interventions based on dormant, former industrial territories as London's East End project, or whether through acupuncture interventions inside problematic and fast-growing cities, as in the case of Mexico and Rio, representation and image are sometimes far more important than the final results. In Latin America, where development is seen always through a short-term perspective, staging the Olympics has become a persuasive media event designed to hide social instabilities, to display a competitive fitness on a global scale and above all to work under a national agenda.

The nearly half a century separating the Mexico City Olympic Games and those of Rio de Janeiro shows that, despite the fact that the Games are an excuse for driving urban transformation, they reinforce the idea that, in the end, all urban planning projects are also a way of doing politics, and it is within this concept that a way of understanding the public realm is constructed. ᴀᴅ

Notes
1. The country's political and social instability, teetering on actual breakdown, was translated into a strong message of national unity – a message that pervaded almost every aspect of creative expression in a sports event that was as much a political and urban one.
2. The urgency due to the inauguration date and financial limitations was a defining factor in the project, led by the architect Pedro Ramírez Vázquez. Mexico 1968 signalled the end of far-reaching modernisation strategies as well as the end of architecture understood as a national project, replaced by isolated actions on a smaller scale in which the public realm has been progressively controlled and fenced in.
3. With architect Oriol Bohigas as the main driving force behind the definition of a new contemporary culture through the formalisation of public space and as the person responsible for post-Franco urban planning in Barcelona, public funds were used to design the empty spaces, the voids in the city. After decades of prohibition of the Catalan language and an active discouragement of the congregation of large crowds, the city began by reinventing itself in a social arena, particularly based on public space.
4. The Olympic Games represent the last major project for the city. The all-encompassing enthusiasm that had made possible projects like Ciudad Universitaria in the 1950s proved unattainable over the following decades.
5. In Mexico, with the modern agenda on the verge of being torn apart after 1968, the representative purpose of construction became increasingly relevant, creating architecture that was as autonomous and authoritarian as the regime to which it owed its existence.
6. In time, however, Barcelona gradually moved towards an atmosphere that glorified architecture and restricted the public realm in favour of private initiatives, with the Diagonal Mar project in 2004 built as the new paradigm of regenerating the city, which received mixed reviews.
7. It is the first time that a South American city is to host the greatest event in world sport and will also site the World Cup two years earlier.
8. The prospectus talks of redeveloping the decaying port area, and cleansing the polluted Guanabara Bay, but whereas Barcelona built its Olympic village in a derelict part of its port, in Rio it will be sited in Barra da Tijuca, a neighbourhood at the wealthiest end of the city. See 'Rio´s Expensive New Rings', *The Economist*, 8 October 2009.
9. 'Urban Age' conference, São Paulo, December 2008.
10. Juan Arias, 'Rio de Janeiro', *El País*, 1 December 2010.
11. Juan Arias, 'Un nuevo Río para 2016', *El País*, 5 October 2009.
12. Richard Neutra, *Architecture as Social Concern in Regions of Mild Climate*, Gerth Todtmann (Chicago), 1948, p 190.
13. Juan Arias, 'Rio de Janeiro', op cit. See also 'Rio de Janeiro, a Magic Moment for the City of Good', *The Economist*, 10 June 2010.
14. 'Brazil Takes Off', *The Economist*, 12 November 2009.

Text © 2011 John Wiley & Sons Ltd. Images: p 52(l) © RIO2016/BCMF Arquitetos; p 52(r) © RIO2016/BCMF Arquitetos/LUMO Arquitectura; pp 53-4 © Ramón Reverté Collection; pp 55, 57 © Augusto Roman; p 56 © Tatiana Bilbao

Jorge Mario Jáuregui

ARTICULATING THE BROKEN CITY AND SOCIETY

Jorge Mario Jáuregui of Metrópolis Projetos Urbanos (MPU) has been responsible for more than 20 projects for the Favela-Barrio (slum-to-neighbourhood) Programme implemented by the Rio de Janeiro city government, and two large-scale urban redevelopment projects for President Lula's PAC (Growth Acceleration Programme). Here Jáuregui describes the strategies behind his work and specifically the transformation of public space that was undertaken at the Complexo de Manguinhos in northern Rio as part of the PAC scheme.

Jorge Mario Jáuregui, Center for Generation of Work and Income, Rio de Janeiro, 2010
opposite: This building for the inhabitants of Complexo do Alemão and its surroundings includes a business incubator and support services for small businesses and entrepreneurs.

Jorge Mario Jáuregui, Complexo de Manguinhos, Rio de Janeiro, 2008
below: Masterplan.

Jorge Mario Jáuregui, Park-Library Manguinhos, Complexo de Manguinhos, Rio de Janeiro, 2010
bottom: External view of the Park-Library Manguinhos with relocation buildings and a public square.

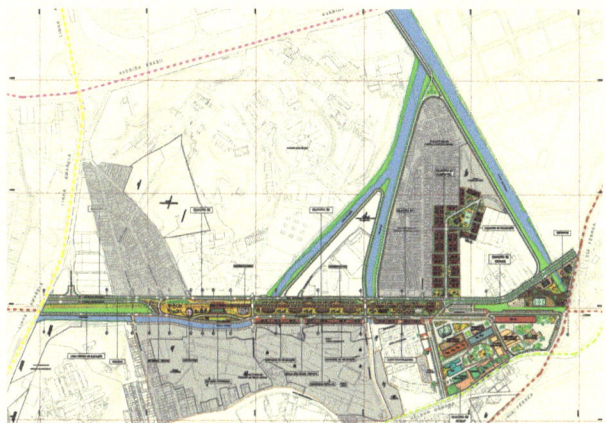

The contemporary metropolis is constantly moving between conflicts, contaminations, interferences, transformations, political decisions and economic interests. Today we recognise two conditions: on one hand, the intensification of urban issues – everything from urban violence and inequality between the formal and informal city, as in Rio de Janeiro, to endless suburban expansion and lack of power of the city centre, as in Bogotá, to the disconnection of parts and fragmentation of the city, as in Mexico City. On the other hand, the inevitable necessity of the coexistence of differences in which we must find a way to work together.

These contemporary conditions are manifested in three types of urban space:[1]

1 Spaces generated through a long process of accumulation and substitution, where the background of some architectural parts is unknown and other parts can be identified as having specific 'authors'. When the accumulation of functions and histories reaches a certain critical mass, it constitutes a recognisable identity. These urban sectors, identified as barrios (neighbourhoods), create a condition of structural regularity that defines them as visual pictures belonging to the city as a whole; for example, the neighbourhoods of Palermo in Buenos Aires or Urca in Rio de Janeiro.

2 Spaces that escape public control, which usually occupy great expanses and peripheries of cities constituting areas of impunity that have no traditional legal and juridical societal code. In some cases, action in this condition would require a certain degree of planning for disasters or war confrontations. To urbanise the peripheries and favelas (shantytowns) means to inscribe points of consistency and singularity with the capacity to produce wide-reaching effects in the communities and their surroundings. These pieces of the urban network – the favelas, which in many cases are not even registered in the city's plans, such as the Manguinhos Complex in Rio de Janeiro – depict the *noir* aspects of society. However, they can also be seen as spaces open to new possibilities for creativity, urban innovation and social experimentation. Places where what is 'in process' is in permanent experimentation.

> The studio of Metrópolis Projetos Urbanos (MPU) in Rio de Janeiro has been working on urbanisation projects in dozens of favelas around the city for the last 15 years.

3   Spaces produced at the will of a large corporation – be it national or multinational, public or private – which are organised around various spatial 'themes' such as the entertainment parks of Celebration, Florida, the international 'exhibition' of the Beijing Olympics in 2008, or the artificial revitalisation of the historical centre of the Pelourinho in Salvador, Brazil. These spaces are disconnected (whether voluntarily or not) from the urban structure, generally constituting what could be considered 'islands of fantasy' in the archipelago of the city.

Through a sequence of urban development projects in Rio de Janeiro – first the Favela-Barrio programme in 1995, then the urban development plans for the Manguinhos Complex and Alemão Complex in 2004, and the Programa de Acceleração do Crescimento (PAC), also the Growth Acceleration Programme, – established by President Luiz Inácio Lula da Silva (2007) and the ongoing development of PAC II, – it has been possible to create a reference base of strategies that address a wide range of urban-scale interventions. This knowledge of concepts and methods can be applied to similar situations in other Latin American countries.

The aim is to articulate the divided city and society by providing greater accessibility, investments in infrastructure, new public social facilities (such as hospitals, public libraries, technical schools, centres for the generation of work and income, and community and youth centres) and environmental revitalisation, connecting the formal and the informal parts, and thus improving the quality of life for residents.

The studio of Metrópolis Projetos Urbanos (MPU) in Rio de Janeiro has been working on urbanisation projects in dozens of favelas around the city for the last 15 years. The strategy and methodology it has put into practice for several of its projects – including the Manguinhos Complex (2010) – have consisted of various stages including: site visits to understand the genius loci and existing conditions to determine the appropriateness and feasibility of the proposal; listening to the 'desires' of the local residents (through the Freudian method of free association and fluctuant attention), and talking with different community representatives, local leaders and residents;[2] research into historical, cultural, economic, social and environmental conditions, as well as technical site surveys; envisioning the future potential of the site; establishing dialogues with significant institutions involved in the intervention area; considering the support of interdisciplinary input including education, health, transport, labour, legal aspects and housing; and formulating the 'urban scheme' by reinforcing existing focal points and introducing new ones to reconfigure the sense of place.

Psychoanalysis is an important instrument to help distinguish the manifest and latent desires of the inhabitants in the process. Architects have the ability and responsibility to propose an ideal to stretch the limits of expectation and imagination.

The Manguinhos Complex, Rio de Janeiro

The Manguinhos Complex is made up of 11 informal communities – favelas – with a total population of 32,000 residents on 400 hectares (1.5 square miles) of land. The project affects a broader area of the North Zone of the city, 1,400 hectares (5.4 square miles) in total, and intersects major access points for the city of Rio de Janeiro. The site includes a major highway and other principal roads, a river and a railway line. The railway line acts as a barrier, dividing the area into various disconnected fragments.

Historically, the complex is home to a variety of uses: old industrial parks, educational and research institutions, commercial areas and a portion of the principal port area. It is also a stronghold of one of the city's three drug-trafficking factions, and the neighbourhoods within the complex are subject to high levels of drug use, crime and violent police raids. The physical-territorial issues addressed by MPU's architectural approach for the project are symptoms of the reality of severe social problems.

The main challenge was to restructure an area historically stigmatised and environmentally degraded with a proposal that could be feasibly implemented under the PAC programme within the four-year term of the federal government, which took control of the process of urbanisation and formalisation of the large complexes of favelas in Rio, through PAC, in 2007. For the first time, the federal, state and municipal governments are working together and investing an unprecedented amount of money and resources in the favelas. The previous urbanisation programme, the Favela-Barrio, addressed these issues on a neighbourhood scale on a municipal level. PAC represents a similar urbanisation process, but on a significantly larger scale,

Jorge Mario Jáuregui, Rambla Manguinhos, Complexo de Manguinhos, Rio de Janeiro, 2008/2011
below: The train line is elevated, eliminating the division established by the existing walls in a place known locally as the 'Gaza Strip', and creating a permeable boundary instead.

Jorge Mario Jáuregui, Relocation buildings, Complexo de Manguinhos, Rio de Janeiro, 2010
bottom: Green public square between the relocation buildings.

By 2004, the MPU architecture team had completed masterplan proposals for two communities – Complexo do Alemão and Complexo do Manguinhos – and was thus selected to realise the projects under the PAC programme three years later.

working in areas that include a broader urban scale throughout the city, and with federal support and funding. Due to this large level of investment, physical, social and ecological issues can be addressed simultaneously, along with aspects of policing and public security. Numerous social programmes and efforts to regulate land tenure now run parallel to the physical architecture project.

By 2004, the MPU architecture team had completed masterplan proposals for two communities – Complexo do Alemão and Complexo do Manguinhos – and was thus selected to realise the projects under the PAC programme three years later. At Complexo do Alemão, the introduction of a cable-car system (to be inaugurated in 2011) will connect six of the *morros* (hills) and each station includes elements of social and economic interest such as small libraries, commercial spaces, classrooms and outdoor public gathering spaces. The project in Manguinhos elevates a divisive and dangerous railway line and transforms it into a linear park for recreation and commerce.

The first step in the proposal for Manguinhos was to define the boundaries of the area of intervention, and analyse and respond to its complex geographical (the convergence of a river, highway and railway line), topographical (treatment of edges of rivers, canals and landfills) and social (the complex social realities of life in Rio's favelas) aspects, such as the circulation and spatial patterns, and the established cultural and social conditions of both the informal and formal areas of the site. The team addressed the adjacent neighbourhoods in terms of accessibility, infrastructure and the reorganisation of urban nodes and centralities.

In addition to the overall development plan, the architects focused specifically on the area around Leopoldo Bulhões Avenue, the most conflict-ridden sector, known locally as the 'Gaza Strip', which was divided, both spatially and socially, by the railroad. The proposal elevates the railway to unite the two divided neighbourhoods with a linear public space underneath connecting the new civic centre with the Manguinhos train station. This public walkway, known as the Rambla, creates an active urban street facade along a major avenue and a new 24-hour transportation interchange connecting the train, bus, taxi, motorcycle taxi, van shuttle service and bicycle routes.

The new landscape design consists of a series of commercial kiosks and work spaces, areas for recreation, social meeting spaces, and abundant plantings and vegetation. It was inspired by the highly successful Flamengo Park, a linear waterfront park

Jorge Mario Jáuregui, Cable-car stations, Complexo do Alemão, Rio de Janeiro, 2011
opposite: Aerial view of the Complexo do Alemão and the cable-car stations.

Jorge Mario Jáuregui, Complexo do Alemão, Rio de Janeiro, 2008
below: Masterplan.

Jorge Mario Jáuregui, Relocation buildings, Complexo do Alemão, Rio de Janeiro, 2010
bottom: Relocation buildings constructed using ecological bricks.

in Rio de Janeiro designed by landscape architect Burle Marx (1965), which embodies the values of a modern democratic urban space, serving as a place of relaxation, recreation and culture for all to enjoy. The Rambla design carefully took into account the potential benefits and uses of different sectors of the local population: culture and recreation opportunities for children and families as well as commerce and income-generating activities for workers. Particular emphasis was placed on providing alternative activities for the local youths, who are all too often seduced into the prevalent drug-trafficking activities that unfortunately generate a large number of jobs in the low-income areas of the city.

This multifunctional programme at Manguinhos transforms a once dangerous and abandoned sector into an active public space, converting the site from divider to connector. It promotes a type of public space that has the power to act as a social articulator, integrating residents internally, within the favela, as well as externally with the larger city as a whole.

The existence of enormous areas in our cities where the inhabitants are excluded from the benefits of urbanity affects everybody. We know that when we try to exclude from ourselves something that we wish to expel, it always returns. However, we can broaden our horizons by recognising the limits and incorporating the excluded ones within our lives, within our cities and within the world. Whether it is the recycling of garbage, reforestation politics or the creation of conditions to generate work and income, the question remains the same: How can we reinsert humanity into ourselves through the recognition of the 'other'? ∆

Notes
1. These parts of the city remain unarticulated between each other, maintaining distance in their interaction. Thus, articulating the 'broken city' implies that we have to consider the intersection of physical aspects (urban, infrastructural and environmental), social aspects (economic, cultural) and ecological aspects (mental ecology, social ecology and environmental ecology).
2. The participation of local residents is usually organised into four stages: 1) an on-site meeting with representatives of the project team, at the beginning of the project; 2) exchange of local knowledge with community representatives in the first stages of the project design; 3) as informal inspectors, and labour during the construction process; 4) as representatives of community interests in the POUSO (Urban and Social Orientation Center) established by the city government to address potential conflicts after project completion.

Text © 2011 John Wiley & Sons Ltd. Images: photos © Jorge Jáuregui, photos Gabriel Jáuregui; drawings © MPU

FORMALISATION
AN INTERVIEW WITH HERNANDO DE SOTO

The Peruvian economist **Hernando de Soto** is internationally renowned for his writings on the informal economy. Through his work as the President of the Institute for Liberty and Democracy (ILD) in Lima, he has effectively advocated the creation of a legal system to help the poor access property rights. In his latest book, *The Amazon is not Avatar*, he makes a significant shift away from the problems caused by massive urban migrations to cities to focusing on the benefits of property and business rights for resource-rich indigenous communities in the Amazon. **Angus Laurie** interviews De Soto on his current thinking and highlights why he has had such an important influence on social housing in Latin America.

After a bloody conflict between indigenous Amazonians and national security forces on 5 June 2009, the remote Peruvian jungle community of Bagua was making international headlines.[1] The conflict started as a response to new policies providing petroleum, mineral and forestry companies with easier access to the resource wealth of the Amazon Basin.[2] The death of more than 30 people and injury of a further 155 marked with an exclamation mark the arrival of globalisation to the unprepared heart of Latin America.

This was a window into a region set to change immensely over the coming years.

Shortly after the clash, the Peruvian economist Hernando de Soto travelled through the region to discover the roots of the conflict. De Soto is the president and founder of the Institute for Liberty and Democracy (ILD), a Lima-based think tank devoted to property and business rights reform in developing countries, and his findings will form the content for his forthcoming book, *The Amazon is not Avatar*.[3] His new work marks a departure from the problems caused by massive migration into the cities throughout the developing world to the benefits of property and business rights in the predominantly rural Amazon – and similar resource-rich indigenous communities elsewhere in Latin America and Africa.[4]

James Cameron's film *Avatar* (2009) serves De Soto as a useful metaphor; but unlike in the film, he does not think leaving the region alone is a viable option. Firstly, most of the miners are informal and come from the region itself. Secondly, he says the Amazonians 'should not be treated as museum pieces, and I believe that those who say leave them alone – maybe that argument was relevant 450 years ago. I'm not saying it was correct to do what the Spaniards did, or what the Republic did. I'm not saying that at all. But the fact is we've got what we've got. And at this time, most of them are talking about integration: integrating into modernity so that they, too, can start and grow businesses, protect those assets, afford a decent education for their children and healthcare.

'[People] talk about them as if they were living in splendid isolation. They are not living in splendid isolation. They are already integrated in the Peruvian economy, and they've got the raw side of the deal. I'm sure there must be a few tribes who are isolated and don't want to integrate, and that's fine. But again, they still need rights, otherwise somebody's going to come and take away from them the valuable natural resources they have that could benefit their communities – the gas, lumber and agricultural land.'

According to De Soto, all Peru's Amazonian communities are currently in litigation,[5] and their lack of property rights or titles leaves them in a precarious position. A great deal of resource wealth is being discovered in their areas, and they are at risk of not benefiting from this boon as they do not understand, or indeed have, a system of law which protects them. They are living 'extralegally', without the legal tools that we take for granted: property rights, formats for organising their businesses productively, ways to expand their markets.

For De Soto: 'There is no possibility of progress unless they have their rights well spelt out.' This is what he means by 'legally empowering the poor'.

In contrast to expert-led consultation, where outsiders advise local people on what they need, De Soto is trying to draw the Amazonian communities into a position where they can propose things on their own, giving them a level of legal autonomy that would allow them to govern – and to prosper from – their region. His goal is to help the people of this volatile region to adapt, and to provide them with the tools necessary to participate and direct how globalisation will affect their lives. While De Soto is not against government or NGO provision of physical infrastructure such as roads, sewerage or electricity, he says they do not help in getting communities organised in a way to protect their assets and benefit economically from their natural resources. Organisation will come through a process that begins with holding legal titles for land, resources or businesses. In this way, people can participate in the judiciary with legitimate documents in order to resolve disputes. This will help to empower remote communities and bring them closer to democratic participation.

Once organised in this way, the Amazonian people 'can even start getting to their own natural resources. I mean here you've got these big mining companies and big oil companies. What's the difference between those and the indigenous people? That the big companies are organised in legal ways that make them productive – and prosperous. That's the difference … What [the indigenous] have got is land, and the bushes that grow on land, and that's what they fight and die for. So first of all, why not give them control. The advantage of doing that is it's an exercise that allows them to understand the importance of organisation and rules.'

Some have criticised this aspect of De Soto's work, claiming that titles will weaken the position of indigenous people in settling disputes. They argue that De Soto is parcelling land and therefore dividing indigenous communities in their fight against would-be invaders.[6] Furthermore, some state that land in the Amazon is generally held communally, and that parcelling land goes against indigenous people's cultural identity.[7]

For De Soto, these critiques miss the main point: 'Essentially, as time has gone by, the concern is not so much private property as such or even public property, but the importance of being precise about control. In other words, I really, deep inside, don't very much care if people decide to organise something collectively or they do privately. For me the important thing is … how much of your destiny can you control if you live in a world where the law asks you for definitions and you have none.'

De Soto goes on to explain that the 'so-called collective rights' held by the Amazonian people are not property rights, but have to do with giving a form of sovereignty to certain ethnic groups or communities. The problem with community organisation through these collective rights is that there are around 5,000 communities in the Amazon. 'How successful

Entrance to the Torres de San Borja (completed in 1983), one of the large-scale social housing projects initiated by ex-President Fernando Belaúnde Terry (in power between 1963 and 1968, and 1980 and 1985). The project was predominantly residential, with segregated movement of pedestrians and cars through an internal network of pedestrian-only streets.

> De Soto's work is decidedly in the realm of economics and law; yet here he is being featured in an architecture publication. His relevance spreads well beyond the immediate field of his work into policy, housing and urbanism.

do you think you're going to be with 5,000 sovereign systems with an average of between 200 and 250 people per sovereign system?' he asks. 'Do you really want to be sovereign on such a small scale? What does that do to your economics, what does that do to your capacity for getting organised productively?'

For De Soto, then, it is not just about property rights: it is about control. The people of the Amazon have no control over their territory. They need to be legally empowered to take advantage of what they already have.

De Soto's work is decidedly in the realm of economics and law; yet here he is being featured in an architecture publication. His relevance spreads well beyond the immediate field of his work into policy, housing and urbanism. He says that the self-built informal cities of Latin America were admirable and beautiful, but very expensive for their inhabitants. The cost of informal self-construction is three times as high as the same construction carried out by a developer. For this reason, in *The Mystery of Capital* he advocates the development of mass housing for the poor through economies of scale, where inhabitants could build more for less cost, and receive titles and utilities from the inception of their project.[8]

This idea, along with De Soto's broader work in providing titles, has influenced how city governments and architects approach housing issues in Latin America and throughout the world. In Mexico City, for example, recent housing policies have tried to reduce the amount of self-built construction, and to lower construction costs for poorer residents through economies of scale, create jobs and allow a new group to enter into the capital market.[9] This is done through the government's Prosavi programme, which provides mortgages for families who earn less than five times the minimum wage. The construction of the actual houses is done for profit by developers who build small houses, provide infrastructure, give titles and help negotiate mortgages for potential buyers. Images from these projects show rows of identical detached houses stretching across vast areas of the city. They have been criticised by the Mexican architect Arturo Ortiz Struck among others for selling 'credit rather than housing', leaving some families indebted for years with a final cost more than three times that of the original house.

Alejandro Aravena from Elemental in Chile has also quoted and taken inspiration from De Soto's work, the result being something totally the opposite of the housing projects of Mexico (see pp 32–7). Elemental's Quinta Monroy project in Iquique provides a flexible design where units are constructed as a shell left for residents to finish over time. The design facilitates a wide range of uses and inhabitants, and judging from the metamorphosis of the housing units since their inception, they have been a success.

On being shown one photo of Quinta Monroy and another of a mass housing project in Mexico to illustrate how his ideas

opposite top: Mototaxis wait for a fare outside the informal market in San Juan de Miraflores, one of Lima's many informal *barrios jovenes*.

opposite bottom: Example of an informal, self-built house in Medalla Milagrosa, one of Lima's consolidated informal *pueblos jovenes*.

below: Main public space at the San Felipe housing development (completed in 1966) in Lima. Photograph by Philippe Gruenberg and Pablo Hare.

bottom: Arturo Ortiz produced and handed out these four stickers as a critical political statement against mass affordable housing programmes in Mexico (2009).

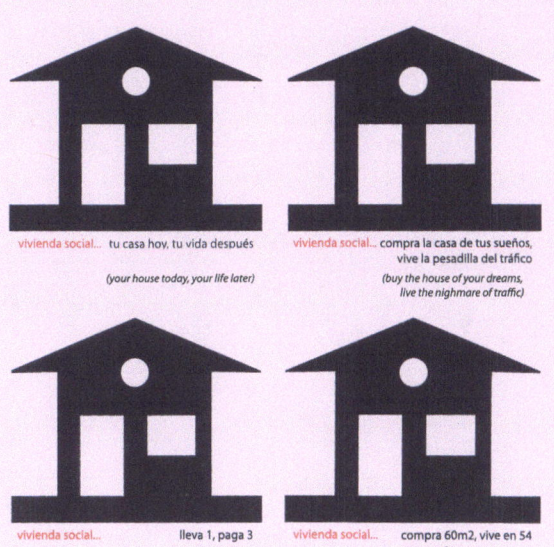

are being made manifest, De Soto recalled another occasion when he was presented with two similarly contrasting photos: 'I remember talking to [the Peruvian ex-] President Belaúnde when our ideas first started coming out and he called me in. He was a trained architect and an eminent public housing specialist, and he brought out a big picture and said, "This is something I've done – the Torres de San Borja – and this is the kind of thing that you're promoting". He showed me an informal settlement, a Lima shantytown, and said, "What do you think about these two pictures?"

'I replied, "Well you're looking for a fight … so I like the informal settlement better." He asked why, to which I responded: "To begin with, the thing that you did before, Residencial San Felipe, you did it for these people – supposedly the poorest – and after two years 90 per cent of them had moved out … because you didn't figure out right the social housing. It was too expensive for them. They would have rather had part of that income go towards a smaller house, probably not so well located, but also have an automobile, or have some education. So that's why 90 per cent moved out in two years. That's a lot of moving out." So the question is, how much demand can you satisfy according to a government's idea of what looks like an orderly city?

'But I tell you, I don't go into those things. What I do go into is the general idea that you've got to ask what [people] want, and it's never exactly what you would like them to have.' ∆

Notes
1. Simon Romero, 'Protesters Gird for Long Fight Over Opening Peru's Amazon', *The New York Times*, 11 June 2009.
2. Simon Romero, '9 Hostage Officers Killed at Peruvian Oil Facility', *The New York Times*, 6 June 2009.
3. Due to be published by Grupo Editorial Norma in Autumn 2011.
4. Fourteen years have passed since the publication of *The Other Path*, the book that launched De Soto into international recognition. It was a direct challenge to the terrorist movement The Shining Path and largely invalidated the terrorists' claims that Peru's poor lived communally. The conflict in Bagua is a reminder that there is still underlying frustration among Peru's poor. Hernando de Soto, *The Other Path*, Harper & Row (New York), 1989.
5. Unless otherwise stated, all figures and quotes are from Hernando de Soto during his interview with the author on 23 September 2010.
6. Argument of Margarita Benevides of the Instituto de Bien Comun (IBC) from her interview with Ricardo Marapi in the video *El Misterio de Hernando de Soto*; CEPES Peru, Lima, September 2009.
7. Ibid.
8. Hernando de Soto, *The Mystery of Capital*, Basic Books (New York), 2000, p 194. De Soto also writes in *The Mystery of Capital* that elites will benefit financially through housing reform that brings the extralegal into the formal market. The Mexican housing developer, Consorcio ARA, proves this point, having made a return of 25 per cent on its progressive units (under $20,000) and 29 per cent on affordable housing units (under $35,000) in 2005. See www.consorcioara.com.mx.
9. Housing Situation in Mexico, 2005, Centro de Investigacion y Documentacion de la Casa (CIDOC) and Sociedad Hipotecaria Federal. See www.jchs.harvard.edu/publications/international/som2005.pdf.

Text © 2011 John Wiley & Sons Ltd. Images: p 64 © Hernando de Soto; pp 65-6 © Angus Laurie; p 67(t) © Philippe Gruenberg & Pablo Hare; p 67(b) © Arturo Ortiz Struck/ Taller Territorial de México

Gary Leggett

This map shows some of the failed agendas discussed in the article: Herman Khan's 'great lakes' proposal, Ford's rubber towns, Roosevelt's expedition, as well as current projects, such as the Transoceanic Highway and the Inambari Dam Project.

PLAYGROUNDS
RADICAL FAILURE IN THE AMAZON

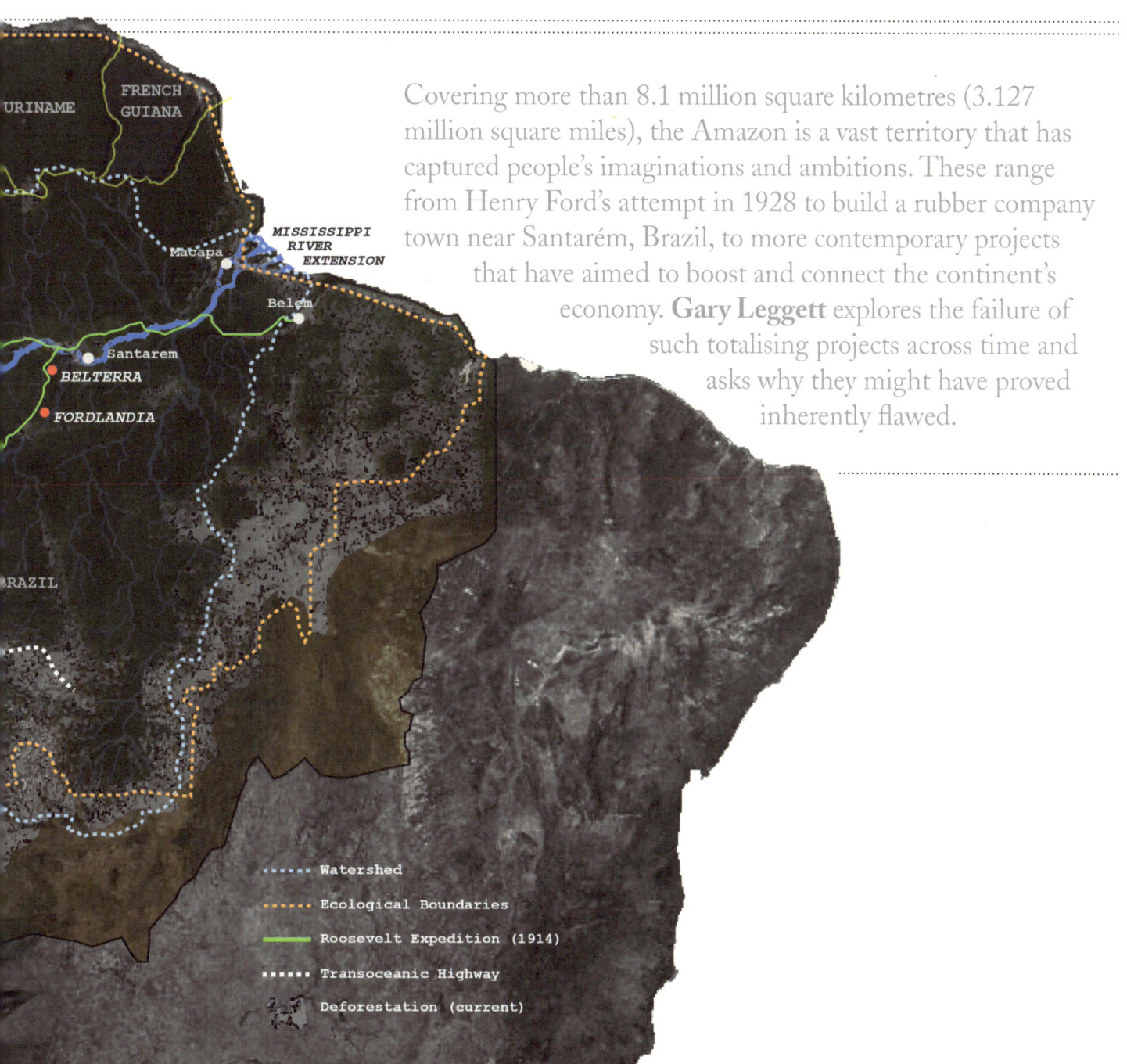

Covering more than 8.1 million square kilometres (3.127 million square miles), the Amazon is a vast territory that has captured people's imaginations and ambitions. These range from Henry Ford's attempt in 1928 to build a rubber company town near Santarém, Brazil, to more contemporary projects that have aimed to boost and connect the continent's economy. **Gary Leggett** explores the failure of such totalising projects across time and asks why they might have proved inherently flawed.

Fordlandia houses on Riverside Avenue, Fordlandia, Brazil, c 1933.

Stanley Kubrick based part of Dr Strangelove's character on the well-known neocon strategist and thermonuclear tsar Herman Khan, a theorist at the RAND Corporation, founder of the Hudson Institute and coiner of Kubrick's Doomsday Machine. In 1965, Khan proposed the creation of five 'great lakes' – South America's own Third Coast – in the Amazon Basin.

Dr Strangelove's closing remark in his namesake film of 1964 comes right before the world presumably ends. He stands up from his wheelchair, addressing the president (*Mein Führer! I can walk!*), and the film cuts abruptly to a sequence of atomic blasts. A bomb is jockeyed overseas by a wild-eyed pilot. Dr Strangelove bursts out, right before the nuke hits the ground: *Sir! I have a plan!*

Stanley Kubrick based part of Dr Strangelove's character on the well-known neocon strategist and thermonuclear tsar Herman Khan, a theorist at the RAND Corporation, founder of the Hudson Institute and coiner of Kubrick's Doomsday Machine. In 1965, Khan proposed the creation of five 'great lakes' – South America's own Third Coast – in the Amazon Basin.[1] The initiative was meant to curb the expansion of communism in Latin America and shore up local economies with a steady flow of hydropower; a single dam, 30 to 50 kilometres (18.6 to 31 miles) long, would have produced around a quarter of the US-installed electrical capacity. The idea never came to a head, of course; it was intended more as a casual napkin sketch than a full-blown development plan based on a napkin sketch (as was Brasilia).

In any case, this kind of totalising gesture was not uncommon. The list of failed projects and proposals for the Amazon is eye-dryingly long. Theodore Roosevelt organised an expedition there in 1914 with his son Kermit – a kind of rite of passage, we assume, into Teddy's Rough Rider manhood – and among other things (15 pages of poisonous snake talk, for one), Roosevelt wrote that the Amazon, if properly reined in, would make for a generous food basket or global manufacturing centre.[2] He almost died of a flesh-eating bacterial infection during the trip.

Years before, Matthew Fontaine Maury, the US Navy lieutenant-cum-cartographer, astronomer, historian, meteorologist, geologist, oceanographer and all-round Confederate powerhouse, writing under the pen name 'Inca', claimed that the Amazon Basin was 'but a continuation of the Mississippi valley', an appendage, a natural extension of the Union's interrupted destiny: 'What one lacks, the other supplies. Together, they furnish all those products and staples which complete the list of articles in the circle of commerce.'[3] One of Maury's more unhinged proposals was to relocate Confederate slave-owners to the Amazon Basin, arguing that in the same way that the Mississippi valley had been 'the escape valve for the slaves of the Northern States, so will the Amazon valley be to that of the Miss'.[4]

What we begin to see then are variations on a theme, a kind of do-it-yourself Manifest Destiny that will use the Amazon, time and again, as a projection screen or fairy-tale mirror writ large. The sheer size of it – 8.1 million square kilometres (3.127 million square miles), occupying 60 per cent of the total area of the eight Amazonian countries, 6 per cent of the planet's land surface, and holding 25 per cent of the world's water supply – produces the illusion of an infinite field of speculation.[5] And so the list of failed projects goes on and on: missionaries, entrepreneurs, explorers, presidents, Nazis, environmentalists, all chipping in on one of the globe's longest-standing debacles.

The Crudest Machine in the World

But perhaps the best example of ideological failure (or inadvertent self-critique) that transpired in the Amazon is Henry Ford's attempt in 1928 to build a rubber company town near Santarém, Brazil, a couple of hours downriver from Manaus. Ford sent the Michigan-based botanist Carl LaRue to 'find a good area somewhere to plant rubber' in an effort to free his company from British-owned Asian rubber (vertical integration, Ford *dixit*).[6] The town was developed to the image of an American suburb – it looks a bit like Frank Lloyd Wright's Broadacre City (1932) from the air – and no sooner had the first foundations been built and the first batch of trees than planted things began to go awry. Within the first year, a diehard fungus ravaged nearly 607 hectares (1,500 acres) of *Hevea* trees, thriving in the crop's monoculture.[7] It was quickly concluded that LaRue, despite his expertise in Midwestern plant life, had 'picked the wrong place'.[8] The town was relocated a couple of miles downriver to Belterra in the hope that a better location would yield better crops, but it didn't.

The Taylorist perfection of Fordlandia was ill-equipped to deal with the social and environmental demands of the Amazon.[9] 'Paved roads, cement walks, comfortable homes, electric lights, telephones – this might be any Midwestern town. But it is Belterra, buried deep in the jungle of Brazil … Yes, there is even a golf course – a sporty 18 holes … Beautiful clubhouse, tropical foliage – and 700 miles from civilization.'[10] Sure enough, shanties began to spread along the river, clustered around the town, just past the 18th hole, like blight on *Hevea* leaves, and the inviolability of Ford's private Eden was swiftly shattered. 'If anybody had any property right where we were going to clear,' claimed one of Ford's emissaries, 'their land would just be purchased and they would be moved elsewhere.'[11]

Intra muros, the town was hardly the agro-industrial utopia it was made to be. 'In a program reflecting Ford's back-to-the-earth philosophy, workers were encouraged to grow their own vegetables for a healthy and well-rounded diet,' which included banning the consumption of alcohol and replacing milk with soya milk (because Ford hated cows, 'the crudest machine in the world').[12] But there was only so much soya milk his employees were willing to gulp down before they snapped. A riot broke out when the company tried to install a cafeteria system in order to shorten lunchtime breaks: 'As the workers filed down the serving line with trays for the first time, one of them suddenly stopped and shouted, "I'm a worker, not a waiter!"'[13] The final stroke came with the widespread commercialisation of synthetic rubber in 1944, though by this time it was already clear that the project was a total failure even if it was touted, like Mao's Dazhai Village in the 1960s, as a model 'to learn from' and to follow.

What Fordlandia revealed, or rather reiterated, was not only the inhospitable nature of the Amazon rainforest but also, by attempting to reproduce an order that was by any measure foreign to the Amazon and its inhabitants, it exposed several flaws (overlooked assumptions, really) in the Fordist model. For one, a labourer is not always, under any circumstance a consumer of his own labour. Ford's Five Dollar Day initiative, even if brought down to local standards (37 cents a day), was a huge flop in Amazonia. Most plantation workers would live in Fordlandia for a couple of months, enough time to rake in a year's worth of income, and then head back to their homes, miles away, sometimes not even in the Amazon, to live off their earnings. The Fordist model, extricated from the American context, lost its Samsonian brawn. It failed to provide a vertical order to an otherwise horizontal, diffused reality. The land was sold back to the Brazilian government at 3 per cent of its estimated value. Ford never visited Fordlandia. A thousand cattle now graze on its golf course.[14]

Continental Drifts

Today we have a string (though calling it a string may be too generous; it is more like a puzzle of jagged edges assembled in the dark by a group of drunk nine-year-olds with ADHD and hammers) of infrastructural projects, social movements, extractive operations, global investments, conservation efforts and illegal activities that have transformed the Amazon into one big steamy soup of speculation. One of the 500-plus projects that the so-called Initiative for the Integration of Regional Infrastructure in South America (IIRSA) comprises

Gary Leggett, P.A.I.D (Project in Assistance of International Disasters), Jan Van Eyck Academie and Yale University, 2010
opposite: The sequence of image describes a proposal to transform the Amazon into a giant virtual billboard. By overlaying a grid on an area with overlapping jurisdictions and interests (oil blocks, native communities, deforestation, national parks, and so on), a zero-level value map is generated based on the number of conflicting claims in each cell. The resulting matrix serves as the basis for an online initiative that allows users to buy and bid for real-estate using aerial images of the Amazon as an interface. The funds accrued by the initiative would subsidise conservation and energy projects within the pixel area or elsewhere (even outside the Amazon). Constant updates of aerial images would allow for a near real-time follow-up on such investments.

– projects that are meant to bolster and connect the continent's economy, Fitzcarraldo-style – is a highway dubbed the Road to China (officially, the Transoceanic Highway), which bisects the Amazon, connecting Brazil to the Pacific seaboard. The highway has not been yet completed and the Peruvian Ministry of Energy and Mining is already spearheading (reviving, really) an initiative to build a dam, the fourth largest in the continent, over 110 kilometres (68.3 miles) of unfinished road.[15] Brazil needs hydropower. It also needs to get its soya to China. The solution: flood your own roads. Build a railway instead. Maybe an elevated highway. Or a soya milk-powered hydroelectric plant with a floating cattle ranch and a jungle theme park. Because that is what integration means these days: do whatever you have to do to keep the continent spit-stuck together, like a political Pangaea, and make sure it doesn't drift too far into the left. God forbid.

Part of the problem lies in how scales are defined. The local is only the local if there is a set of rules and conventions that makes the category useful and practicable, and differentiable from any other particular definition of scale. But there is, of course, an inherent fuzziness in this procedure; we cannot cleanly cut off any political action according to its imagined structure (say, a national park), nor can we say that something only occurs at a given scale. So in this sense, when we are dealing with a territory like the Amazon that defies easy categorisation or is really a patchwork of jurisdictions and constituencies conflicting with each other, it is hard to use words like 'local', 'regional' and 'global' in a meaningful or accurate way. When projects are 'locally' deployed, they rarely go beyond a half-baked environmental impact statement or a ready-made commission to pocket outside funds. And when the initiative does comes from the central government, as it sometimes does, it comes as a far cry, a technocratic echo, quickly dampened by the exactions of everyday life.

A major flaw with Peruvian economist Hernando de Soto's position regarding the Amazon (see pp 64–7) is precisely that in an attempt to debunk certain myths that for him stand in the way of progress, he reinforces such a disconnect, revealing, by way of disguise, his own myths in the process. His arguments in favour of land titles – that is, that property titles provide poor individuals access to credit and free enterprise – reinforce an idea that now seems dated: namely, that the market is already there, that it is a latent attribute of collective life, inescapable and omnipresent, natural, like ether, and that we can, or rather should, allow it to express itself. This is pure ideology – as ideological as claiming that indigenous communities are better off in voluntary isolation. Amazonian communities are not poor because they do not have land titles. Some of the poorest ones, in fact, do. They are poor – trapped in poverty, that is – because they lack the conditions, the framework, the territorial requirements that would even make a land title useful. This does not imply, by extension, that we should try to change such conditions to fit the purported usefulness of a land title, but rather, that we should see in what ways the current fabric of these communities raise different, more positive, approaches to development.

This has little to do with an indigenous people's so-called worldview. The whole armature of their subsistence does not allow for an easy 'transition' (a politically correct way of saying they are pretty much hurled into the global economy); that we can all agree upon. However, to think that what facilitates the movement of capital in one setting, namely property titles and legal institutions, can be readily transposed to another, producing similar results (which are not exactly golden) is a bit facile. Who is it, after all, that seeks to have the upper hand here: the locals, who are mostly migrants anyway (some cities, like Puerto Maldonado in the Peruvian Amazon, see a 15-person-per-day migration rate from the Andes), or the central state, whose policies have time and again failed to include (involve, engage) the Amazon in its nation-building/resource-extracting efforts?[16] And if it is the latter, why do we pretend otherwise?

Besides, there is no such thing as an Amazonian community. No sample is representative enough. De Soto conjures up the Second Law of Thermodynamics along with Charles Darwin's 'warm little pond' and Aristotle's concept of 'abiogenesis' or spontaneous generation (mice come from dirty hay, moths from the air pockets between sheets, and so on) to make the point that indigenous communities have to behave more like permeable membranes, in accordance with natural laws, that is, if they are to survive the globalist siege (he calls it the globalist 'tide').[17] This simply distracts us from the main point: that the siege itself has to be addressed as a totalising failure and one that is good (read: successful) at sustaining itself. And while De Soto may say, with good reason, that illegal activities such as small-scale mining and informal logging account for some of the more insidious threats the Amazon faces today, there is no reason to believe that well-regulated large-scale operations will actually produce, *in toto*, a rosier outcome.

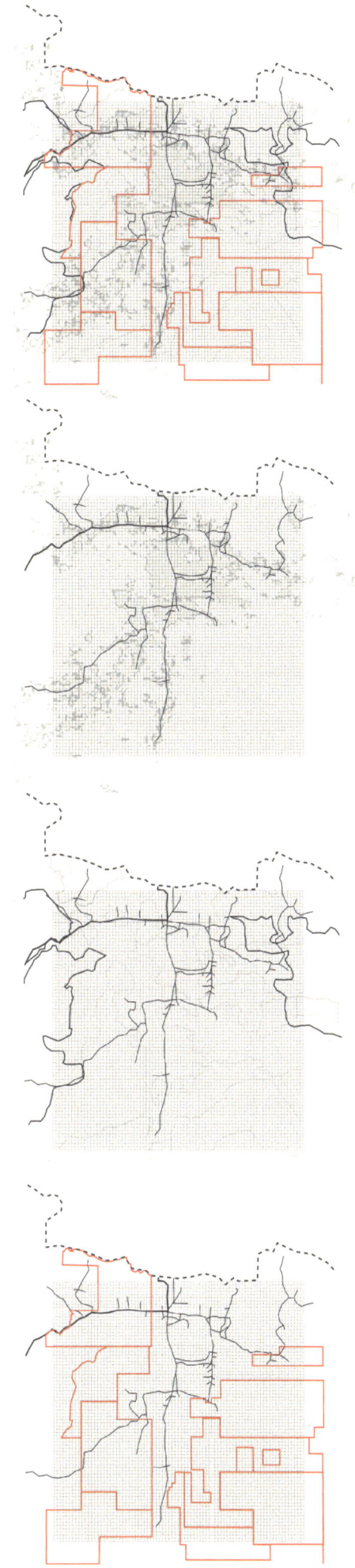
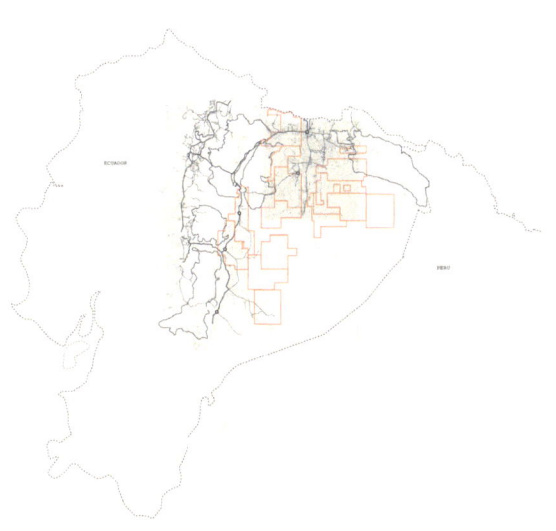

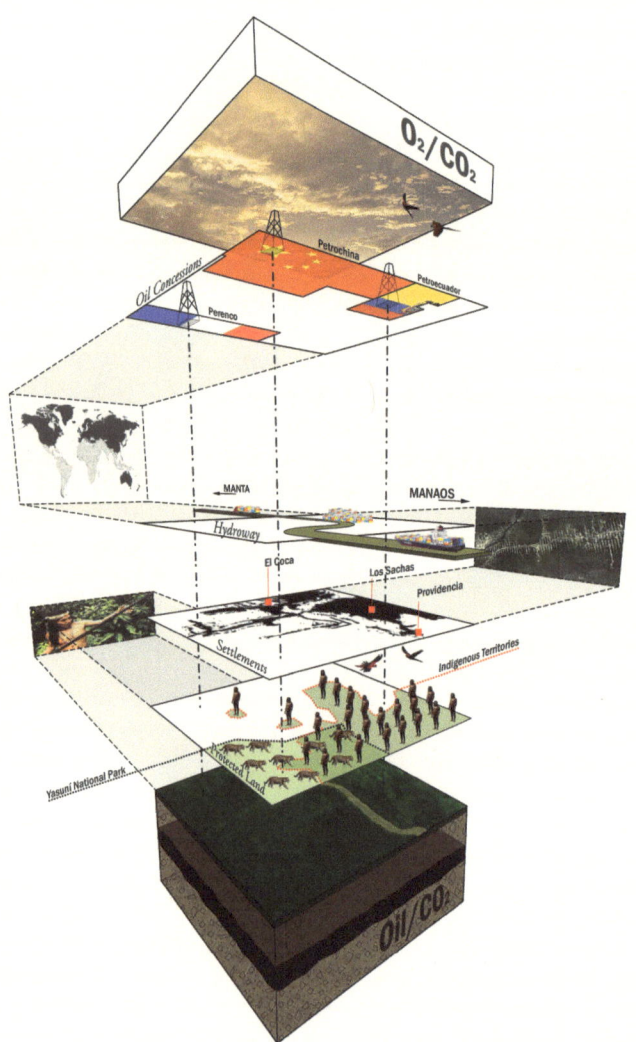

Santiago del Hierro and Gary Leggett,
Planes of Violence, 2010
Sectional perspective depicting the layering
of conflicting jurisdictions – oil blocks,
native reserves, national parks – on a
single patch of land.

What seems far more interesting is to ask what forms of failure we are actually talking about. Who or what fails exactly? Nature, technology, language? Is there anything not failing that we should be paying more attention to? Are there better ways of being destructive? Do all deforestation patterns necessarily produce negative feedback effects? Apparently not. A recent paper by a meteorologist at the University of Illinois at Urbana-Champaign tries 'to reconcile the discrepancy between the decrease in precipitation predicted by general circulation models and the observed increase in precipitation due to specific deforestation patterns, like fishbone deforestation, which [paradoxically] produce more clouds and rain over the deforested patches.'[18] But is there really a middle ground between development and conservation or is this only a useful myth that validates the debate's polarity and hence its bias towards development? 'The danger here,' David Harvey writes, 'is of accepting, often without knowing it, concepts that preclude radical critique. One of the most pervasive and difficult to surmount barriers … is that which insists on separating out "nature" and "society" as coherent entities.'[19] In the case of De Soto, the danger – his weakness – lies in using one as the metaphor for the advancement of the other.

Nature Morte

Consider the architectural rendering. Trees are cut, feathered and pasted with such ease and confidence that it makes nature seem like an exercise in ornament. We spray-paint trees on our facades, we vegetate our roofs and walls, we render a view, a moment, a snapshot of a process of change that is, for lack of a better word, natural, and we say to ourselves, apodictically: Nature. Nature is what is natural.

But it is also dead. In his critique of Malthus, Harvey addresses the question of natural limits: 'To say that scarcity resides in nature and that natural limits exist is to ignore how scarcity is socially produced [I would add, in the line of Robert Nozick, that it is only socially produced insofar as it is ostensibly tied to a market price] and how limits are a social relation within nature (including human society) rather than some externally imposed necessity.'[20] Any view that defines nature as a superstructure, framing and controlling human activity, sustains the illusion that there is in fact something inherently natural about it, some thing-in-itself or Holy Ghost that draws necessary limits to our growth and feeds, at once, our sense of progress.

The question of scale is inextricably linked to this problem. Nature, as substance or essence or what-have-you, is predicated on the assumption that there is in fact such a thing as continuity between measurable phenomena. Things happen *there* only if they also happen *here*. Everything (as every *thing*) is only qualitatively different if it is quantitatively variable. But this also glosses over an important ontological distinction: the possibility that certain phenomena become entirely different animals when observed at different scales or, more precisely, when described as occurring in distinct spaces (registers, conventions) of representation.

Instead of assuming, then, that an economic community is empowered and able to transcend itself, to navigate between scales, simply by virtue of holding legal tenancy over its land (the degree zero of capital accumulation, let's say), it seems far more interesting to ask how such titles could be spatially arranged or distributed to ensure more radical results. We could imagine, for example, that certain state incentives, like standpipes and power lines, the infrastructural blueprint of a community, could be laid out in predetermined areas (*squat here!*), producing – pardon the expression – more efficient results than a single damp 80-gram A4 document stamped a posteriori by a man who could not care less what you do with your new-found right. The point is that titles, in and of themselves, do not guarantee anything if they do not, at once, dictate and reconfigure the behaviour of the group that gives them sense in the first place.

If there is an underlying theme to the problems discussed so far, it would therefore have to be this: whether we think of nature, capital, culture, politics or any other broad-brush category we use to describe processes that are essentially formless, the problem lies in our assuming that there is something intrinsically whole in the world simply because it can be described. The Amazon is one example among many – albeit of an exceptional size – where our assumptions about human development, assumptions that depend on such categorical wholeness, can hardly hold their own. And if there is anything positive about the failures we have encountered here it is precisely that, in an effort to foist order on to the world, they have added a layer of disjunction, distance and self-reference to the very chaos they sought to tame. ⌁

Notes
1. Michael Goulding, Nigel JH Smith and Dennis J Mahar, *Floods of Fortune: Ecology and Economy Along the Amazon*, Columbia University Press (New York), 1996, p 47.
2. Theodore Roosevelt, *Through the Brazilian Wilderness*, Charles Scribner's Sons (New York), 1914.
3. As quoted in Hilgard O'Reilly Sternberg, '"Manifest Destiny" and the Brazilian Amazon: A Backdrop to Contemporary Security and Development Issues', *CLAG Yearbook* 13, 1987, p 26. Lansford Warren Hastings, a fellow Southerner, did follow up on Maury's ideas and founded a settlement of Confederate emigrants in 1867 in Santarém. Needless to say, it was a failure.
4. See Matthew Fontaine Maury, 'The Amazon, and the Atlantic Slopes of South America: A Series of Letters Published in the National Intelligencer and Union Newspapers, Under the Signature of "Inca"' [1853], Cornell University Library, Digital Collections, August 2010.
5. 8.1 million square kilometres corresponds to the definition of Greater Amazonia according to three criteria: political, ecological and hydrographic boundaries. See *Geo-Amazonia: Perspectivas del Medio Ambiente en la Amazonía*, The United Nations Environment Program, Organización del Tratado de Cooperación Amazónica, Centro de Investigación de la Universidad del Pacífico, 2009, p 38.
6. 'In 1922 the British Stevenson Plan restricted Asian plantation rubber exports by means of cooperation between British and French planters. Thus they created an artificial rubber shortage and inflated the price of this commodity on the international market.' John Galey, 'Industrialist in the Wilderness: Henry Ford's Amazon Venture', *Journal of Interamerican Studies and World Affairs*, Vol 21, No 2, May 1979,7.'Grown in their natural environment, rubber trees are protected from the spread of the disease by the shelter of other plant life and the distance between them. Ford, having planted the trees in rows on barren land, could not stop the fungus once it started.' Elizabeth Esch, 'Shades of Tarzan!: Ford on the Amazon', *Cabinet*, Issue 7: Failure, Summer 2002.
8. The quote is by one Dr Emerick Szilagyi, a Henry Ford Hospital surgeon who ran the Fordlandia plantation hospitals in Amazonia from 1942 to 1945, in reference to the location chosen by Carl LaRue to build the town.
9. See Greg Grandin, *Fordlandia: The Rise and Fall of Henry Ford's Forgotten Jungle City*, Picador (New York), 2009.
10. Esch, op cit.
11. Grandin, op cit, p 110.
12. Galey, op cit, p 268. For Ford's low opinion of cows, see See Grandin, op cit, p 60.
13. Galey, op cit, p 277.
14. Fordlandia and Belterra, valued at $8 million, were sold back to the Brazilian government for $244,200 in 1945. Grandin, op cit, pp 350, 360.
15. The Inambari Dam Project. See Bank Information Center at www.bicusa.org/en/Project.aspx?id=10078.
16. The statistic was gathered in an interview with the regional president of Madre de Dios in November 2008. The National Statistics Institute (INEI) can only vouch for annual population rates across the entire Peruvian basin, which it estimates above the national population growth rate. See *Geo-Amazonia*, op cit, p 68.
17. Hernando de Soto, 'La Amazonia no es Avatar', *El Comercio*, 5 June 2010.
18. See Somnath Baidya Roy, 'Mesoscale Vegetation-Atmosphere Feedbacks in Amazonia', *Journal of Geophysical Research*, Vol 114, D20111, 2009.
19. David Harvey, *Justice, Nature and the Geography of Difference*, Blackwell Publishers (Cambridge, MA), 1996, p 140.
20. Ibid, p 147.

Text © 2011 John Wiley & Sons Ltd. Images: pp 68-9, 73 © Gary Leggett; p 60 © The Henry Ford Collection; p 74 © Gary Leggett and Santiago del Hierro

URBAN RESPONSES TO CLIMATE CHANGE IN LATIN AMERICA
REASONS, CHALLENGES AND OPPORTUNITIES

Cities in Latin America have a crucial role to play in climate change. Urban areas are the main emitters of greenhouse gases, while being vulnerable to severe weather conditions such as floods, heat waves and tropical storms that environmental shifts are expected to trigger. **Patricia Romero-Lankao** outlines the background to greenhouse gas emissions and climate change, while highlighting how development in Latin America presents unique opportunities for mitigating potential damage to the environment.

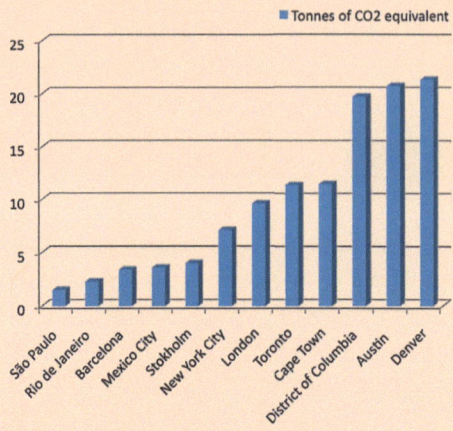

The world currently faces a very dangerous threat if strong action is not undertaken to reduce greenhouse gases (GHGs) and promote more sustainable patterns of development. Urban areas in Latin America play crucial roles in the climate change arena, not only as key sources of greenhouse gases, but also as hot spots of vulnerability to floods, heat waves and other hazards that climate change is expected to aggravate. These roles create a unique opportunity for urban mitigation and adaptation responses.

Urban GHG Emissions

Cities are key sources of GHGs. Yet just as Latin American cities have followed unique paths of development, they also follow trajectories of emissions that are different from, and often lower than, those prevailing in other nations. For instance, carbon emissions per capita in Austin, Texas, and the District of Columbia are 6- to 20-fold those in São Paulo, Rio de Janeiro and Mexico City

Different factors account for the diverse levels and sources of urban GHG emissions. Cities such as Rio de Janeiro and São Paulo have lower levels of emissions not only because they are located towards the tropics, thus requiring less energy for heating purposes, but also because they depend

on hydropower as a key source of energy. The lower level of economic development of Rio de Janeiro and Mexico City lies behind their relatively lower per capita emissions compared to those of Los Angeles and Denver. (The respective GDP per capita of the four cities are US$12,087, US$13,470, US$44,114 and US$40,031).[1] Equally important factors, however, are urban form, transportation layout, technologies and wider governance settings.

The Urban Face of Climate Risks

Climate change has a variety of urban implications. Changes are expected in the frequency and intensity of heavy rains, droughts, heat waves, wildfires and other extreme events. Higher risks are, therefore, expected for urban areas that are already exposed to these threats, such as to tropical storms (the Caribbean and Central America) or to water shortages (northern Chile, the Brazilian northeast, northern Mexico)[2] as the frequency and intensity of these events increase with climate change.

This increase in severe weather will create two distinct tales of water problems: too much or too little. Large cities and growing cities that are currently facing serious problems obtaining sufficient freshwater supplies will be especially affected on the too little water side – for example, Quito in Ecuador and Huancayo in Peru, which depend on water from the glaciers in the Andes.[3]

As illustrated by the December 1999 floods in Venezuela, excess of water is as problematic as too little. Flash floods and landslides killed nearly 30,000 in Caracas, and higher than average and more extreme rainfall events will be related to further flood hazards, increased landslides and mudflows.

Other effects of climate change are increases in mean temperatures, decreases in precipitation levels and increases in sea level which will impact the energy sector, will impair the draining capacities of sewage systems and the viability of low-lying coastal cities, where 7 per cent of the regional total population is located. Climate change is but one of multiple societal and environmental stresses facing cities. Heat stress and respiratory distress from extreme temperatures coalesce with a reduction in air quality to create higher mortality in urban areas.[4]

'Adaptive capacity', the ability of the urban population and economic activities to attenuate climate stresses or cope with their consequences, is as key a determinant of climate impacts as exposure is. Latin American cities have been struggling to provide their populations with many of the determinants of adaptive capacity. For instance, 48 per cent of urban workers in Latin American cities are employed in the informal sector, thus lacking access to sufficient and stable sources of income. Under recent state reforms in Latin America, public provision of infrastructure and services was practically abandoned,[5] leaving urban governments unable to provide these key determinants of adaptive capacity to their burgeoning populations.

The deficits in adaptive capacity are compounded by the completely lacking infrastructures in many areas critical to adaptive capacity. Many Latin American cities have no all-weather roads. The proportion of urban dwellers with no piped water supplies ranges between 1.2 per cent in Chile and 42 per cent in El Salvador; the percentage with no drains ranges between 13 per cent in Chile and 77 per cent in Paraguay. About 37 per cent of the housing stock in Latin America is inappropriate to afford protection against disaster and disease. Many homes are situated on illegally occupied or subdivided land which inhibits any investment in more resilient buildings.

Santiago, Chile
opposite left: Under climate change, the health impacts of air pollution and weather extremes might be aggravated.

opposite right: Greenhouse gas emissions per capita for selected cities.

Glacier Perito, Moreno National Park, Argentina
above left: Glaciers like this will disappear as a result of climate change.

Puerto Plata, Dominican Republic
above right: A colourful alley turned into a river due to heavy rains.

Some of the low-income populations live on risk-prone areas because these are the only sites they can occupy within reach of income-earning opportunities. It is, hence, difficult to talk about adapting infrastructure and buildings that are not there.

Linking Mitigation and Adaptation Responses with Development

Although Latin American cities are not big emitters, there are still good reasons for them to pay attention to mitigation and choose development paths with an eye towards wealthy cities such as Stockholm and Barcelona that have pretty low levels of emissions.

While still relatively low, emissions in Latin American cities are growing and these cities will need to address some of the causes of this (urban sprawl, increased commuting distances and the increasing use of private vehicles). Buenos Aires, Santiago and Mexico City, for instance, experienced a polycentric urban expansion of localities sprawling along major highways. A consequence of this is increased commuting distances and decreased speeds (for example, in Mexico City from 3.5 kilometres (2.2 miles) and 16.8 kilometres (10.4 miles) an hour by bus in 1987 to 5.6 kilometres (3.5 miles) and 16.7 kilometres (10.3 miles) an hour in 2000).[6] A 1 per cent increase in the density of urban areas relates to an approximately 0.7 per cent decline in CO_2 pollution at the city level, with other factors held constant.[7]

The second reason, equity and affluence, can be illustrated with data on transportation. The motorisation rate among high-income households is 8.6-fold that of low-income households.[8] In Mexico City, private cars only contribute 18 per cent of the city's daily trip segments, yet they account for 40.8 per cent of CO_2 equivalent emissions. Conversely, public transport accounts for 82 per cent of those trip segments yet emits 25.9 per cent of CO_2 equivalent emissions.[9] A key determinant of GHG emissions, therefore, is the consumption patterns of middle- and high-income sectors – a minority in the region – together with the production systems that benefit from that consumption.

Third, a set of governmental and non-governmental policies and actions in some cities illustrates the constraints but also the opportunities available when responding to climate change. Cities like Mexico City have developed a refined framing of climate change. Policy networks, political leaders and research groups have been critical in launching a climate agenda. Nevertheless, this has not been enough to push effective policies. Policy-making has been constrained by two institutional factors: fragmentation in local governance and lack of institutional capacity; for example, financial resources and well-trained and permanent personnel.

Manizales in Colombia and Ilo in Peru provide good examples of local governments working together with grass-roots organisations, communities and universities to promote urban development – and at the same time reduce vulnerability. The governments in these cities implemented actions to avoid rapidly growing low-income populations settling on dangerous sites. Although not originally driven by climate-change concerns, these initiatives illustrate how pro-development and pro-poor policies can enhance adaptive capacity.[10] Other cities such as Curitiba in Brazil have been able to integrate transportation and land use through the transit-orientated development idea, and thus to reduce emissions.[11]

Many cases also exist of non-governmental initiatives seeking to create more sustainable urban places (for example, river remediation in Morelia and Tuxtla Gutiérrez in Mexico, and land preservation in the peri-urban area of Bogotá). Although not designed to respond to climate change, these projects illustrate how pro-development actions can improve the adaptive capacity of poor populations (for instance, by the creation of low-cost and space-efficient

Laboratório de Eficiência Energética em Edificações (LabEEE) and the Universidade Federal de Santa Catarina (UFSC), Solar Heating and Rainwater Harvesting Tower, Brazil, 2009
above: About 44 per cent of the electricity consumed in Brazil is for the supply of buildings in general, and residential housing demands around 22 per cent of that percentage. In the housing sector the main end uses for electric power consumption nationally are: cooling (27 per cent corresponding to the use of refrigerators and freezers); heating water (24 per cent corresponding mainly to the use of electric showers as a main current source of hot water in the sector); air conditioning (around 20 per cent) and lighting (14 per cent). One promising solution for heating water in single-family residences is the use of solar energy, a renewable source for which the technology is easily accessed and relatively low cost. The main objective of LabEEE's tower proposal is to bring together within a single structure solutions for energy efficiency and the rational use of water for the improvement of low-income housing.

social housing in Mexico City). Development actions may also reduce carbon emissions through innovations such as treating solid waste and the introduction of solar water heating in new housing developments (for example, in São Paulo).[12]

To summarise, there are many reasons why Latin American cities need to address their multiple climate-change issues: like other cities they concentrate on carbon-emitting activities and entities such as industry, transportation and households. Yet these cities are often disproportionately affected by the hazards that climate change is expected to aggravate, and face existing deficits in adaptive capacity. Action therefore needs to be taken to address these deficits and, by doing so, to enhance the adaptive capacity of their urban populations. Although Latin American cities have been faced with many economic and institutional constraints during recent decades, they have also been the sources of many initiatives, policies and actions aimed at mitigating emissions and adapting to climate change.

Notes
1. P Romero-Lankao and D Gnatz, 'Introduction: Urbanization and the Challenge of Climate Change' in UN-Habitat, *2011 UN-Habitat Report on Cities and Climate Change*, 2011, p 60. P Romero-Lankao, 'Are We Missing the Point? Particularities of Urbanization, Sustainability and Carbon Emissions in Latin American Cities', *Environment and Urbanization* 19, 2007, pp 159–75.
2. G Magrin, C Gay, DC Choque, JC Giménez, A Moreno and G Nagy, et al, 'Latin America', in *Climate Change 2007: Impacts, Adaptation and Vulnerability. Contribution of Working Group II to the Fourth Assessment Report of the Intergovernmental Panel on Climate Change*, Cambridge University Press (Cambridge), 2007, Chp 13.
3. Ibid.
4. Romero-Lankao, op cit.
5. M Wilder and P Romero-Lankao, 'Paradoxes of Decentralization: Water Reform and its Social Implications in Mexico', *World Development* 34(11), 2006, pp 1977–95.
6. Romero-Lankao, op cit.
7. P Romero-Lankao, JL Tribbia and D Nychka, 'Testing Theories to Explore the Drivers of Cities' Atmospheric Emissions', *Ambio* 38, 2009, pp 236–44.
8. MF Osses and R Fernandez, 'Transport and Air Quality in Santiago, Chile', *Advances in City Transport: Case Studies*, 2006, pp 79–105.
9. Romero-Lankao, 'Are We Missing the Point?', op cit.
10. J Díaz Palacios and L Miranda, 'Concertacion (Reaching Agreement) and Planning for Sustainable Development in Ilo, Peru', in S Bass, H Reid, D Satterthwaite and P Steele (eds), *Reducing Poverty and Sustaining the Environment*, EarthScan (London), 2005, pp 255–79.
11. UN-Habitat, *Planning Sustainable Cities: Global Report on Human Settlements 2009*, Earthscan (London), 2009.
12. See www.holcimfoundation.org. The mission of the Holcim Foundation is to select and support initiatives that combine sustainable construction solutions with architectural excellence and enhanced quality of life beyond technical solutions.

Text © 2011 John Wiley & Sons Ltd. Images: pp 76(b), 77 © iStockphoto; p 76(t) © Patricia Romero-Lankao; pp 78-9 © LabEEE - Laboratório de Eficiência Energética em Edificações. Universidade Federal de Santa Catarina, Brasil

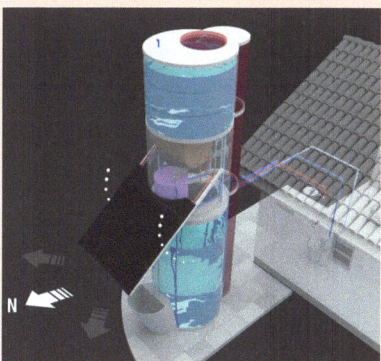

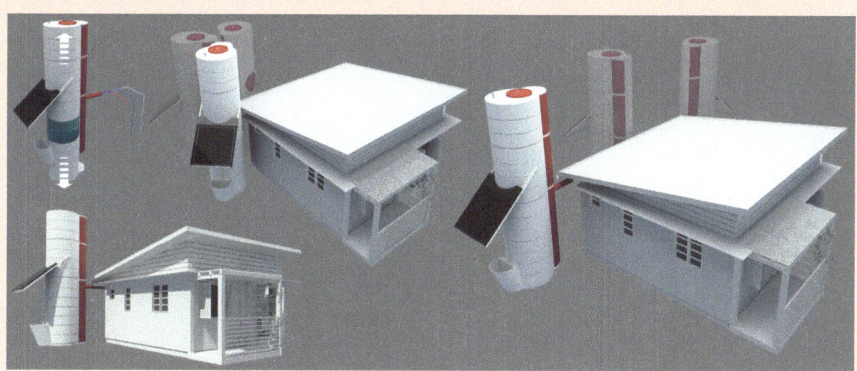

top: Tower prototype constructed using laminated concrete, or ferrocement, on an existing house in a low-income community in Florianópolis, Santa Catarina, Brazil.

above left: The possibility of changing the orientation of the solar collector or panel depends on the house's orientation in relation to the sun or to the north, and on the collector's angle depending on the local latitude.

above right: The tower structure can be modular, adapting to different needs and local situations.

Fernando de Mello Franco

FILLING THE VOIDS WITH POPULAR IMAGINARIES

In the last few years, the emergence of a burgeoning middle class in Brazil has transformed the country into one of the fastest growing consumer markets in the world. For MMBB Arquitetos, based in São Paulo, social mobility and the upgrading of urban infrastructure represent a unique opportunity to develop the city. **Fernando de Mello Franco** of MMBB describes the practice's strategy for 'urbanising' much needed new infrastructure. A canal with a public park can be inserted, for instance, alongside a new drainage system, providing necessary social adhesion in a fragile urban culture.

MMBB, Watery Voids, Pirajuçara Watershed, São Paulo, 2007
Schematic plan for the programming of the Watery Voids on the Pirajuçara watershed. The aim is to offer the voids to the local population to fill them with whatever they wish.

opposite top left: Rainwater reservoir # 1 on the Pirajuçara watershed. São Paulo's social housing and drainage issues are totally connected.

MMBB, Watery Voids, Pirajuçara Watershed, São Paulo, 2007
opposite top right: Schematic proposal for the possible articulation of urban policies.

opposite bottom: The construction of a network of urban voids can be converted into an opportunity for extending the infrastructure on the periphery.

São Paulo is undergoing major transformations common to a number of industrial cities around the world. The process of productive restructuring[1] has released former industrial sites (mainly fluvial plains of the metropolis' three main rivers: the Tietê, Pinheiros and Tamanduatei) for redevelopment and reuse. At the same time, the threat of climate change demands renovation of the general modes of transport. Moreover, the rise in urban land values is boosting growth on the periphery, in the mode of favelas, while the central core of the city is emptying.

The context of an emerging economy also raises specific issues. The upward social mobility of a large segment of the population allows speculation that new demands and values regarding the city will emerge. The challenge then becomes the redefining of objectives, strategies and project tools that are able to act within this process.

Macroeconomic restructuring and social assistance programmes, such as Bolsa Família,[2] implemented consistently by recent government administrations, have lifted approximately 30 million people above Brazil's poverty line. As a consequence, the internal consumer market has expanded significantly. The impact of this new middle class on the city is the generation of values that manifest themselves in the use of urban space.[3] Currently, about 30 per cent of the population of São Paulo lives in informal settlements. Assuming that the current growth rate continues, the informal and formal cities will be mutually reshaped, suggesting a breakdown of the dichotomies between them.

This transformation of the favelas in São Paulo has been carried out by several public programmes – such as the Programa de Aceleração do Crescimento (PAC) and Plano Municipal de Habitação (PMH) – for the regeneration of informal sectors, in terms of both housing and environmental policy. Indeed, informal sectors often occupy the protected areas of springs, rivers and streams of a catchment basin, and their drainage system will be affected the most by climate change. São Paulo's location on a high plateau will protect it from rises in sea level. Nevertheless, evidence shows that an increase in the frequency and intensity of the rainfall cycle will aggravate the risk of chronic flooding. The need to mitigate the economic impacts of flooding is consensual among politicians and the population. This presents an opportunity to develop an integrated approach to tackle housing problems and water resources management as both issues are strongly related.

The articulation of housing, sanitation, flooding and water resources policies is already under way in São Paulo, but despite such public transformation programmes much more needs to be done. It is necessary to rethink the design of the city's infrastructure in order to incorporate urban values into what has been historically conceived only as a technical and functional artefact. Infrastructure should play a role in providing basic services and also in promoting the improvement of the local urban tissues.

Urban infrastructure consists of fixed elements that support and structure the transformation of the city. These provide the departure points for the proliferation of the multiple webs that constitute the urban fabric. For a city with a fragile urban culture, that lacks a socially constructed concept of landscape, it is essential to 'urbanise' its infrastructure.

In this context, MMBB Arquitetos' hypothesis is that the emergence of a new social class provides an opportunity to investigate new demands for the city's urbanity. The practice's approach integrates two fields of this type of investigation: firstly, rethinking the paradigm of infrastructure; secondly, constructing forms of popular imaginary that can impact the use of space – for example, on to a web that embeds value in urban space as a place for living.

MMBB is based in São Paulo and led by architects Fernando de Mello Franco, Marta Moreira and Milton Braga. The office has been working in informal areas since 2007 when it received the Best Entry Award at the 3rd International Architecture Biennale in Rotterdam for its Watery Voids project.

Watery Voids, São Paulo

Watery Voids is a conceptual project that proposes strategies to boost architects' participation in the production of the contemporary city. The key idea is to exploit the social capital employed in the construction of large infrastructure projects in order to obtain better results with the same resources.

The systemic character of such infrastructure works impacts both at the local and at the whole-city scale. The solution to an urban problem often cannot be found in the place one wishes to benefit. Rather, it must be sought in spatially discontinuous, yet interrelated, spaces. This can require a more even distribution of government investment than one would expect, particularly when it occurs in the context of an imbalanced battle for public resources in the uneven context of Brazilian society. This is the case, for example, in the efforts to fight floods in São Paulo: a significant investment is planned for peripheral sites in order to solve a problem that affects primarily the central areas of the city where the main metropolitan transport infrastructure is located.

The solution proposed by the government is to build a set of storm-water retention reservoirs, the main purpose of which is to retain water and delay its onset into the city's main rivers. There are currently about 27 of these facilities, and once completed, this network of reservoirs will be capable of

The solution proposed by the government is to build a set of storm-water retention reservoirs, the main purpose of which is to retain water and delay its onset into the city's main rivers.

MMBB, Antonico Creek Urban Project, Favela Paraisópolis, São Paulo, 2009
below left: Plan.

below right: The design of the main square includes a surface canal that will also carry flood water to encourage the interaction of the local population with the water.

bottom left: Partial plan of the open-space system. The dark areas correspond to the spaces offered to the population for new building fronts. The bike lane and commercial activities are part of the strategy to avoid future illegal occupation.

bottom right: Open space model.

opposite: Sectional diagrams of the proposed hydraulic model.

The perennial waters will be carried by a surface canal, and this will also collect the flooding waters that are compatible with urban activities. The run-off from heavy rain flows will be directed to an underground storm-water retention reservoir.

retaining 15.5 million cubic metres (547 million cubic feet) of water. The reservoirs are distributed throughout all of the metropolis' sub-basins and most are located near informal settlements. This means that tackling the metropolitan dimension of the flooding problem requires the dispersion of public investment in peripheral areas. The starting point of MMBB's Watery Voids project is to reconcile the metropolitan and the local scales of these interventions.

Spatially, these reservoirs consist of large excavations that are temporarily filled during rainy periods. When not in use, they are abandoned spaces. This network of urban voids, however, might be an opportunity to develop a system to structure the peripheries, if well articulated with other sectoral policies.

São Paulo has a deficient potable water supply that demands the remediation of its water resources. Once this process, already under way, is finished, new uses for the reservoirs might be envisioned that will allow the project to integrate these facilities into the urban fabric, giving the population an opportunity to interact with the water. Thus the network of voids might be reprogrammed by the population according to its own values of public realm. The idea is that the embodiment of significant images into the urban landscape will build a strong affection and bond between the city and its inhabitants.

Antonico Creek Urban Project, São Paulo

The Antonico Creek Urban Project is part of the favelas urbanisation programme undertaken by the municipal housing secretary of São Paulo. The site is located in Paraisópolis, the city's second largest favela with an area of about 1 square kilometre (0.386 square miles) and around 60,000 inhabitants, which emerged from the failure of a previous urban project. The creek cuts through an orthogonal grid that was irresponsibly built on highly irregular topography. Currently, it is invisible below the areas of informal building. The projects to be developed by the municipal government will require the demolition of settlements built on these non-buildable areas to create the sites for the slum's main network of public spaces.

The scope of the project is the design of the drainage system and the reconfiguration of open spaces. However, the main challenge is to create a means of appropriation that prevents future illegal occupations. The proposed strategy is to respond to the initial technical requirements through an articulation of popular imaginary forms that govern the use of urban spaces.

Initially, the project investigates hydraulic models that, on the one hand, foster the reconciliation of the slum and rivers and, on the other, protect the fragile urban fabric from the negative impacts of the heavy tropical rains. The proposal will separate these flows. The perennial waters will be carried by a surface canal, and this will also collect the flooding waters that are compatible with urban activities. The run-off from heavy rain flows will be directed to an underground storm-water retention reservoir. The sanitation of the neighbourhood and water cleaning remediation projects promised by the government will allow the population contact with the new stream.

Running parallel to the canal will be a corridor of open space of varying widths for cyclists and pedestrians. This corridor sits on the site's gentlest slopes and will be the main mobility axis for the neighbourhood. These intense human flows will foster the dynamics that activate and safeguard places. The opening of new building fronts along the corridor will be encouraged, boosting the local service and commerce economies that are usually found on a city's main circulation axis.

The project will create a linear centrality comprising a sequence of public spaces, similar to one of the most powerful spatial structures in Brazilian cities: the *calçadão*. This paved corridor is often employed to make the transition between a beach and the urban fabric. Its linear configuration, the possibility of it being experienced in a processional way, and its indeterminacy, give this border a porous character. In the case of Antonico Creek, the presence of a body of water with which one can interact suggests that using the imaginary of beach culture might be successful. Beach culture provides an example of a spontaneous use of space that culturally allows for an active and desirable coexistence, though not totally devoid of conflict.[4]

Both the Watery Voids and Antonico Creek projects investigate possible ways of negotiating the use of space through design strategies. They urbanise infrastructure and expand its values: they consider its role as a structuring system for the city and as a service provider. However, they also open up infrastructure to a variety of popular manifestations that have the ability to transform a technical artefact into an inhabitable place. ∆

Notes
1. David Harvey, *The Condition of Postmodernity: An Enquiry into the Origins of Cultural Change*, Wiley-Blackwell (Oxford), 1990. The term 'reestruturação produtiva' is used to characterise the passage from the Fordist (Henry Ford) productive process to the 'flexible accumulation' process that brings new forms to the use of the territory and the city.
2. The Bolsa Família is a government programme that provides a monthly stipend to allow families to send their children to school.
3. See A Souza and B Lamounier, *A Classe média brasileira: ambições, valores e projetos de sociedade*, Elsevier Editora (Rio de Janeiro), 2010.
4. See Eduardo Aquino and Karen Shanski, 'Beachscape', in *Complex Order: Intrusions in Public Space*, Plug In Editions (Winnipeg), 2009.

Text © 2011 John Wiley & Sons Ltd. Images: pp 80-1, 83(tr&b), 84-5 © MMBB; p 83(tl) © Nelson Kon

CIVIC BUILDING
FORTE, GIMENES & MARCONDES FERRAZ ARQUITETOS (FGMF), SÃO PAULO

São Paulo-based practice **Forte, Gimenes & Marcondes Ferraz (FGMF)** places particular importance on developing relationships between architecture, its environment and the user. This is apparent in its two projects featured here: the FDE Public School at Várzea Paulista, for which the firm created concrete brise-soleils; and the Edifício Projeto Viver, a community building at Morumbi, which it retained as a gateway for the favela it serves.

FDE PUBLIC SCHOOL, VÁRZEA PAULISTA, SÃO PAULO

A foundation for the development of education (FDE), a public agency, regulates the implementation of public schools in the state of São Paulo. One of its recent programmes was for a series of architect-designed public schools to be built using prefabricated and low-cost structures and components.

For the Várzea Paulista elementary school, FGMF aimed to create a relationship between the public and semi-public spaces through a dialogue between indoors and outdoors, and provide an interesting, though low-cost, space for the children to study in.

The project consists of two large volumes – a blue one (made of concrete) that houses a multipurpose indoor sports court, and a brighter one that contains the classrooms, supporting facilities and open space for games and activities. The tension and counterpoint between the volumes have been worked out based on the opacity of the one volume and the translucency of the other. The school's entrance sits between the two volumes, and at weekends when the gates are open for the community to use the building, indoors and outdoors connect with one another.

The classroom spaces are reflected in the main facade, protected by premanufactured concrete brise-soleils. The end result is one large panel that hangs over the local community. At the rear, sunlight is filtered by the perforated metal roofing that shelters the recreation space, allowing it to be fully illuminated during the day and intensifying the sense of connection with the garden (there are no gates or enclosures).

At night, the school is lit inside out, and this impression of a 'lantern' allied to its site on one of the highest points in the neighbourhood creates a referential architectonic element that adds to its significance as a reference point for the community.

FGMF, FDE Public School, Várzea Paulista, São Paulo, 2008
opposite: The school entrance is designated by the contrast between its two main volumes – the heavier, blue-painted volume of the sports court serves as a counterpoint to the main volume of classrooms, closed with concrete brise-soleils: ethereal versus translucent.

above: The concrete brise-soleils have the double effect of shading the interior spaces of the school and allowing vistas over the city.

FGMF, FDE Public School, Várzea Paulista, São Paulo, 2008
top: View of the neighbourhood from the far side of the school.

above: At night, the school becomes a lantern in the Várzea Paulista landscape. Its emblematic site, one of the highest in the neighbourhood, allows the project to read not only as a school but also, when its role changes at weekends, as an important amenity for the whole community.

FGMF, Edifício Projeto Viver, Morumbi, São Paulo, 2005
opposite top: The opening day of the new building served as an example of the architects' intention: that the project and building, and formation of this semi-public space, become a focal point for the favela community.

opposite centre and bottom: The NGO's headquarters has become an important geographical reference point for the Jardim Colombo community. This is partly due to its role as a vehicular entrance to the favela after part of the site was donated to the community to allow the new access.

EDIFÍCIO PROJETO VIVER, MORUMBI, SÃO PAULO

Edifício Projeto Viver was built in 2005 to serve the Jardim Colombo community, a favela (shantytown) located in the southern region of São Paulo, where more than 10,000 inhabitants live within a precarious urban context. The building is the headquarters of the Associação Viver em Família (Living in Family Association), a Brazilian bank employees' non-governmental organisation (NGO) that represents the social development and welfare of the community. Located on one of the last remaining plots in the area, it aims to establish a gateway to the favela that also acts as a central node for the inhabitants and their activities.

The site previously functioned as an informal entrance to the community, for both cars and pedestrians. In designing the project, FGMF chose to retain this function, adding a paved road for vehicular access and creating an open, semi-public square with stairways to form a pedestrian gateway. The square also plays host to a number of community events such as celebrations and vaccination campaigns.

Inside, the building programme facilitates a multitude of uses: offices (medical, dental and legal), computer classrooms, a library, and an experimental kitchen for classes that includes a small street-level store selling the products made in class.

The square below, allied with the space underneath the building's columns and terraced gardens, enables the headquarters to integrate with the site's topography. ᴅ

Text © 2011 John Wiley & Sons Ltd. Images: pp 86-8 © Forte, Gimenes & Marcondes Ferrraz Arquitetos, photos Nelson Kon; p 89 © Forte, Gimenes & Marcondes Ferrraz Arquitetos, photos Editora Pini

Enrique Peñalosa

A CITY TALKS
LEARNING FROM BOGOTÁ'S REVITALISATION

As the Mayor of Bogotá (1998–2001), **Enrique Peñalosa** transformed Colombia's capital from a city without hope to one that is held up as an international example of best practice. This was epitomised by his far-reaching transport policy and the TransMilenio bus-based transit system. Peñalosa describes the ambitious urban revitalisation programme that his administration undertook and how they were guided by the fundamental aim of 'the construction of equality'.

Enrique Peñalosa

Bogotá is a large Latin American city located at 2,600 metres (8,530 feet) above sea level on a high green Andean plateau, and has severe inequality and poverty problems. The new administration came into office on an Independent Party ticket, and during our three-year tenure (1998–2001), implemented a very different urban model from that which had prevailed for decades in our city and in most developing countries. Our strategy contributed significantly to changing the attitudes of Bogotá's citizens from negativism and hopelessness to pride and confidence in the possibility of constructing a better future. It gave a new legitimacy to the social order. And it influenced every city and town, not only in Colombia, but across Latin America and even in countries further afield.

The fundamental criterion guiding our work was the construction of equality. There is a vast difference between creating equality and simply giving aid to the poor: programmes that dole out money or free food to the needy may be necessary but they do not bring about equality.

That *tugurios*, favelas, *bidonvilles* and slums of every conceivable type are found all over the developing world testifies that the problem does not stem from bad government: it is systemic. The poor in developing world cities are forced to build their often precarious housing in the wrong places without public spaces, and at least initially, without basic utilities such as water and sewerage. Almost 50 per cent of Bogotá has sprung up illegally, mainly on steep mountainsides that are often at serious risk of soil erosion leading to potentially deadly landslides, always difficult to access by bicycle and where the provision of transportation and services is energy intensive and thus costly. Yet Bogotá is surrounded by hundreds of thousands of hectares of perfectly level land very well suited to quality urban development.

The city administration initiated massive slum legalisation and improvements. But beyond that we created a municipal land bank company which bought up land that was either sold voluntarily or through the use of compulsory purchase orders. The company, Metrovivienda, produced quality urbanism and private developers built and sold homes within set price and time constraints. The result was some of the best-quality urban development in Colombia.

opposite: Besides cycle lanes and pedestrian corridors, Peñalosa's administration oversaw the creation of a network of protected cycle paths along city streets and roads that led to a significant increase in bicycle use.

above: Where JICA had proposed an eight-lane highway through the city, Peñalosa's administration created the 35-kilometre (21.7-mile) long Juan Amarillo greenway which links some of the poorest to some of the richest neighbourhoods in the city, and through which tens of thousands of people now cycle to work daily.

Towards an Open City

If it works well, a city centre integrates people from all parts of the city and all income brackets. Bogotá's centre was in a state of collapse as illegal street traders had completely taken over crucial public spaces, creating chaos and a fertile environment for crime. Worse, a 24-hectare (59.3-acre) and growing area called Cartucho located two blocks from the Presidential Palace, Congress and the city's main square, was totally in the grip of drug dealers and their clients amid unimaginable conditions of degeneration. It was a no-go area as far as the police were concerned and murder rates were the highest in the world.

Accompanied by massive social programmes and relocations, more than 600 buildings were demolished in order to open up a 23-hectare (56.8-acre) park in the heart of the city, intended to foster a repopulation of the centre; public spaces were reclaimed from the chaos of crime and neglect and Jimenez Avenue, one of downtown's most important thoroughfares, was pedestrianised. In many poverty-stricken, squalid and crime-prone environments, quality architecture attracted, comforted and dignified fragile humans desperately in need of a more protective and beautiful city.

Only about 20 per cent of home-owners owned cars, but they had the most economic and political power. A majority of upper- and upper-middle-class citizens in developing cities

In many poverty-stricken, squalid and crime-prone environments, quality architecture attracted, comforted and dignified fragile humans desperately in need of a more protective and beautiful city.

pull out of their garages in the morning and may go for weeks without walking a block on a city street. They consider the absolute priority for government to be the construction of more and bigger roads. Which is why even in some very poor African cities where most of the population does not even have access to clean water, it is still possible to find highways. Car infrastructure absorbs most of the budget. There is a conflict for funds between the needs of the automobile and the needs of the poor for such imperatives as schools, parks, housing or public transport. And there is a conflict for space between cars, pedestrians, cyclists and buses.

It was clear to us that more or bigger road infrastructure may be convenient, but that it would never solve traffic jams: more than the number of cars, what creates traffic is the number of trips and their length. We rejected the recommendations of the Japanese International Cooperation Agency (JICA) study we received on our arrival at City Hall, which advocated spending billions of dollars on expressways that were to crisscross our city. Instead, we restricted car use in several ways: by establishing a restriction on driving whereby every car had to be off the street for two peak hours in the morning and two in the afternoon, two days a week; the administration also embarked on a crusade to get cars off the sidewalks where they had been parking unimpeded until then. By means of a referendum we established a Car Free Day on the first Thursday of February every year in which all cars except taxis are off the streets; the city has worked fine every Car Free Day with the majority of citizens enjoying shorter travel times. A vision of an urban environment that required restricted car use necessitated the creation of a high-quality public transport system.

Buses in Bogotá were a disaster, almost all individually owned, old and in poor condition, crammed to the point where people would hang out of the open doors; madly racing against each other they were often the cause of fatal accidents, or mired in traffic and hardly moving

Subways are the ultimate dream of car-owners in the cities of developing countries: often not because they have the slightest intention of using them, but because they imagine traditional public transport and its users will disappear into underground tunnels and this will somehow do away with traffic jams. It is not very democratic to put public transport users underground just in order to free up space for cars. Most importantly, rail transit systems were unaffordable, both in terms of investment costs and from the perspective of operational costs, if we were to reach all sectors of a large city.

The administration thus created a bus-based transit system copied from the Brazilian city of Curitiba, where articulated buses operate in dedicated, physically isolated lanes.

opposite: A TransMilenio bus zooming past private cars in its dedicated lane in a traffic jam makes democracy more real and social organisation more legitimate.

above: Alameda Porvenir, a 23-kilometre (14.3-mile) long pedestrian-and-bicycle-only promenade through very low-income areas. In their formidable pedestrian space, citizens feel they are important, their needs respected despite their poverty.

> We are pedestrians, animals that walk: we need to walk, not in order to survive but to be happy. If there is a single piece of infrastructure that distinguishes advanced from backward cities, it is quality sidewalks.

We are pedestrians, animals that walk: we need to walk, not in order to survive but to be happy. If there is a single piece of infrastructure that distinguishes advanced from backward cities, it is quality sidewalks. Lack of them, or the presence of parking bays where there should be sidewalks, is a symbol of inequality, lack of respect for human dignity and insufficient democracy. We built hundreds of kilometres of high-standard sidewalks and put up bollards along many others in order to keep cars off them. As mayor, I was nevertheless almost impeached in the process: well-financed by irate shop-owners whose customers could no longer park on the sidewalk, a campaign to collect signatures to proceed with my impeachment almost succeeded.

Creating a Walkable City

We created or rebuilt hundreds of parks which had been mostly neglected until then. We removed fences which middle-class neighbourhoods had erected illegally in order to privatise public parks, and recovered parkland in the middle of the city given to professional soccer teams by a previous mayor. We waged a difficult battle when we proposed that the country's most exclusive golf club, then situated in the middle of a dense city area, should be converted into a public park. After a lengthy legal fight, finally at least the polo fields gave way to a park for everyone.

above: The Avenida Jiménez sustainable pedestrian corridor in downtown Bogotá is also home to an important TransMilenio interchange.

top and opposite: These library buildings speak, expressing the fact that children are important, something not obvious in a society where one out of every four children born is unwanted at the moment of birth, and in neighbourhoods where some 20 per cent of children do not know who their father is.

Besides cycle lanes and pedestrian corridors, the administration oversaw the creation of a 250-kilometre (155.3-mile) long network of protected cycle paths along city streets and roads that led to an increase in bicycle use from practically nothing to nearly 5 per cent. As important as the safety a protected cycle path affords cyclists is its symbolic power: it enhances the cyclist's social status, since a citizen on a $30 bicycle is as important as one in a $30,000 car.

Despite poverty, the creation of public pedestrian space is not an irresponsible use of scarce funds in a developing country's cities. It is during leisure time that income differentials are most keenly felt. During work time a high-level executive and the lowest-paid company employee may be equally satisfied or dissatisfied, relatively speaking. But when they leave work the high-level executive goes to a large home, has access to gardens, clubs, country homes, vacations, restaurants, cultural activities; while the low-income person and his or her children return to a very small living space; and for recreation the only alternative they have to television is public pedestrian space. The very least a democracy can do for its citizens is to provide quality sidewalks, parks, plazas and other spaces so that even the poorest can enjoy their city.

Changing the Meaning of Access:
From Building Highways to Schools

The funds the administration did not expend on JICA-proposed highways were instead spent on the construction of nearly 50 high-quality schools in the poorest neighbourhoods, their buildings and facilities as good as anything the most expensive private schools in the country can boast; on three beautifully equipped libraries designed by some of the country's best architects, plus 12 small ones; and on state-of-the-art nurseries and community centres.

Iconic, more beautiful than even the most elegant shopping mall, they create value; their presence and form make statements about the importance of education and knowledge, and showcase culture for its own sake. For a child from a very poor neighbourhood whose home may have a dirt floor or at best a rough cement one, free access to a beautiful, almost luxurious library, where admission is not dependent on wealth, educational attainment or social status, but simply on their rights as a citizen, citizenship acquires real meaning. A library in a poor neighbourhood symbolises society's confidence in the intelligence and capacity of the young citizens around it; just as a free food programme, despite its eventual necessity, expresses the opposite. ᴅ

Text © 2011 John Wiley & Sons Ltd. Images © Photos by. Architect Carolina Hernández Galeano. Camera. Canon EOS 400D Digital

Lorenzo Castro
Alejandro Echeverri

BOGOTÁ AND MEDELLÍN
ARCHITECTURE AND POLITICS

In the last 15 years, Bogotá and Medellín, Colombia's two largest cities, have undergone urban renaissances. These are a direct result of a political will to tackle the social, economic and physical segregation caused by the large-scale urban migrations of the 1970s and 1980s, which resulted in informal developments that were often isolated from central urban areas with no infrastructure. **Lorenzo Castro and Alejandro Echeverri** describe the shared experiences and distinct approaches of each city.

TEP/ Departamento Administrativo de Planeación Distrital, Plaza de San Victorino, Bogotá, 2000
opposite: Located in the popular city centre, the Plaza de San Victorino demonstrates the possibility of transforming the city through the recovery of public space.

Municipality of Bogotá, Cycle path network, 1999
below: At almost 400 kilometres (248.5 miles) in length, Bogotá's network of cycle paths offers an alternative way to move around the city.

Rogelio Salmona, Centro Cultural García Márquez, Bogotá, 2008
bottom: The historic centre of Bogotá serves as a backdrop to this project, a gift from the Mexican government to the city as a vote of confidence in its future consolidation.

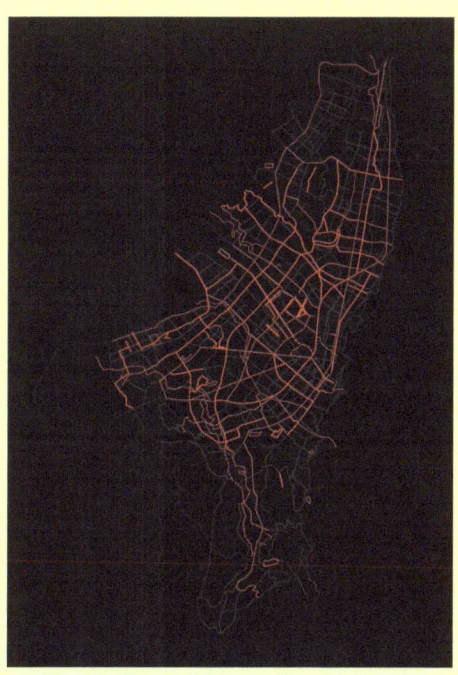

Following global trends, the majority of Colombians today live in cities. The republic's five largest cities are each home to over one million inhabitants, and eight are home to more than half a million.[1] So, unlike Chile with its capital Santiago, or the UK with London, Colombia does not have one dominant city, but like Germany a network of interconnected cities.

In recent years, its two largest cities, Bogotá and Medellín, have become exemplars of urban and social transformation following their renaissance in the 1990s. Based on local management, and driven by a succession of independent mayors working along the margins of traditional politics, their famed improvement has seen these two cities referenced by numerous architects and city mayors around the world. Without the political will to challenge mainstream ideas, their transformation would have been impossible.

Both cities have made considerable strides towards creating a more accessible and democratic urban environment. Common in their approaches towards improvement were strategies to mitigate the strong social, economic and physical segregation typical of Latin American cities. Both have adopted a bus rapid transit (BRT) system based on the model of Curitiba in Brazil. In Bogotá, the first phase of the BRT has been operational since 1999 (84 kilometres/52.2 miles of a projected circuit of 250 kilometres/155.3 miles). In Medellín the system is currently being implemented, and will deliver high-capacity and high-quality mass transit at a fraction of the cost of a subway. In parallel to providing access through public transport, both cities improved access to public services through the formation of new parks, libraries and other public amenities spread across the entire city rather than concentrating them in formal middle- and upper-class enclaves. This transformation led to Bogotá receiving the Golden Lion Cities Award at the 2006 Venice Architecture Biennale. A decade before, however, the story was much different.

Bogotá: An Urban Renaissance

Throughout the 1980s and the early 1990s, prior to its transformation, Bogotá was inhabited, but uninhabitable. In 1973, the city's population was 2.85 million, in 1985 4.2 million, and by 1993 5.5 million,[2] reaching a scale that seemed impossible to plan and give form to. Much of the city's growth came as the result of informal construction, which today covers over 50 per cent of

the city's urban area. These settlements, while rich through their intensity of urban activity, lack basic infrastructural services, suffer from their unstructured form, and tend to be located in marginal areas where poverty leads to segregation and violence.

Things began to change between 1995 and 1997 during Antanas Mokus' run as mayor of Bogotá, during which he implemented a programme of civic and cultural restructuring that aimed to change the general behaviour of citizens through promoting a culture of mutual respect. This paved the way to reigniting civil society in the city, and improved its citizens' perception of their city and its public realm; moreover, it led to a significant drop in the level of violent crime. During the previous period, Jaime Castro reorganised the city's finances, making the bureaucracy run more efficiently and allowing taxation revenue to be used more productively.

Between 1998 and 2000, under the mayoralty of Enrique Peñalosa, there was a fundamental shift in terms of how city-making occurred in Bogotá and, one could argue, across all of Latin America. At the time, Colombia was facing a severe economic crisis that deeply affected architectural offices hitherto comfortably devoted to the development of projects for real-estate speculation with an absolute disregard for the city. Peñalosa called on the best architects, aware of the importance of their participation in the construction of a beautiful and dignified environment and in achieving a more human-scaled city.

Beginning with quality architecture, a city can generate a culture that permits a harmonious and inclusive urban existence for an entire society. In Bogotá, this quality civic architecture was then overlapped with a network of public transport and cycle routes, along with other specific projects, to generate a city that is integrated, continuous, open and accessible to everyone, inclusive, environmentally sustainable and capable of facilitating a sense of civic pride and stewardship among its citizens. This, in turn, helped to ensure the continuity of such programmes and their adoption by different local authorities.

Given the size of Bogotá, both in terms of population density and surface area, and its physical and social fragmentation, the intention was to create a complete and unique image of the city that, rather than ignoring socioeconomic differences between its territories, was capable of bridging these through the design of a series of iconic urban elements associated with cross-city systems. In the case of the TransMilenio, an articulated BRT system, a national public architectural competition was held to define those elements with a specific identity that were spread across the entire system and the entire city. It was accompanied by the development and construction of a network of bicycle paths, aimed at mobilising 10 per cent of people through this city-friendly transportation. This strategy helped in saving energy, reducing fuel consumption, reducing both air and noise pollution, and in providing a healthy, low-cost and democratic means of private transportation. Under these conditions it was possible to rethink the use and spatial qualities of the city, a fundamental task for the architects involved.

In parallel to the design of cross-cutting urban elements, a second form of democratisation came through the development of a manual for the construction of public spaces which aimed to achieve a consistency in the elements that make up such spaces, from furnishings to paving and urban plantings.[3] These started to be developed prior to Peñalosa's term as mayor, but it was not until then that they were developed with the required significant technical details to be put into practice. Through repeated use the manual can be employed to construct the materiality and the specific image of the city, while allowing for local variations and creating spaces in which all citizens feel welcome and treated as equals. It has become a fundamental reference, used by each project architect to produce a coherent image of the city through a consistent standard of design, and has allowed for the recovery of hundreds of kilometres of sidewalks previously occupied by street pedlars and parked cars.

Despite the role of the public space, and in particular the plaza as the place where we construct the identity and culture of a society, for many years Bogotá, despite its population growth, generated no new spaces of this type and, what is more, neglected those it already possessed. In response, a plan was formulated for the recovery of existing public plazas and the construction of new ones, such as Plaza de San Victorino, Plaza España, Plaza-Monumento a los Caidos, Plaza de La Rebeca and Plaza de La Hoja. At the same time, a plan for parks and green spaces was developed focusing on three different scales: the metropolitan, the urban and the neighbourhood. The plan saw to the improvement of over 700 parks through masterplans or projects by more than 120 architects. Consideration of

Daniel Bermudez, Biblioteca Pública El Tintal, Bogotá, 2000
opposite: This library, located in the southwest of the city, was envisioned on a site where a former and unused garbage collection plant used to be located. It forms part of the network of libraries planned for Bogotá that have already been built.

Leonardo Álvarez, Colegio Porfirio Barba Jacob, Bosa, Bogotá, 2009
below: The Porfirio Barba Jacob College is part of a programme for the construction of more than 70 public schools in different parts of the city.

TEP/Departamento Administrativo de Planeación Distrital, Alameda de Bosa, Bogotá, 2000
bottom: This public space project, which functions on two levels, was assisted by the consolidation of the existing working-class neighbourhoods along the Tintal 3 Canal. It also led to the creation of a network of tree-lined promenades.

> Under the Peñalosa mayoralty, many architects regained a civic conscience, realising that they could play a fundamental role in creating a city worth inhabiting.

parks as a system allowed for the recovery of the geographic relationships between the Eastern Hills and the Bogotá River to the west, with a new primary ecological structure. While the interventions were very basic, such as the design of trails, urban boundaries, sports facilities, playgrounds, furnishings and plantings, they restored the architects' ability to propose areas that dignify the lives of citizens, generating a significant impact.

This approach worked to improve neighbourhoods through a system of participative planning where communities developed their own projects with technical assistance offered by over a hundred young architects. The project led to the construction of wells, stairs, neighbourhood access roads, sidewalks and local parks as part of the Obras con Saldo Pedagógico (Works for Educational Purposes) programme. Surveys were made of conditions in different neighbourhoods, and the neighbourhoods were then formalised through the development of basic infrastructures.

As in the case of public infrastructure, the importance of architectural design was carried across to the development of public buildings in order to transmit civic values and to help ensure their appropriation by the city's inhabitants. A network of public libraries was created in metropolitan parks or in new parks designed by architects. The libraries were intended as cultural centres and strategically located to be accessible to poorer neighbourhoods. Another plan saw the development of new schools to serve 100 per cent of all school-age children, using international standards and in many cases surpassing the architectural quality of the city's existing private schools, fuelling children's imagination with architecture worthy to be upheld as the future of the city. Other new constructions included centres for senior citizens, nurseries and playgrounds, together with cultural centres.

Under the Peñalosa mayoralty, many architects regained a civic conscience, realising that they could play a fundamental role in creating a city worth inhabiting. This opened up an important space for the participation of architects in many cases as leaders or participants in interdisciplinary groups working to define systems, or as designers of quality public buildings. The transformation of Bogotá over the last 15 years, and above all during Peñalosa's period in office, resulted from a number of progressive policies and projects. During this time a host of public competitions led to the redesign and renewal of more than 1,300 parks and 57 schools.

Lorenzo Castro and Ana Elvira Velez, Jardin Botanico, 2008
right: The Jardin Botanico (Botanical Gardens) are located in a strategic renewal sector, together with projects destined to be part of a system of facilities along the metropolitan fringes of the Medellín River. The urban redevelopment of the surrounding sector involves the margins, once defined by high walls that defined enclosures, obscuring visibility by 100 per cent.

La Quintana Library Park, 2008
opposite top: The library connects two districts with the linear park creek La Quintana.

Carlos Pardo, Public School, Santo Domingo Savio, Medellín, 2009
opposite bottom: The school redefines the urbanity and public services of this hillside neighbourhood.

Medellín: Social Urbanism

As in the case of Bogotá, metropolitan Medellín, home to some 3.5 million inhabitants, is plagued by profound physical, social and economic segregation. The north and the highlands of the eastern and western slopes are home to half the population, who live in conditions of extreme poverty. This is contrasted by the middle and upper classes in the centre and south of the valley, who inhabit the flat areas that make up the formal city.

During the 1990s, civil society began to organise itself, initiating an important series of social and cultural projects as a reaction to the violence in the city, and beginning a process of urban renewal in the centre. In 2004, under the leadership of Mayor Sergio Fajardo, the city began to implement structural changes integrally combined with educational, cultural and entrepreneurial programmes designed to 'change the skin' of various neighbourhoods located in the most critical areas of the city.

Today, Medellín's is a 'tale of two cities' – and two opposite realities. Social urbanism was proposed as a tool to mitigate these serious problems of inequality and segregation, and to connect, integrate and coordinate the city through an instrument of physical and social inclusion. Architecture and urbanism were the primary tools for working with the community to implement a process for the recovery of the city's neighbourhoods. Through multidisciplinary teams, these projects sought the best-quality designs, and improved the relationship of design with its context through combining actions at the large scale, such as public transport infrastructures and facilities, with actions at the small scale, such as trails, pedestrian bridges and neighbourhood parks.

In order to precisely identify the areas in which to intervene and to define an order of priorities, designs evolved from a deep understanding of the territory in its broadest and most complex sense, and of the relationship between natural, cultural and urban conditions. Each project was required to start with a holistic vision to form a connecting strategy to physical, programmatic and social interventions. Physical continuity was sought between different interventions to ensure complementarity. Through adding programme, the city sought to build new networks of public facilities for low-income neighbourhoods strategically located throughout the territory. From a social perspective, the goal was to identify processes and dynamics that emerge from the community and from different stakeholders, working to foster local participation and appropriation before, during and after the interventions.

The interventions, in turn, were defined through strategic urban projects, each with its own project manager responsible for opening up channels of communication and coordinating relations between the different actors and institutions involved. These projects were developed by a decentralised public institution that formed part of the organic structure of the city and which offered special dedicated multidisciplinary technical teams. Since 2004, the city has developed architectural and urban projects including libraries, educational facilities, social housing in risk areas, and a number of parks.

At the local scale, Medellín looked to construct the best possible buildings in some of the city's poorest neighbourhoods, claiming the symbolic value of architecture as a physical expression of new public policies for education and culture. Border regions of exclusion were converted into permeable places for integration. The new facilities, awarded through public tenders, focused on the creation of spaces of encounter that serve as urban landmarks and gathering spaces for the community. The first phase of the programme included five library parks: Belen, España, La Ladera, La Quintana and San Javier, catering for 72 of the city's districts, creating 21,393 square metres (230,272 square feet) of built space, including playgrounds, internet access and reading rooms, and 71,643 square metres (771,158 square feet) of public space. The project also included 10 new public schools and the renovation of 132 existing schools that are part of the Open School programme, benefiting 418,000 students, and generating 65,000 square metres (699,654 square feet) of built space and 189,300 square metres (2,037,608 square feet) of public space. Educational programmes were developed to activate and manage these new spaces, such as entrepreneurship, sustainability and art programmes.

At the urban scale, integrated urban projects (IUPs) were executed in areas of elevated marginalisation and violence, identifying and prioritising a set of neighbourhoods as early intervention models, framed within a six-year programme. The Northeastern zone of Medellín was selected as the first stage for the implementation of the pilot project in five areas. This sector presented the lowest quality of life and human development

Architecture and urbanism were the primary tools for working with the community to implement a process for the recovery of the city's neighbourhoods.

EDU Design Workshop, Medellín, 2008
below: The city's urban development institute created this pedestrian bridge connecting the neighbourhoods of Andalucía and La Francia.

EDU Housing Workshop, Northeastern Integrated Urban Project (IUP), Medellín, 2008
bottom: Interventions focused on mitigating risks and improving environmental conditions, the construction of new four- and five-storey residential buildings in the valley for relocated families, and improvements to dwellings that were not in a critical condition.

Alejandro Echeverri, Explora Science and Technology Park and the Carabobo Promenade, Medellín, 2008
opposite: One of the flagship projects is the Carabobo Urban Promenade in the city centre; 3.5 kilometres (2.17 miles) in length, it connects the traditional city centre with the 'New North'.

The intention was to provide the city with a network of public spaces that improved pedestrian mobility, allowing people to meet and move through a quality public realm.

index (HDI) in the city. The area was chosen for the creation of the first public gondola lift system integrated with the subway. The new base stations were essential in defining the overall strategy of physical intervention.

With the aim of enabling a physically and socially sustainable model of implementation for a city in which the majority of slopes and valleys are occupied by marginal housing, the first pilot housing project was developed along the Juan Bobo stream. Such natural environments, including hills and streams that have been invaded by informal settlements, are referred to as 'invaded urban ecosystems'. The intervention in this area increased the quantity of public space from 0.5 square metres (5.3 square feet) per person to 6 square metres (64.5 square feet) per person, and succeeded in legalising 100 per cent of housing, 80 per cent of which was informally constructed.

The intention was to provide the city with a network of public spaces that improved pedestrian mobility, allowing people to meet and move through a quality public realm. For those neighbourhoods located on the slopes, inhabited by populations with the lowest incomes in the city, a gondola lift system and an articulated BRT were developed, both of which were integrated with the existing subway network and aimed to improve the quality of life and accessibility in these communities.

All of the strategies mentioned above were part of a broader policy of social urbanism that sought to generate a qualitative leap forward from the traditional understanding of neighbourhood improvement. The policy employed such tools as IUPs to bring structural changes to strategic sectors of poorly consolidated neighbourhoods, and the design of habitats within fragile natural systems to achieve the definitive integration of marginalised communities. Currently, these programmes continue to develop under the political leadership of Mayor Alonso Salazar.

Conclusion

New strategies for intervention flourished through the processes of independent political leadership beginning first in Bogotá (inspired by the revitalisation of Barcelona's neighbourhoods in the 1980s and 1990s) and thereafter Medellín (largely inspired by the Favela-Barrio project in Rio de Janeiro that began in 1993). Today, Sergio Fajardo, Antanas Mokus and Enrique Peñalosa belong to the green party, but all were first elected as independents. The technical teams, including architects and urban designers, were similar in both cities; however, it is important to note that architecture and urban interventions were not an end in themselves, but were tools to express the political intention of municipal programmes.

In Medellín there was a greater focus on specific territories with a singular architecture, or 'protagonism in pieces and its connections'. Integral urban projects and punctual interventions sought to improve public spaces and housing, and to generate a new image of the city through providing new symbolic references. In particular, interventions improved frontier areas, converting them into permeable and more desirable neighbourhoods. This approach differed from that of Bogotá, where the focus was more on systems or networks and included cross-cutting systems of transport, like the TransMilenio, pedestrian corridors and cycle routes, always emphasising the quality of the new civic buildings and public spaces that act as icons in the reinvention of the city's image.

Despite their different approaches, the end result was similar in both cities. In the past 15 years, both have played host to a dramatic democratisation through enabling a level of social integration. In both cases, providing quality urban infrastructure and amenities in the poorest and most violent neighbourhoods has provided those residents with a sense of equality and a feeling of stewardship within their own city. This change in residents' image of their city, and their new-found sense of belonging, have transformed Bogotá and Medellín from being 'uninhabitable' to today being the hip and trendy belles of the ball. ∆

Notes
1. Bogotá 8,840,000; Medellín 3,370,000; Cali 2,730,000; Barranquilla 1,950,000; Cartagena 1,200,000; Cúcuta 920,000; Bucaramanga 566,000; Ibaqué 518,000.
2. See www.banrep.gov.co/blaavirtual/revistas/credencial/enero2001/colmundo.htm.
3. The Manual de diseño y ubiación de elementos en el espacio público (Manual for design and location for elements in the public space) was developed in 2000, during Enrique Peñalosa's term as mayor, and was composed of three parts: 1) Cartilla de Andenes (streetscape design); 2) Cartilla de Mobiliario Urbano (urban furniture); and 3) Cartilla Manual Verde (green landscape).

The authors would like to thank Juan Sebastian Bustamante and Natalia Castaño for their collaboration on this text.

Text © 2011 John Wiley & Sons Ltd. Images: pp 96, 97(b) © Enrique Guzmán García; pp 97(t), 99(b), 100 © Lorenzo Castro; p 98 © Diana Moreno; p 99(t) © Carlos Naranjo; p 100(t) © Luis Adriano Ramírez; p 100(b) © Alcaldía de Medellín; p 102 © Oscar Santana; p 103 © Andrea González

FROM PRODUCT TO PROCESS
BUILDING ON URBAN-THINK TANK'S APPROACH TO THE INFORMAL CITY

Adriana Navarro-Sertich interviews a pioneer of the informal in architecture, co-founder and co-director of Urban-Think Tank (U-TT) **Alfredo Brillembourg**. Brillembourg explains how U-TT's work seeks to connect informal settlements with the formal city, enabling inhabitants to access services and infrastructure. U-TT is now taking the lessons it has learnt in working in Latin American cities, such as Caracas and São Paulo, elsewhere in the world with the aim of 'working globally and acting locally'.

U-TT, Vertical Gymnasium Petare, Caracas, 2007–11
This Vertical Gym has a ground-floor commercial base level with small shops for informal vendors.

Social and cultural responsibility is returning to the forefront of contemporary architecture. We are now witnessing spectacular libraries in depressed neighbourhoods, cable-car systems in marginalised areas and museums in informal settlements. Through interventions that acknowledge and legitimise the potentials of urban informality, designers have begun to adopt the 'informal city' as a new paradigm. Alongside the increasing traction of this paradigm, analyses of key issues and questions, as well as short- and long-term outcomes of such interventions, are critical. One pioneer in this field is co-founder and co-director of Urban-Think Tank (U-TT) Alfredo Brillembourg.

Starting out as an NGO (Caracas Think Tank) conducting research in the barrios (informal settlements) of Caracas, founders Brillembourg (a Venezuelan architect educated at Columbia University) and Hubert Klumpner (an Austrian architect also educated at Columbia) soon started making proposals for the city, in the process transforming their practice into the architecture firm Urban-Think Tank in 1998. With work including a series of Vertical Gymnasiums, the first of which was constructed in 2004 in Bello Campo (Caracas), the Metro Cable in Caracas (2010), the FAVA autistic children's school and the community centre proposal for Paraisópolis (São Paulo) projected for 2012, they view themselves as 'contemporary architects working in conflict zones'. Although many of these interventions are relatively new, exploring the approach, methodology and impact is essential to further both the discourse and practice.

Brillembourg began by explaining that U-TT's projects seek to 'connect the formal and informal city'. The main objective is to give the inhabitants of the local communities better accessibility and services, and to bring some of the infrastructure from the formal city into the informal city.

'We have developed an "In Your Face" methodology because cities in the developing world are legitimately in a crisis. We can be working in Jordan, where we are doing a project in Rusaifah, a Palestinian refugee camp; it could be in a Moroccan community in Utrecht, in Kibera where we have been doing some work, or in São Paulo … Those places and people are very much on the edge, so you really have to engage the informal systems in these big metropolises.'

Working in Caracas, São Paulo, Rusaifah and Kibera, among other places, U-TT has been clear in its push to establish a global practice, 'working globally and acting locally'. In doing so, Brillembourg states that the aim is 'to develop best practices of typologies that can be repeated in different areas of the world, but which get adapted locally'. In an article entitled 'Slum Lifting',[1] U-TT hinted at these 'best practices', listing a number of challenges within slums followed by a set of solutions. For example, for transportation and infrastructure, U-TT suggests decentralised public service systems, modular stairs and cable-car systems; or for the socioeconomic wellbeing of dwellers, encourages sustainable development, urban agriculture, prefabrication and modular design. Working in what he terms 'territories of speed and need', Brillembourg clarifies that U-TT creates a framework, hands it over to municipalities, and welcomes re-adaptations from local communities. 'We don't pretend to control the project up to the last screw,' he affirms.

The idea of establishing best practices highlights the importance of transferring knowledge and supporting transnational analyses in research and urban practice. It also raises questions about the transferability of projects. When asked about the differences and similarities in U-TT's approach to the multiple projects and contexts, Brillembourg says: 'We try to start our projects from an ethical position, but there are different cultural frameworks depending on the context … Culture greatly modifies what type of technology or design we attempt to make. Generally, we engage the community profoundly in discussions and meetings, and we bring this community development practice to each place, though often with different methods of implementation.'

Declaring that 'the idea of transferring knowledge from the comfortable distance of a New York office is a big problem', Brillembourg stresses the importance of being on the ground and engaging with the social, political and economic aspects of the local community. For this reason, U-TT has established offices in Caracas, New York, São Paulo and Zürich. He adds: 'Architecture is much more interesting if you attack it from the grass-roots community perspective because sustainability really means focusing on the user and his or her connection to a building. Thus it is not about the formal aspects, but about the way it works, the programme.'

Cultural specificities, in addition to the politics of place with its particular socioeconomic dynamics, set up very different conditions and value systems that are embedded within the urban fabric. Although physical challenges might be similar from place to place, the manner in which these challenges are addressed needs to be very specific to the context. Will projects be received and used in the same manner in different areas and situations? When we speak of use, we also speak of associated socioeconomic outcomes. For example, will the impact of a metro cable in Caracas or Medellín be the same in other places? Can projects in São Paulo's favelas be relevant solutions for Johannesburg's townships?

Contingent on this, in speaking about 'connecting the informal to the formal', we need to understand that the informal city is not disconnected from the formal city. Quite the opposite: informality is not a product but a process, constantly in the making, shifting and redefining relationships

Working in what he terms 'territories of speed and need', Brillembourg clarifies that U-TT creates a framework, hands it over to municipalities, and welcomes re-adaptations from local communities. 'We don't pretend to control the project up to the last screw,' he affirms.

U-TT and Guy Battle, Baruta Vertical Gymnasium #2, Santa Cruz del Este, Caracas, 2007–11
opposite: This second version of the Vertical Gymnasium incorporates the use of recyclable materials, wind towers, solar panels and rainwater collection as part of the design complying with the Kyoto Protocol.

U-TT, Metro Cable Station and Vertical Gymnasium, San Agustin, Caracas, 2010
below left: Integrated within the La Ceiba metro cable station, this Vertical Gymnasium is made of prefabricated bolted channel steel.

below right: Rendering and diagram of La Ceiba metro cable station and Vertical Gymnasium.

with the formal.² As such, when considering the informal, we need to acknowledge multiple dynamics, including income levels and employment, the value of real-estate, tenure and legality. By looking at informality as a product, or as merely an issue of form and morphological conditions, physical design interventions ignore critical factors related to the process. The importance of linking design to policy is testimony to the significance of these factors.

One of the biggest obstacles for many of the practices and projects dealing with informality is a failure to integrate with the policies of government agencies. When asked his opinion on the latter, Brillembourg replied that a large amount of U-TT's time and attention is dedicated to engaging cities' mayors within the process and communicating the power of design in bringing visibility and awareness: 'The engineering of practical quick fixes is necessary, but if innovative design is not integrated then we lose the opportunity to create a sense of pride. If there is no pride, the community won't feel integrated with the building, and over time the project loses its potential and gets sucked back into the informal fabric.'

Moreover, reinforcing the idea of best practices, Brillembourg affirms that the purpose of 'paring back architecture to its elements, and making it simple and repeatable,' is to convince mayors, who are only in office for three to five years, to implement a project. 'The only way that you can convince them is if they can cut a ribbon, because they are looking for political capital,' he explains.

In addition to getting politicians onside is the need to directly engage with city policy and planning. For these projects to be effective, they need to be part of the larger city plan, thereby becoming integral to strategies of social inclusion, mobility, security and environmental protection. They will become instrumental in restitching the city, providing the necessary opportunities for economic growth and sustainable development. Currently, some of the more striking interventions have been manifestations of continuous and integral government policies and planning strategies, with some private-sector support. Clear examples are Medellín's Social Urbanism, Guayaquil's Malecón 2000 urban regeneration projects, or Rio de Janeiro's well-known Favela-Barrio programme.³ In contrast, the delicate political climate and centralised government structure in U-TT's home country, Venezuela, have impeded the implementation of similar strategies there, with the result that the 1990s Physical Habilitation of the Barrios Program culminated in punctuated and disconnected projects.

Despite the difficulties in Venezuela, U-TT continues to look for new ways of reconfiguring the city, pushing for experimentation and redefining the role of the architect: 'Hubert and I identify with the role of film producers, activists or even social entrepreneurs. We attempt to put together communities, design ideas and urban actors on the ground who are the

U-TT, Metro Cable, San Agustin, Caracas, 2010
below left: The metro cable is located in the San Agustin barrio, adjacent to Caracas city centre. The design of the station incorporates, at the base of the buildings, programmes for social, cultural and sports activities. Currently, due to lack of funding, the building bases are walled off and the stations only function for the cable-car system.

below right: Transportation systems, such as the metro cable in San Agustin, have the possibility of becoming a catalyst for urban and social change if they are well integrated with the transportation infrastructure of the city and are accompanied by programmes focusing on socioeconomic factors.

San Agustin's cable-car system is so new that its real impact and sustainability are yet be seen. The painted houses (using the colours of the Venezuelan flag – yellow, blue and red – are the work of the Misión Tricolor, the national initiative for barrio development.

In the world of the informal city, where choices are limited and informality is sometimes the only option for survival or resistance, these interventions and design-centred approaches are opportunities for the local people to gain recognition and to claim their rights to the city.

U-TT, Rusaifah Community Centre Vertical Gymnasium #5, Amman, Jordan, 2010–12
opposite bottom: Designed as a network of youth centres for the city, the design includes a Vertical Gymnasium and social centre that are to be modified depending on the site.

U-TT, Vertical Gymnasium Chacao, Caracas, 2004
below left: The Chacao gym was developed with U-TT associate partners M Pinto and consists of welded pieces with square steel-tube sections.

U-TT Sport Spot, Hoograven, Utrecht, The Netherlands, 2008–10
below right: The Hoograven Sport Spot is integrated with the Dutch Rowing Club.

stakeholders in order to produce high-quality architecture … We look at bringing together different people, different disciplines and coming up with new products.'

In this experimentation, it is also critical to look to the past. An important lesson learnt from previous projects, practitioners and theorists is that we cannot de-politicise the question of informality, solely focusing on packages of physical transformations. As practices like U-TT reflect, dependence on time and space makes the concept of best practices obsolete if it is disengaged from a more holistic approach which engages the local community, and acknowledges internal hierarchies, cultures, values, race, gender, local aesthetics and functional standards, as well as working directly with sociologists and anthropologists, and becoming more ethnographic in its approach.

'This is the paradoxical problem of today's designers – how to address contemporary crises with future-oriented solutions. But unlike the paradigms of last century's architects, we must not seek one solitary answer to our complex problems. Instead we must embrace the idea that good products and processes will only arise when the discourse that births them consists of both words and actions.'

In the world of the informal city, where choices are limited and informality is sometimes the only option for survival or resistance, these interventions and design-centred approaches are opportunities for the local people to gain recognition and to claim their rights to the city. As we continue to follow and perhaps mirror work such as that of U-TT, we need to understand and evaluate the impact and use value of our strategies and interventions to avoid falling into the trap of adopting an image of social good instead of addressing the social and economic realities of everyday life. 🅐

Notes
1. A Brillemburg and H Klumpner, 'Slum Lifting', in *Sustainable Living Urban Model Laboratory (S.L.U.M. Lab)*, SPAE São Paulo Edition, Columbia University Graduate School of Architecture, Planning and Preservation (New York City), 2010, pp 12–13.
2. Manuel Castells and Alejandro Portes, 'World Underneath: The Origins, Dynamics and Effects of the Informal Economy', in *The Informal Economy*, Johns Hopkins University Press (Baltimore, MD), 1989, pp 11–37.
3. To give some background on the examples cited: Medellín's Social Urbanism, part of former mayor Fajardo's 'Medellín la más educada' (Medellín the most educated), has resulted in an extensive network of libraries and public spaces (proyectos urbanos integrales) in depressed areas of the city. Guayaquil's urban regeneration projects, such as Las Peñas and El Malecón Salado, are part of a larger beautification scheme for the city that began with the downtown waterfront renovation project, Malecón 2000. The interventions are designed, constructed and maintained by a private organisation that works directly with the municipality, the Fundación Malecón 2000. Finally, Rio de Janeiro's Favela-Barrio programme, with the financial support of the IDB, focused on infrastructure and public space interventions in medium-sized favelas. Today, through the national PAC, or Growth Acceleration Programme, a similar strategy to the Favela-Barrio is being implemented in Rio's larger favelas.

Text © 2011 John Wiley & Sons Ltd. Images: pp 104(t)-105, 106-7, 108(b), 109 © Urban-Think Tank; p 104(b) © Joost Bataille; p 108(t) © © Adriana Navarro-Sertich

LATIN AMERICAN MEANDER IN SEARCH OF A NEW CIVIC IMAGINATION

Teddy Cruz reviews the shifting political landscape of the last two decades in Latin America. Breaking from US dependency, the continent has charted an alternative course as municipalities have reconnected public policy, social justice and civic imagination. In order to address inequality, new models of urban development have been produced on sites of scarcity, and city mayors and administrations have been prepared to learn from each other through best practice.

I lived the first 20 years of my life in Guatemala City, until early 1982 when I migrated to the US to continue my architectural studies. During those convoluted years in Latin America – Guatemala being one of its epicentres of social injustice – I never imagined that the oppressive regimes consolidated by military dictatorships, rooted oligarchy and US Cold War interventionism that atrophied social and economic progress throughout this continent would transform so rapidly. Latin America has in fact radically reconfigured itself sociopolitically and economically in the last years, becoming one of the main sectors in the world, breaking away from US-style globalisation, charting instead its own idea of social and economic progress.

The institutional transformations that have been taking place in many South American capitals, including La Paz, Brasilia, Caracas, Lima and La Asunción have been altering the previous established protocols of control and influence that had traditionally aligned many of these countries with Washington DC, pointing at a very different political landscape that was hard to imagine barely 15 years ago. It has been surreal, for example, during this time to see the ascension to power of counter-establishment civic figures such as ex-union leader Ignácio de Lula in Brazil, who just ended a successful two-term presidency in this country, and Bolivian Evo Morales who, in an unprecedented way, opened the possibility for the under-represented aboriginal class of Bolivia to claim the presidency of that country.

In the context of the history of US-Latin American relations, I have found that this transformational process produced a strange cultural reversal: the institutional deficiency and corruption, the chronic illegality and infrastructural precariousness that generally shaped the US perception of Latin America have now mutated to Washington DC and Wall Street. In other words, the consolidation of the US-led neoliberal, freemarket policies that culminated in the recent global economic collapse have been, at their very base, defined by unprecedented 'illegality' (the unchecked abuses of Wall Street are well documented by now, and continue to be emblematised by the mortgage crisis that drove millions of people to lose their homes) and 'uneven development' (in the US, recent years have been defined by an abandonment and de-funding of public institutions and infrastructure, as seen with the Katrina disaster in New Orleans and the polarisation between enclaves of economic power and the sectors of precariousness that surround them).

Furthermore, the instalment of this institutionalised, greedy individualism that has widened the gap between wealth and poverty so dramatically today also yielded hyper-nationalist protectionist strategies which, fuelled by politics of fear and paranoia, defined a radically conservative social agenda that has had a fundamental impact on urban planning policy and legislation, yielding the incremental privatisation and erosion of public culture in the US. It is somehow against this US-driven sociocultural closure of the last years, polarising the individual and the collective, that Latin America, generally speaking, has begun to chart a very different course, an alternative future: Latin American governments, from Brazil to Colombia, have produced a paradigm shift in matters of urban development, seeking – like no other place in the world – to reconnect public policy, social justice and civic imagination.

New Sites of Experimentation:
An Urbanism Beyond the Property Line

While the world's architecture intelligentsia – supported by the glamorous economy of the last years – flocked en masse to the Arab Emirates and China to help build the dream castles that would catapult these enclaves of wealth to being global epicentres of urban development, many of these high-profile projects have in fact only perpetuated the exhausted recipes of an oil-hungry, US-style globalisation, camouflaging with hyper-aesthetics an architecture of exclusion based in many cases on urbanities of surveillance and control. Other than a few isolated protagonist architectural interventions whose images have been disseminated widely, no major ideas were advanced here to transform existing paradigms of housing, infrastructure and density, and resolve the major problems of urbanisation today which are grounded in the inability of institutions of urban development to engage with informality, socioeconomic inequity and lack of affordable housing and infrastructure.

While the attention of the world had been focused on those enclaves of abundance, the most radical ideas advancing new models of urban development were produced on sites of scarcity, across Latin American cities. Challenging entrenched neoliberal urban logics of development founded on top-down privatisation, homogeneity and exclusion, visionary mayors in cities such as Porto Alegre, Curitiba, Bogotá and Medellín began to enable new institutional protocols by producing new interfaces with publics and unorthodox cross-institutional collaborations, rethinking the very meaning of infrastructure, housing and density, and mediating top-down development and bottom-up social organisation. I cannot think of any other continental region in the world where we can find this type of collective effort led by municipal and federal governments seeking a new brand of progressive politics to produce an urbanism of inclusion.

Different to the other epicentres of development in the world that in recent years relied on conventional planning approaches 'from above', sponsoring stand-alone experimental architectural gestures supported by large capital and corporate branding, many of these Latin American cities were experimenting, in fact, by reconfiguring socioeconomic relations first, uncovering the potential of informal systems and social networks to rethink urbanisation, negotiating formal and informal economies and large and small scales of development. Much of this experimentation began a few years ago with unorthodox public policies and economics, which have already become mythical.

These experiments ranged, for example, from the decision by the municipality of Porto Alegre in Brazil to enact 'participatory budgets', enabling communities to decide the distribution of municipal budgets; to Brazilian president Ignácio de Lula's economic policy awarding property titles to thousands of slum dwellers in Rio de Janeiro and declaring the intervention into slums as a vital part of his urban development agenda, not by erasure but by retrofit; to the announcement by President Evo Morales that he would insert illegal coca production into the Bolivian national economy to subsidise social housing; to Bogotá's ex-mayor Antanas Mockus' mobilisation of a civic culture founded on a massive urban pedagogical project that paved the way for one of the most successful public transportation systems in the world, Colombia's TransMilenio project; to Mayor Sergio Fajardo's decision that he would transform his violence-ridden city by building an infrastructure of public library parks in the slums of Medellín; and also even to Venezuelan Hugo Chávez's demagogic proclamations promising to give huge oil revenues to the poor of his country towards the formation of the new socialist city. All have become paradigmatic gestures during recent years.

Even though much has been written about these important realised projects in Latin America, there is still a lot of missing information. Most of the descriptions behind these projects focus on the achievements themselves, as final products, but very seldom, if not at all, can we find specific narrations that convey the sociopolitical and economic processes behind many of the transactions, exchanges and negotiations that took place across institutions and with the public to make these projects happen. In other words, beyond the images emerging from these success stories I have been seeking to understand the main sociopolitical and economic procedures behind many of these emblematic projects. While these processes of negotiation across institutions are natural to the institutions of planning, the stories behind these projects are much more complex, as these depended on generating new socioeconomic protocols that would in turn produce a new public domain.

There is not the space here to elaborate on the specificity of such procedures –an essential part of my research practice is in fact the retroactive mapping of the processes emerging from the global South, translating not their images, but their operative procedures so that those urban operations can enable public policy and activism in the US. But it is important to mention a couple of revelations that in my mind emerged from some of these projects and have been inspirational to my practice as an architect working on the border between Latin America and the US. The revelations have to do primarily with identifying a couple of major conceptual strands that framed these models of possibility: an investment in urban pedagogy – the transfer of knowledge across governments and publics – and the pursuit of a civic culture and social justice as the basis for an inclusive urbanisation.

One major idea that is seldom discussed about these projects is the way in which they informed each other, from Brazil to Colombia. The exchange of knowledge across successive governments, from federal to municipal, learning from one another and in so doing refining the tactics and strategies of the other. It is impossible, for example, to think of the success story of Enrique Peñalosa's TransMilenio bus rapid transit system in Bogotá without the lessons transferred from ex-Mayor Jamie Lerner's experiments with public transportation in Curitiba, whereby retrofitted existing roads were retrofitted to eliminate cars, allowing an uninterrupted flow of buses that would operate as a metro system on the surface, by also producing elevated bus stations so as to increase the accessibility and time frequency of the system. Peñalosa took these urban logics to another level of refinement and complexity in TransMilenio by layering it with other infrastructural categories, enabling a system of transfers to move across different scales of mobility, from pedestrian to bicycle to bus, and interconnecting a network of public spaces, libraries and housing projects, between the centre and the periphery of the city, between enclaves of wealth and sectors of informality. In turn, this experience ended up informing ex-Mayor Sergio Fajardo in the creation of Library-Parks, a unique typology of public space he injected into the slums around Medellín, as an antidote to fight violence with education.

Another major aspect behind this transfer of knowledge that ultimately enabled critical interfaces between governments, from the top down, and social activism, from the bottom up, is the fact that all of these projects began with a committed investment in education at the scale of the metropolitan: an urban pedagogy that would close the gap between institutions and publics. The success of the Participatory Budgets policy in Porto Alegre depended on the formation of a civic culture, where the dissemination of information across community activists would enable a citizen-led political will that intensified public participation in the distribution of economic resources at the scale of communities. The visualisation and democratisation of information became the tool to enable this public policy. Similarly, Jamie Lerner in Curitiba famously rallied the elementary schools of the city to lead a pedagogical project towards environmental sustainability, which would be guided by children putting pressure on their parents to become accountable for recycling. Learning from many of these precedents, one of the most effective campaigns elaborating on the relationship between urban pedagogy and the formation of a civic culture that would enable a very different idea of public spending and infrastructure occurred years later in Bogotá.

Former mayor of Bogotá Antanas Mockus led one of the most comprehensive public policies to promote a civic imagination, by enacting idiosyncratic public legislature inclusive of social activism. A fundamental reorganisation of social systems occurred here that capitalised on the creative intelligence of communities and activists, mobilising mutual support and volunteerism in the shape of citizen-led collaborations to face the most pressing urban problems in the contemporary city, including violence, political apathy, social indifference, environmental degradation and lack of economic resources. This massive mobilisation of the citizenry allowed the most intangible of factors in the shaping of the next urban revolution to enter the collective imaginary: that communities themselves can, in fact, be participants in the shaping of the city of the future; and that the identity of this city is based not on the dominance of private development alone and its exorbitant budgets to sponsor the image of progress, but it can also emerge from the value of social capital and incremental layering of urban development, enabling a more inclusive idea of ownership.

So successful did this campaign of strengthening a civil society in order to reduce urban violence become that it prompted the willing participation of particular socioeconomic sectors in 'pay-as-you-want' capital contributions that would increase the city's tax base for enabling urban infrastructural improvements. It is very seldom discussed, but it is this fundamental reframing of sociopolitical and economic protocols that enabled the materialisation of Peñalosa's vision in shaping the TransMilenio project. Similarly, Antanas Mockus built upon the intelligent work of previous administrations that by the early 1980s had begun to shape a comprehensive progressive political document, a conceptual scaffold for dealing with Colombia's anticipated urban growth, called POT, the Territorial Organizing Plan. This document was founded conceptually on issues pertaining to complexity theory sprinkled with progressive politics, aspiring to a civic humanism based on the Rights to the City movement. This document and its subsequent iterations have framed many of these achievements, moving from the large scale of the territory all the way to the scale of neighbourhoods and communities, connecting the abstraction of large-planning logics with the specificity of everyday practices within communities.

Sergio Fajardo enabled this level of specificity when designing a policy that would redefine the conventional idea of public space at the scale of community. His famous Library-Parks in Medellín opened the critique that our conception of public space is too abstract and neutral: the naive idea that if we simply design a nice looking plaza we would magically assure socialisation. Instead, he proposed levels of specificity by injecting tactical programming into open space. Each park or public space in this city would be plugged with pedagogical support systems hybridising social space with knowledge. This was a powerful message, in my mind, that moved the discussion from the neutrality of public infrastructure to the specificity of urban rights: the radical democratisation of space by enabling access and concrete civic rights to diverse publics and communities.

The translation of these processes into new urban paradigms that can be replicated at other scales and even with different sociopolitical actors is an essential point of departure for my work. The conceptual legacy of these projects and the sense of possibility they engender to produce a different approach to a more democratic form of urban development, away from the selfish recipes of urbanisation that have permeated the world in the last two decades, have inspired the transformation of my practice in recent years, as I have been researching the impact of the Latin American immigrants in the transformation of many US neighbourhoods, using the US–Mexico border as a laboratory to rethink affordable housing and infrastructure.

Seeking expanded models of architecture practice and a new role for the arts and humanities in shaping new public policy is the primary effort we need to engage in these times of crises. In this context, it is very telling that many of the visionary mayors in Latin America discussed briefly here have, in fact, come from the arts and the humanities, such as Mockus and Fajardo, for example, who are both philosophers and mathematicians, and Lerner is an architect. When asked about their move from pedagogy into politics they usually respond that their incursion into the political arena sprang from a necessity to engage a new brand of progressive politics. Here they suggest that to engage the political is not to be a 'politician' but to enact a course of action.

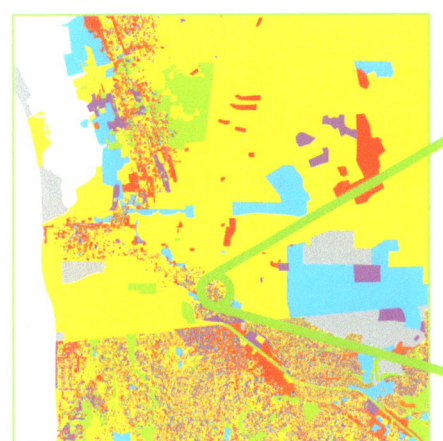  

An Urbanism of Retrofit
The multicoloured 'confetti' of a transborder migrant urbanism deposits itself in many older California neighbourhoods – pixelating the large with the small. Mono-use parcels are transformed into complex, micro socioeconomic systems. While the global city becomes the privileged site of consumption and display, the immigrant local neighbourhood remains a site of production, of new cultural and socioeconomic relations.

Top Down Institution
Economic value as seed of development for the city.
Private developer sees ...

| **Housing Development** as market owned |
| **Profit** as an individual's right |
| **Density** as maximum amount of units and minimum investment in public infrastructure |
| **Inhabitants** as generic customers |

the power of
Economic Capital

- City Official
- Financing
- Designing Collaboration
- Community Activist
- Neighbourhood Participant

the power of
Social Capital

Bottom Up Agency
Cultural and social value as economic engine for the neighbourhood
Community Activist sees ...

| **Housing Development** as neighbourhood owned |
| **Profit** as the community's right |
| **Density** as maximum social exchanges per acre embedded in public infrastructure |
| **Inhabitants** as participants |

Casa Familiar Micro-Policy

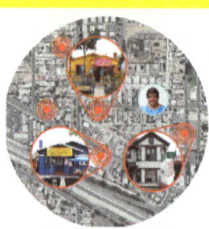 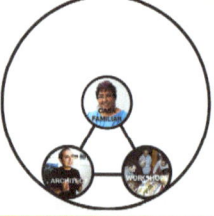

1 Translating the Informal
Casa Familiar coordinates mapping and documenting of all non-conforming additions and mixed uses.

 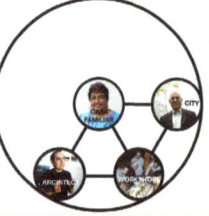

2 New Zoning Categories
City Hall legalises non-conforming units through a new affordable housing overlay zone and authorises their reconstruction.

3 Casa Familiar: Informal City Hall
NGO facilitates the design and production of plug-in additions. City Hall prepackages new units' construction permits and allows NGO to manage process.

4 Casa Familiar: Facilitator of Micro Lending
NGO manages prepackaged tax credits and other subsidies and facilitates micro credits by breaking large construction loans. Residents partner NGO to co-own resources.

1. **The Neighbourhood as a Site of Production**
Designing political and economic processes
2. **An Urbanism of Coexistence**
Redefining density as the number of social exchanges per acre
Redefining housing as a system of economic and cultural interactions

Tax credit subsidies do not support small development; existing land uses prohibit alternative mix uses and small plot housing densities.

No advances in housing design and affordability can be achieved without advances in housing policy and economy.

Micro Infrastructures for Coexistence

 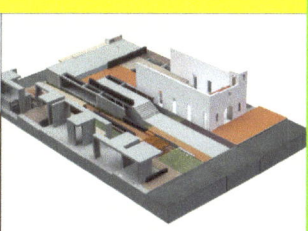
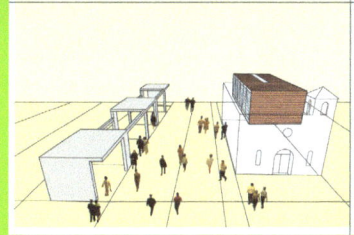 

Small public rooms, a community garden and the retrofitting of a historic church serve as a social framework for housing.

FLEXIBLE UNITS FOR YOUNG | ARTISTS LIVE-WORK DUPLEX | CASA FAMILIAR HUB FOR | EXTENDED FAMILIES ACESSORY | LARGE FAMILIES LIVING WITH

Flexible units for young adults and single mothers + Artists live-work duplex + Casa Familiar Hub for social infrastructure + Extended families acessory buildings + Large families living with grandmothers.

The tactical distribution of diverse housing building types within a small infrastructure of collective spaces supports different housing economies and demographics.

Casa Familiar Programmes		Informal Uses/ Time Scenarios
Tues 3:30 PM	ARTS WORKSHOPS	
FARMER'S MARKET	Sun 9:30AM	
Sat 7:30 PM	QUINCEÑERA	
COLLECTIVE KITCHEN	Wed 6:00 PM	
Mon 10:30 AM	CATERING LEASE	
PUBLIC SYMPOSIUM	Sat 4:00 PM	
Sun 1:00 PM	GARDEN ORIENTATION	
GALLERY SHOW	Fri 8:00 PM	
Wed 7:30 PM	COMMUNITY MEETING	

A small frame, co-owned by residents, is conceived as a social service infrastructure threaded into housing. Plugged with electricity and collective kitchens, the frame is activated across time with specific social, cultural and economic programming tactically choreographed by Casa Familiar.

CASA FAMILIAR: THE PERFORMANCE OF A SMALL PARCEL

Located in the border neighbourhood of San Ysidro, community-based NGO Casa Familiar has evolved from a social service provider into an alternative developer of affordable housing. Estudio Teddy Cruz's collaboration with Casa Familiar has conceived the neighbourhood as a producer of new housing policy and economy, focusing on designing parcels as small infrastructures that mobilise social entrepreneurship into new spaces for housing, cultural production and political participation.

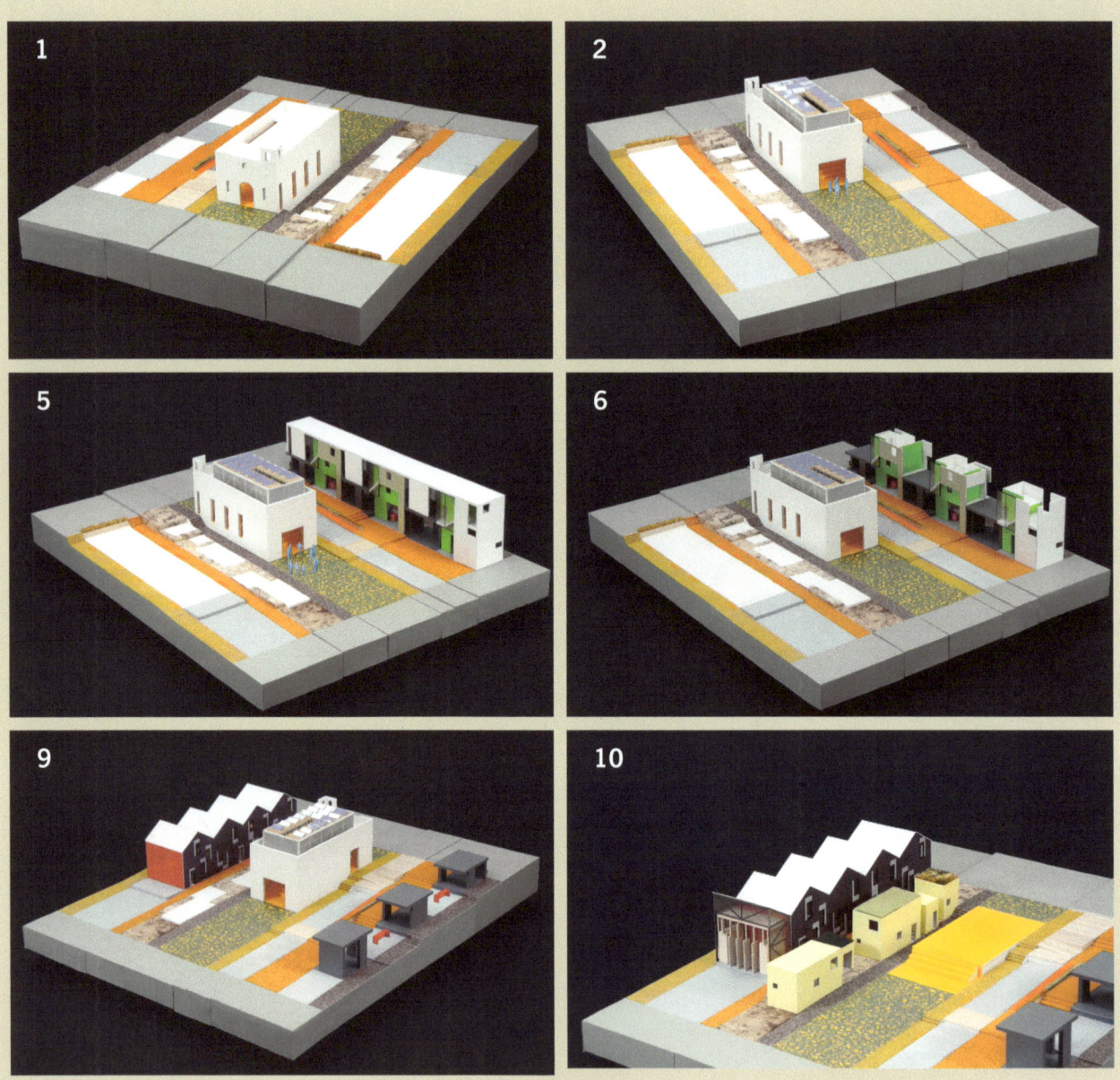

(1) Casa Familiar acquired a large parcel with an old church and then subdivided it into smaller slivers, anticipating a finer pixelation of property and circulation. **(2)** The church is retrofitted into an incubator of cultural production where Casa Familiar will generate new categories of socioeconomic programming. For Casa Familiar, housing is not sustainable as units only. It needs to be plugged with economic and cultural support systems. **(3)** Open frames, conceived as social rooms, are equipped with electricity, collective kitchens and movable urban furniture. Casa Familiar injects them with specific cultural and economic programming. The church, social rooms, collective kitchens and community gardens are the small infrastructure for housing. **(4)** Here, the void is more than open space for private housing growth; it is the site made available for injecting specific collective programming to support informal economies and social organisation. Such tactical programming enables new interfaces with the public, across time (Thursdays: new community workshops; Saturdays: framing Informal markets; every day: collective kitchens) supporting entrepreneurship. **(5–6)** Housing type 1: Young couples, single mothers with children. More than just renting or owning units, dwellers are participants in co-managing socioeconomic programmes. **(7)** Housing type 2: Live–work duplex for artists. The exchange of rent for social

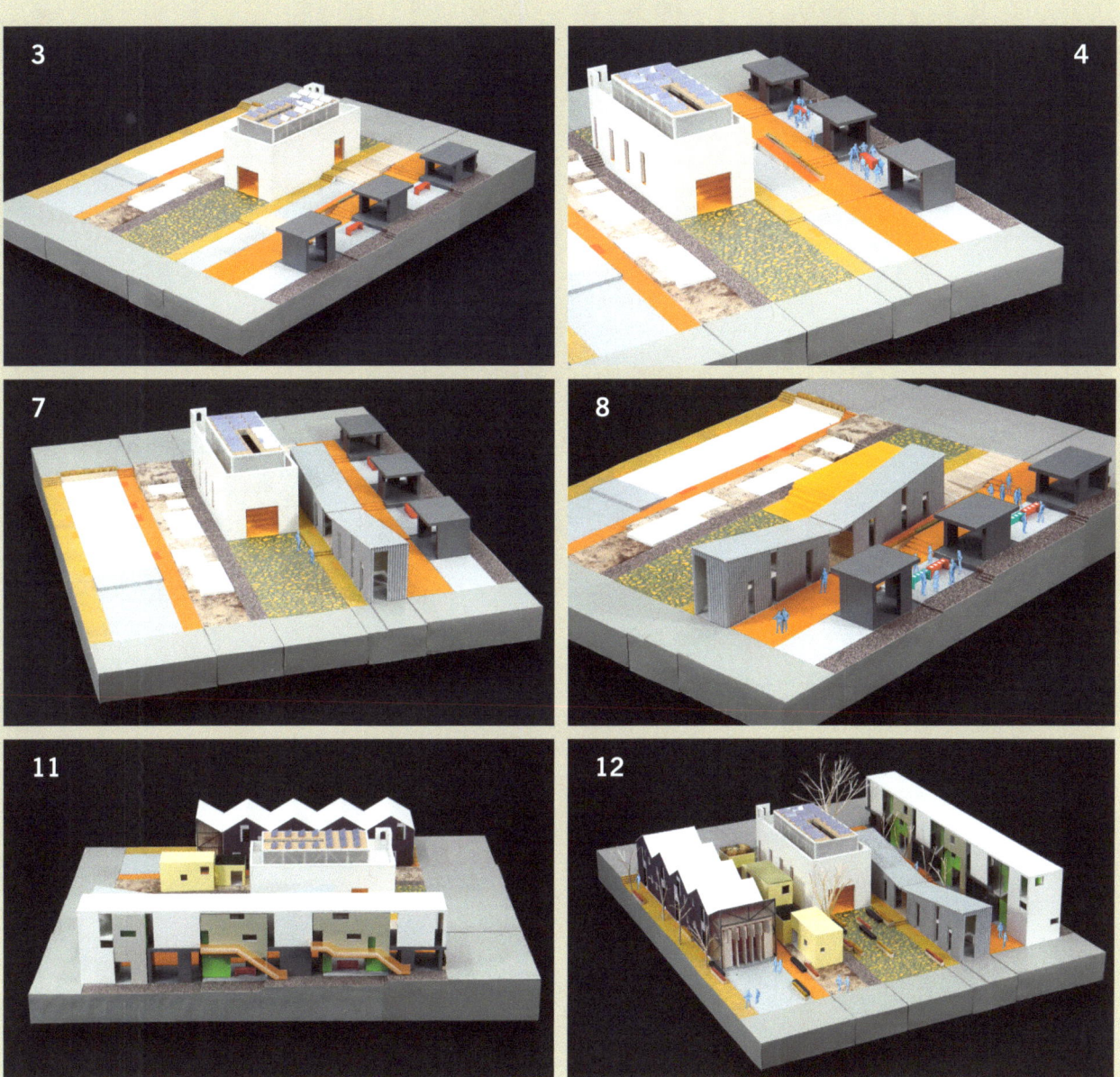

service: artists and Casa Familiar choreograph pedagogical interfaces with children and families, plugging education and other resources. **(8)** Integrating artists within new models of financing, social contracts and unconventional mixed uses. Artists engage urban pedagogy as well as partner with dwellers as co-producers. **(9)** Housing type 3: Large families with grandmothers. Housing equipped with shared kitchens to support two small extended families. Casa Familiar partners with families, promoting economic entrepreneurship **(10)** Housing type 4: Accessory buildings as alternative housing. Small sheds become flexible spaces for extended families. For example, a nephew studies at a local community college, and rents studio and living space; a niece, recently married, rents a studio temporarily and uses a small shed for office space; and Casa Familiar subsidises a room for the gardener who collaborates with dwellers to maintain vegetable beds. **(11)** Density and housing are no longer sustainable as an amount of objects per acre: 1. Redefining density as an amount of social exchanges per acre. 2. Redefining housing as a system of economic and cultural interactions. **(12)** Casa Familiar: The performance of a small parcel. A social infrastructure of small buildings and spaces produces a gradation of housing economies and social interactions, activating small plots into economic and social systems.

Text © 2011 John Wiley & Sons Ltd. Images 2010 Estudio Teddy Cruz

Supersudaca

SUPERSUDACA'S
(AKA AT HOME IN THE FIRST, SECOND,

The architecture network **Supersudaca** is best known for its research projects on Latin America and the Caribbean. Here they describe their experiences as they shifted their focus to Asia and the Middle East in a super-tour that took in Kuala Lumpur, Tokyo, Dubai, Mumbai, Dhaka, Phnom Penh, Singapore and China.

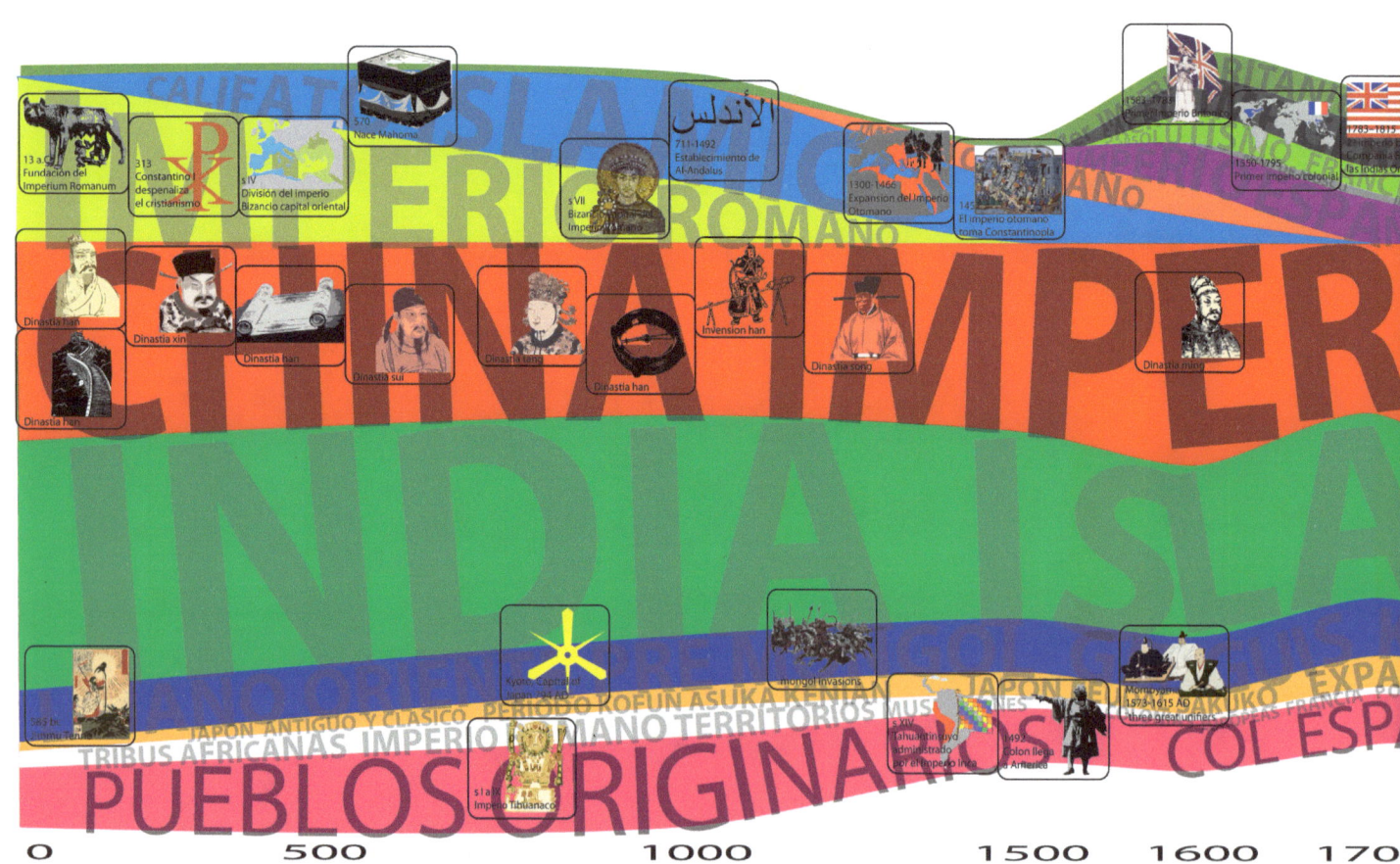

After two centuries of unalloyed, aggressive global domination by the West, Asia is getting back its throne. Should Latin America embrace the new Asian throne?

ASIA STORIES
(THIRD, FOURTH AND FIFTH WORLDS)

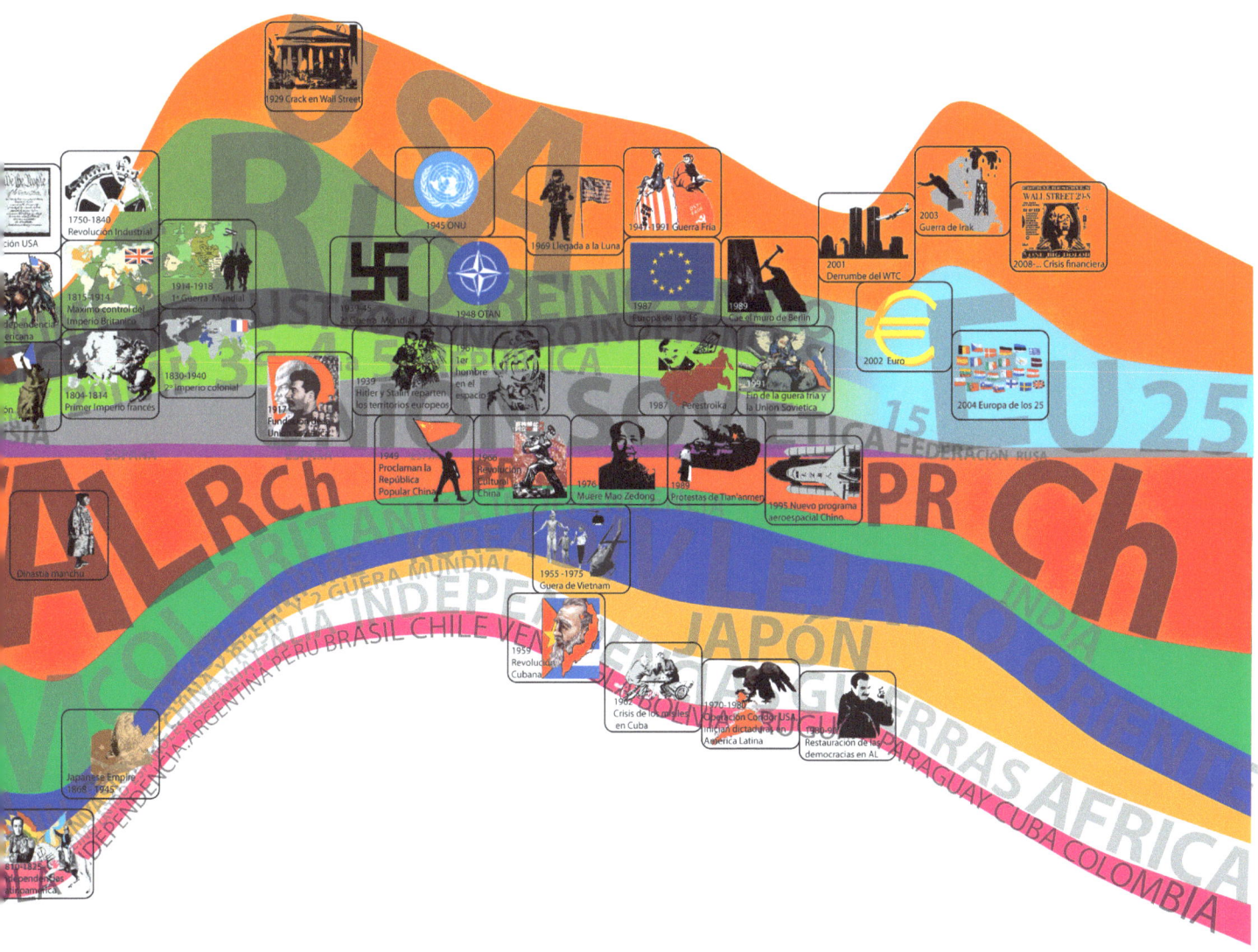

Invitations to the collective to run workshops started in familiar territory – Buenos Aires, Talca, Lima – cities where we dealt with the usual daily round of problems and possibilities: illegality and irresponsibility; opportunity and ingenuity. Gradually we moved into an area in which we have become almost specialists: the Caribbean. Over the past few years collective members have organised several workshops, competitions and research projects in that part of the world, where the most beautiful places have become all-inclusive package destinations for mass tourism.

But can't these single-subject Latinos deal with somewhere else? Perennial local crises seem to predicate our fixation with the local, while we appear content merely to read about the rest of the world in someone else's magazine or website. Yet, strangely enough, a new period for Supersudaca has recently dawned and, almost by accident, has seen our increasing involvement in Asia.

Let Asian Stories begin.

Kuala Lumpur Fix

'Malaysia … truly Asia,' that CNN tune went round and round in our heads for the entire duration of the 30-hour flight from Buenos Aires until our landing at Metabolist Kurokawa's airport, when the gentle voice of the flight attendant announced: '… 32 degrees Celsius. Death penalty for drug trafficking and please enjoy your stay ….' Malaysia – where it's all about standards, rules and quotas. X% Malay, Y% Chinese and Z% Indian. This non-melting pot strangely enforces its diversity but discourages mixing. On every level 'positive discrimination' ensures x%, y% and z% – for university grants, jobs, political representation. The same goes for the city where a futuristic monorail public transport system hovers above streets without sidewalks that run alongside open sewers. No in-between. Seems like renovation doesn´t exist as a concept. 1+1 will always be 1+1 and never 2. For instance, the government decision to create a better city resulted in a new city … somewhere else: Putra Yaya. A brand new town with all the government buildings and amenities. The architecture there is X% Islamic, y% Tuscan, z% High Tech … diversity, but no mix.

Tokyo Bittersweet

We were asked to go to Tokyo on a very strange mission: to help save the lively arty neighbourhood of Shimokitazawa. Save it not from greedy developers as we initially thought, but from the highly efficient Japanese government planning department that, according to its uncontested 50-year-old plan, contemplates building a road through it. To save it, to beat the heavy planning machinery at its own game, we thought the neighbourhood should become a legend in its own right, insulate its aura so completely that it becomes a gizmo. Fetishism seemed the only deadly bullet capable of piercing the hermetically sealed Japanese dogged perseverance. September 2010, and Shimokitazawa is still standing.

Dubai Boat

Don't be fooled. Dubai isn't really a city, it's simply the largest, most extraordinary, best, first-class cruise ship on earth – yes, instead of the sea it sails the desert. Don't make a claim for public space because there's nothing public about it; it's all private, it's owned not governed. It's where credit cards could easily replace passports. Nothing is produced in Dubai. Everything is carefully selected and brought on board: from Swiss cheese to German cars, from Italian suits to Russian escorts. It all ends here. And, unbelievably, it all seems to work.

Marketing? Outside 40°C; inside, malls with ski slopes. Check. Engineering? Artificial islands with every extravagant shape imaginable – palm trees, world map. Check. Planning? Airport to highway, to hotel, to marina, to highest tower; the future flows. Check. Branding? Interior and graphic design as ultra-efficient atmosphere reinforcements producing a just-in-time palimpsest of familiar occidental brands, even those with which you are unfamiliar. Check.

What about architecture? Anything interesting? What's cool? … Nothing. So many buildings, erected at such speed, so much hype and yet not a single remarkable architectural experience. Despite our Latin frivolity/tolerance, our *Learning from Las Vegas* training and trademark Supersudaca open-mindedness, we couldn't believe to what extent we were both fascinated by this consummate achievement in

opposite: View from the artificial beach at the tip of Dubai's artificial Palm Island towards the artificial skyline. Don't be fooled. Dubai isn't really a city. It's a cruise ship sailing in the desert.

top: Shovels of the world, unite! There are as many ways to dig as there are countries. Still, such local customisation comes from the global factory, China (in its showroom: Yiwu).

centre: An architectural masterclass. The imposing geniality of Louis Kahn's parliament building in Dhaka doesn't reside in its celebrated tectonics but rather in its ability to create a monument – and in that process the notion of a nation.

bottom: Billboards advertising enormous new developments have started to invade Phnom Penh's prime locations at a time when Cambodia's obsession with its tragic past obscures any collective vision for the future.

Don't be fooled. Dubai isn't really a city, it's simply the largest, most extraordinary, best, first-class cruise ship on earth – yes, instead of the sea it sails the desert.

human entrepreneurship and simultaneously repelled in the face of such a coherent assemblage of perverse fakeness at such social, economic and environmental cost. Dubai is *Baywatch* pending season 12. Hot and hollow. Maybe the global financial crisis is to Dubai what the iceberg was to the *Titanic* … but maybe just Dubai is a real city with the capacity to reinvent itself before sinks.

Love and Hate in Mumbai

Invited as guest professors to participate in a workshop, we once again felt the collective had much to learn rather than anything to impart. We were immediately suspicious of the grass-roots, NGO, poverty-glorifying approach. No more surveys. 'In order to be good you have to be evil' was to be our take on what must surely be the most densely inhabited slum in Mumbai … in India … in the world.

What if a trumped-up top-down approach has a better chance of succeeding than a genuine bottom-up one? Can research targets be explored with fictional tools?

Although Supersudaca embraces bottom-up strategies, we felt that politeness from all sides (curious architects versus humble inhabitants) would cloud the issue, masking any real wishes or needs on either side. In the first place, what were we actually doing there?

An article found on the flight in *The Economist* entitled 'Rising Slum' helped orient us. It described Dharavi's complexity, mega congestion and how people are incredibly busy recycling Mumbai's garbage. Yet what impressed us even more was the discovery that the speculators' price tag for the slum starts at U$9 billion! Our task was to disguise ourselves as developers with the aim of seducing the inhabitants with the promise of high-rise apartment life post-slum. At the end no one was nostalgic for his or her picturesque neighbourhood; instead they were curious about the renders illustrated in our spurious brochures. In any case the slum dwellers should know they are sitting on top of a gold mine that only looks like garbage. Private initiatives seemed more effective than well-intended state interventions. Change is certain and fast, and everybody wants to be a part of it – it's got all the dynamism of Bollywood choreography.

Bangladesh is the most densely inhabited country on earth. When one imagines density one thinks of congested urban realms; however, hyperdensity here in countrywide terms means rural density.

below: Putra Yaya – Malaysia's newly built government city – strangely plays host to the most diverse collection anywhere of streetlamps per hectare. To each block its own lamp design; likewise every government building has its architectural style. Malaysia is truly Asia.

bottom: Phnom Penh is emptied out in 1977. A few years later people slowly return. Only some have houses to go back to, most take anonymous apartments; the weakest take the last option – cultural buildings such as churches or pagodas. The worst dwelling proposition has to be a cinema: a favela with a dark roof becomes the living space for dozens of people. The tragedy continues 33 years later.

opposite left: Exact (yes, exact!) scale replica of Singapore at the Urban Redevelopment Center. The ultimate urbanism theme park.

opposite right: Promotional material from the Supersudaca workshop in Dharavi. When slum dwellers became aware of the enormous value of their land, they happily gave in to imagining the same kind of future as your local eco-developer.

Home of one of the great archaeological wonders of the world (the temple of Angkor Wat) with 400 kilometres (248.5 miles) of coastline and coral reefs. Yet its turbulent past still exerts a powerful break on the country's future. The real horror for Cambodia lies in ignoring its potential.

Dhaka Kahn

Bangladesh is the most densely inhabited country on earth. When one imagines density one thinks of congested urban realms; however, hyperdensity here in countrywide terms means rural density. Even though Dhaka – the fastest-growing megacity in the world – is super-chaotic and dense, it is similar to other third world cities that expand at random. What makes the impact is when one travels through the country; when one experiences the sheer number of people everywhere one goes. Nowhere is there 'nobody'. And programmatical mix per hectare is astonishingly high; rice paddies, fishponds, villages, brick factories with their tall chimneys, more villages, more rice paddies. Land is an ever-scarcer commodity after every monsoon season ... within such a context we were reconciled with an old master, Louis Kahn's parliament building. A magnificent contrast that makes so much sense in its isolation and boldness. The masterstroke we learned? The grand gesture is the way forward in an incredibly unstable, heavily fragmented environment.

Cambodiasyndrome

When we got to Cambodia, its complex history of wars, revolution and genocide finally became more comprehensible: not just Pol Pot and Khmer Rouge, but Americans (Kissinger; Nixon), Vietnamese, Chinese. The country was in the wrong place at the wrong time (viz the Vietnam War) just at what should have been its brightest moment (King Sihanouk and modernisation). Dragged from its rural Marxist utopia, its people were forced to abandon Phnom Penh in a hurry. When the city was reoccupied, incomers settled in the abandoned buildings regardless of their former uses, so temples, schools, cinemas, etc turned into micro neighbourhoods. Formerly private corridors and stairways became public streets. Architecture became urbanism.

A tuk-tuk (motorised rickshaw) culture had emerged: a city made out of small reversible elements set against a hard background. But so too a new wealthy class of triumphant generals emerged: the Lexus culture of big cars and beautiful young escorts again. Speculation on a vast scale, ballooning real-estate prices, corruption that ties land concessions to private

capital; the country's geography is being transformed (lakes drying up, land reclaimed from the river).

Yet the outside world only knows about this place when they wear a T-shirt. The reality of our 'Made in Cambodia' clothing is to be found in the textile factories that proliferate on the outskirts of Phnom Penh attracting enormous numbers of female workers who arrive by the truckload. History in reverse. Cambodia is perhaps too conveniently located in the heart of Southeast Asia, neighbour of booming Vietnam, Thailand and Malaysia. Home of one of the great archaeological wonders of the world (the temple of Angkor Wat) with 400 kilometres (248.5 miles) of coastline and coral reefs. Yet its turbulent past still exerts a powerful break on the country's future. The real horror for Cambodia lies in ignoring its potential.

Singapore Amnesia
From Kuala Lumpur we arrived at Singapore. Somehow it seems hard to recall any street or name from Singapore, probably because the English toponym confuses it all, or maybe because there's a strange scale disorientation effect: a country, a city, a neighbourhood, a building compressed into a single visual experience. Like a big scale model. And of course in this ideal Lego city it is forbidden to leave any trace of mess, so no chewing gum, no smoking, no jaywalking. Here, where supposedly hybrid programming projects were finally realised, there is an awkward and seductive feeling of stability. Our invitation was to the Urban Redevelopment Center, a place where planning actually works and is proudly demonstrated even in amazing interactive games for school kids.

Planning meets Pixar. It seems to work like this: some urban concern is raised, a competition might be opened to the best qualified professionals and the winning scheme triumphantly publicised. Then it is painstakingly built and officially inaugurated. In the Center's centre there's a huge model of the city; it bears a quite shocking resemblance to the real thing. Just so you can see for yourself, they've even installed a periscope so you can check with the outside how similar they are. But wait! There are buildings missing … or pieces. Those are the upcoming projects to be finished in a perfect cadence of timing.

A unique, strangely anonymous experience; one impossible to forget but just like the models: the streets have no names.

China tu madre! China Your Mother
We arrived in China with little background knowledge but a wish list that included playing ping pong with Chinese masters, having a foot massage, and finding out where everything is actually made; we wanted to see if you can really feel the 300 million people.

We were directed by our hosts to the epicentre of our every wish and, particularly in two cases, we caught a glimpse of what we can already see happening in our part of the world. Yiwu and Thames Town were examples of contrast and power. Yiwu is the biggest market in the world, hosting 100,000 shops that sell quite literally everything from around the world. The most important alongside the most trivial items, from Christmas decorations to surveillance cameras. Everything that you have in your house comes from Yiwu.

Thames Town, or James Town as we called it, is the epicentre of a brand new 970,000-inhabitant city just finished and half empty. James Town is English style and could be part of any London area with its red telephone boxes, brick houses and old-style traditional pubs. We couldn't stop imagining the contrast between a Latin American politician proudly opening a new library and a Chinese one opening just another brand new 1-million-inhabitant city.

Shortcuts
Nowadays there are endless combinations of nation groups – G-2, G-7, G-8, G-20 – but the one which is really missing is G-ALL minus the 7. Maybe if we could circumvent the usual triangle where Europe and the US play the central role, Latin America, Africa and Asia could learn and profit from each other in several and surprising new ways.

An insider joke is that Supersudaca is slowly becoming a travel agency. The most frequent question we are asked after lectures is: 'How can I become a Supersudaca?' It seems everyone wants to join the tour. ∆

Text © 2011 John Wiley & Sons Ltd. Images © Supersudaca

Saskia Sassen

WHEN CITIES BECOME STRATEGIC

The 1980s saw the rise of cities as strategic economic spaces. This was driven by the emergence of intermediate services, such as IT and finance, which tend to be located in cities regardless of whether or not they serve the manufacturing sector. **Saskia Sassen** describes both the direct result that cities becoming strategic had on built form and how the growth in the informal economy was in fact a response to this shift in late capitalism.

Hilary Koob-Sassen, *Endless City*, 2008

For much of the mid-20th century, cities were above all centres for administration, small-scale manufacturing, and commerce.[1] While the major cities in each country have their own particular histories, these trends are shared by much of the Americas and Europe. There are important exceptions, notably Bogotá, given a militarised conflict, and the period of South America's military dictatorships. But, generally, cities were mainly spaces for rather routine activities. The strategic spaces where major innovations were taking place were the government (the making of social contracts, such as the welfare state) and mass manufacturing, including the mass construction of suburban regions and national transportation infrastructures.

This contrasted with the previous century and the early part of the 20th century when cities were cauldrons within which new economies were made, where populations were hybridised, and where struggles for social justice often succeeded. In the 1980s, cities once again became strategic, and thereby a lens into the larger economic and political struggles of an emergent new global epoch.

The Territorial Moment of Global Capital

The most common and most basic answers as to why cities became strategic in a global corporate economy are the ongoing need for face-to-face communications and for creative classes and inputs. But these are surface conditions that cannot fully explain the new phase. The rise of cities as strategic economic spaces is the consequence of a much deeper structural transformation evident in all developed economies. It affects cities at multiple levels, from the provincial to the global. And at the heart of this deep structural trend is the fact that firms in even the most material and non-urban economic sectors (mines, factories, transport systems, hospitals) are today buying more insurance, accounting, legal, financial, consulting, software programming and other such services. These so-called intermediate services tend to be produced in cities, no matter the non-urban location of the mine or the steel plant that is being serviced.

Thus even an economy centred on manufacturing or mining will feed the urban corporate services economy. Firms operating in more subnational markets increasingly buy these service inputs from more local or regional cities, which explains the growth of a professional class and associated built environments in cities that are not global. The difference for global cities is that they are able to handle the more complex needs of firms and exchanges operating globally. It is only in its most extreme forms that this transformation feeds into the growth of global cities and cuts across the national–global binary.

The outcomes of this structural condition get wired into urban space, and sooner or later become evident in all major South American cities. The growth of a high-income professional class and high-profit corporate service firms becomes legible in urban space through the growing demand for state-of-the-art office buildings and all the key components of the residential and consumption sphere. The growing demands for both kinds of space has generated massive and visible displacements of the more modest-income households and more modest profit-making firms, no matter how healthy these may be from the perspective of the economy and market demand. In this remaking, urban space becomes one of the actors producing the outcome, and it becomes the lens through which we can see this remaking.[2]

In this mix of conditions lies a politics: the politics of the new city-users, a politics built in stone. But also the politics of claiming rights to the city by the expelled, who are often the long-term residents.

This remaking of urban space partly explains why architecture, urban design and urban planning have each played such critical and often new roles in this period, even as an anti-government and anti-planning ethos was part of the neoliberal shift. Beginning in the 1980s we see the partial rebuilding of cities as platforms for a rapidly growing range of globalised activities and flows, from economic to cultural and political. Further, it explains why global cities become an object *of* investment, beyond being a place for investing *in* building an office for one's firm, and why the number and types of cities that became such objects expanded rapidly with globalisation in the 1990s and onwards.

The visual order that emerges from these dynamics suggests a much greater autonomy of the new 'glamour zone' in the larger city and its more modest spaces than is in fact the case. This is especially the case with the new so-called 'intelligent cities'.[3] Beneath the clash of extremely unequal spaces and their distinct visual orders there are multiple articulations. This obscuring, and even camouflaging, of articulations between the glamour zone and the rest of the city is also a potential source for a politics of reclamation – especially by the displaced and those workers who matter to the glamour zone but are never recognised as mattering.

Fragmented Topographies and Underlying Connections

The topographies of global cities obscure the multiple connections between advanced and so-called backward sectors that are assumed not to belong in an advanced urban economy and which are thus seen as an anachronism. But many of these sectors are in fact servicing the advanced economic sectors and their high-income employees. Parts of the traditional small-enterprise sector, and of the informal economy, service particular components of a city's advanced sectors. The visual orders and topographies of global cities do not help make visible these articulations. The state-of-the-art glamour zone speaks the language of disconnection with poverty zones. In its most extreme format, each global city has a global slum, either on its outskirts or in its centre. However, no matter how different the urban spaces within which they are located, there are multiple articulations between backward and advanced sectors.

The novel spatial and social inequalities mentioned earlier take concrete and specific formats, two of which are discussed below: first, a generally overlooked sector we refer to as urban manufacturing, and second, the more general and by now familiar subject of the informal economy.

Urban Manufacturing

Urban manufacturing is very much part of today's urban service economies, including the most advanced ones. It is geared to design sectors of all types: customised jewellery, designer furniture, architecture, interior decoration, cultural industries (theatres and opera houses need sets and costumes, museums and galleries need display settings for their collections, and so on); building trades (customised woodwork and metalwork) and their sectors are very much part of advanced service-based economies (the staging in luxury shops and restaurants, displays in corporate headquarters, and so on). A very advanced and rapidly growing type of urban manufacturing is emerging out of the diversity of projects to green our economies.

Urban manufacturing has several characteristics: 1) it needs an urban location because it is deeply networked and operates in contracting and subcontracting chains; 2) it is often fairly customised and hence needs to be in close proximity to its customers and to a diverse pool of first-rate craftworkers; 3) it inverts the historical relationship between services and manufacturing in that it serves service industries (services originally developed to serve the needs of manufacturers).

The Informal Economy

A new type of informal economy is emerging in global cities, one linked to advanced capitalism. This is highly visible in cities of the global north, but less so in the global south, where the new informal economy is submerged beneath the vastness of the older informal economy.

Three trends signal that much of today's growing informalisation is actually linked to key features of advanced urban capitalism. One is the sharp emergence and growth of informal economies in the major global cities of the north – in North America, Western Europe and, to a lesser extent, Japan. We also see this new type of informal economy in global cities of the south, from Latin America to Asia; these coexist with the traditional long-term informal economies of these cities.

A second trend is the mostly overlooked proliferation of an informal economy of creative professionals – artists, architects, designers, software developers, event choreographers, working in these cities. This new creative professional informal economy greatly expands opportunities and networking potentials for these artists and professionals, even if this is mostly a partial informality. It allows them to function in the interstices of urban and organisational spaces often dominated by large corporate actors, and to escape the corporatising of creative work. In this process they contribute a very specific feature of the new urban economy: its innovativeness and a certain type of frontier spirit. Conditions akin to those in global cities of the north may also be producing a new type of informal economy in global cities of the south, including a professional creative informal economy. Their emergence may be far less visible than in the north because they are partly submerged under the old informal economies that continue to operate in the global south, and are still more a result of poverty and survival than of the needs of advanced economic sectors.

A third trend is that the new types of informalisation of work actually function as the informal equivalent of the formal deregulation in the new advanced sectors – finance, telecommunications and most other advanced economic sectors pursued in the name of 'flexibility and innovation'. The difference is that while formal deregulation was costly, and was paid through tax revenue as well as private capital, informalisation is low cost and sits largely on the backs of workers and informal firms themselves.[4]

In brief, the same politico-economic restructuring that led to the new urban economy emerging in the late 1980s also contributed to the formation of new informal economies and the demand for urban manufacturing. The decline of the manufacturing-dominated industrial complex that prevailed over most of the 20th century, and the rise of a new, service-dominated economic complex, provide the general context within which informalisation and urban manufacturing need to be placed; this is critical to take the analysis beyond a mere description of instances of informal work and manufacturing that services design industries.

These trends raise a number of questions about what is and what is not part of today's advanced urban economies. One way of capturing these somewhat invisible dynamics is to think of the urban economy as traversed by multiple specialised circuits.

Thus an analysis of the diverse circuits that connect a given sector to various urban activities shows us that even finance, when disaggregated into such circuits, is linked to urban manufacturing suppliers, often through the design and building trades; an example is the installation of advanced security devices in corporate office buildings.

Conclusion

The rebuilding of central areas in all of these cities, whether downtown, at the edges or in both, is part of the urbanising of more and more economic activities. Rebuilding key parts of these cities as platforms for a rapidly growing range of global activities and flows, from economic to cultural and political, also explains why architecture, urban design and urban planning have all become more important and more visible in the last two decades. This rebuilding, in turn, has generated a clash of visual orders and topographies in cities – the glamour zone and the poverty zone – which obscures the multiple articulations of the advanced economy with poorer economies in the city. It also explains the growing competition for space in these cities and the emergence of a new type of politics, one centred on the right.

Whether all of this is good or bad for the larger social fabric of cities and their countries is a complex matter, and the subject of many debates. But the fact that global firms need cities, and indeed groups of cities, should enable political, corporate and civic leaderships to negotiate for more benefits for their cities from global firms. This could lead to overall positive outcomes if the governing classes can see that these global economic functions will grow better in a context of a strong and prosperous middle class rather than the sharp inequality and polarity we see today.

The newly emerging global cities of the south are experiencing the now familiar trends of the north: growing numbers of the very rich and of the very poor, along with the impoverishment of the old middle classes. What there will be less of in these cities are the modest middle classes and the modest profit-making economic sectors that once dominated these cities. But these are critical to the urban economy because they are most likely to recirculate their incomes in the city's economy. Their presence is a built-in resistance to the spatial and social reshaping of cities along extreme class lines.

This is a whole new urban era – with its share of positive potentials and its share of miseries. What are usually referred to as our global governance challenges become concrete and urgent in cities. But existing modes of urban governance mostly do not help us change these dynamics and their negative outcomes. There is much work to be done. 𝕠

Notes
1. For detailed information on the issues discussed in this article, see Saskia Sassen, *Cities in a World Economy*, Sage/Pine Forge Press (Thousand Oaks, CA), 4th edn, 2011.
2. The most pessimistic scenario is that conflict is now wired into urban space itself, partly due to gentrification and displacement and the resulting politics of competition for space, and partly because of asymmetric war, see Sassen, 'When the City Itself Becomes a Technology of War', *Theory, Culture & Society*, Vol 27(6), 2010, pp 33–50.
3. On intelligent cities see: http://whatmatters.mckinseydigital.com/cities/talking-back-to-your-intelligent-city.
4. For one of the most detailed accounts on four favelas in São Paulo and how they are connected to the new economic trends, see Simone Buechler, 'Deciphering the Local in a Global Neoliberal Age: Three Favelas in São Paulo, Brazil', in Sassen (ed), *Deciphering the Global: Its Scales, Spaces, and Subjects*, Routledge (New York), 2007, pp 95–112.

Text © 2011 John Wiley & Sons Ltd. Image © Hilary Sassen. Original publication in Ricky Burdett and Deyan Sudjic (eds), The Endless City, Phaidon Press, 2008

Enrique Martin-Moreno

ORGANISING COMMUNITIES FOR INTERDEPENDENT GROWTH

Recognising interdependence provides unique opportunities for small businesses to grow and communities to flourish. **Enrique Martin-Moreno** urges architects, as they are presented with opportunities in Latin America, to participate in the building of social projects to understand the potency of trust and shared self-reliance.

Imagine the world without trust? It does not even seem human; we would not be able to carry out the simplest tasks if they required someone else. How have we evolved and generated so much value in the world collectively? Other species cannot even be around unfamiliar members of the same species without an outbreak of violence. We have certainly come a long way from that reality. Yet, picture a group of owners of small restaurants from the same district of a large Latin American city. Invited by an NGO, they get together to plan a joint strategy for the improvement of their individual businesses. They understand economies of scale, but fail to implement the most basic plan for buying their supplies in bulk, bypassing several intermediaries that could result in great savings for all, due to a lack of trust among them. Or imagine a large mining consortium having to build and operate its own rail lines to ensure its minerals reach the market. This particular rail system will not grow beyond the specific needs of the mining company, and the region will not fully profit from this enormous investment, but the corporation feels it cannot trust anyone else to reliably transport its goods.

Trust is built through relationships of fair exchange. It has allowed for the division of labour, specialisation and the constant increase in our standards of living. Fair and honest exchange teaches us to recognise that enlightened self-interest lies in seeking cooperation. It helps us to develop a culture of fairness and respect for individuals that helps us to develop that uniquely human attribute of being able to deal with strangers, even our enemies, in a civil fashion.[1]

Latin America is indeed the land of opportunities, some of which lie in its social structure. In analysing the public (government and bureaucracies) and private (corporations, business enterprises, a market culture) sectors of society, we find that there is also a robust and cohesive social sector (people, when they are acting as citizens and not as part of the other sectors). As governments and private developers struggled to cope with the demands of rural to urban migrations and of the demographic explosion of the 20th century, the social sector organised and began to fill the voids, creating strategies and emergent systems of urbanity. But we have not developed the proper instruments (legal and financial) to help unleash the social sector's entrepreneurial potential and to create fluid, upper-social and economic mobility.[2]

Corruption, unsuccessful public policies and government bureaucracies have diminished the power of the state and left governments disenfranchised; and in recent decades this void in the power structure has often been filled by organised crime cartels that in some countries occupy and control entire territories, challenge the hegemony of the state and render the countries in a state of war. Organised crime extorts money from the rich and lures labour from the poor,[3] contributing to a culture of fear, dehumanisation and lack of trust that results in a more dangerous polarisation of society, in which violence almost inevitably grows. The result in most cases is a divided city, fragmented well beyond the binary divisions of rich and poor, formal and informal. A polarising 'us versus them' mentality divides

> It helps us to develop a culture of fairness and respect for individuals that helps us to develop that uniquely human attribute of being able to deal with strangers, even our enemies, in a civil fashion.

Alberto Kalach, FARO de Oriente, Mexico City, 2000
opposite: The Fábrica de Artes y Oficios + de Oriente (Arts and Trades Factory of the East) urban development project began by rescuing an abandoned government building and transforming it into a new public focal point with cultural production as its priority. Conceived by Alejandro Aura, the FARO de Oriente opened its doors in June 2000 in an area with the highest crime rate and the lowest level of infrastructure and urban development in Mexico City. It developed into a workshop for artistic creativity that also offers cultural events such as concerts and multimedia performances.

Rodrigo Alcocer, María Alós, Gustavo Artigas, Torolab/Raúl Cárdenas, Teddy Cruz, Minerva Cuevas, Iván Hernández, Jonathan Hernández, Homeless, Moris, Tercerunquinto, Wakal, and Taro Zorrilla, Vacíos Urbanos, Lisbon Architecture Triennale, 2007
above: The Mexican contribution to the Lisbon Architecture Triennale consisted of diverse urban tactics distributed throughout Lisbon – tactics that do not make a unit, but remain interconnected. It is in the so-called 'urban voids' where incidentally unrelated parts of the city coexist in a never-ending interplay of differences.

Community is an emergent property of the system. It requires participation and empathy. It has to be carefully planted in each of us and diligently cared for in order to grow.

society into all sorts of petty groups based on religion, race, ancestry, socioeconomic level, class, political views, gender, sexual preferences or even something as simple as soccer-team affiliation. Dehumanisation occurs when one stops seeing 'the other' as human.[4] The result is a self-destructive, fear-based society. This is our struggle.

In examining which sector has the most power, we would find that almost across the board the private sector and the market have the most ability to act, and the capacity to direct or influence the behaviour of others or the course of events. National and multinational corporations (legal or illegal) push governments around, and certainly have more power than people. In turn, the public sector has more power over the social sector. Their powers are dependent on the very fragmentation of society. The problem is not the very few at the very top or the very bottom of the ethical/moral scale, but a mass of atomised, terrified individuals who are easily manipulated and pushed around. Through consumption or taxes, every dollar we spend gives a vote for that business or government to exist. The power, then, is ours, if we choose to seize it.

After eight years of trial and error through academic projects,[5] private practice and involvement in the Inlak'ech movement in Mexico, where communities are being organised to reduce fear and violence through participation, expression and community work,[6] it has become apparent that the greatest adversaries we face are our fear, entitlement and lack of trust. They represent the most limiting conditions to our continuous growth and to greater complexity and the

---

Ines Linke and Louise Ganz, Empty Lots Occupation Project, Belo Horizonte, Minas Gerais, Brazil, 2006
above: In this experimental occupation project, vacant sites were used as provisional public spaces with cows, swimming pools, living rooms, flowering fields for picnics and spaces to rest and read. The use of vacant lots makes it possible to produce, and live in, a sphere other than speculation, fear or segregation.

Giacomo Castagnola/Germen estudio, Banca Ambulante, Tijuana, 2006
opposite top: Felipe Zuñiga from Consultorio de Cultura Pública describes Banca Ambulante as a project that arises from a simple and genuine inquiry: the possibility of 'being' in a place – 'being' as opposed to 'occupying' a space or making it one's own. It suggests a brief stay, an experiential occupation of space, and responds to a seemingly simple gesture, that of hospitality.

Raúl Cárdenas/Torolab, Coma, Puebla, Mexico, 2006–7
opposite bottom: Coma culminated in creating a new food product, a type of bread containing all the nutrients absent in a typical Mexican diet. For the project, Torolab collaborated with local gastronomy students, musicians and artists, creating a system of distribution with the design of a transformable vehicle that is basically a moving oven.

production of value. There is a tension between the objective world as it is and the subjective world as it should be[7] that by definition is unreal. Yet, we seem determined for the world to be as we want it to be.

Through phrases like 'the government should take care of that', or 'it is not our job to …', we make ourselves victims and continuously find someone to blame to evade our responsibility for our own participation in the system. We might agree that the particular genius of the city is its ability to provide high standards of living through public facilities and public spaces. However, a city whose citizens are afraid of each other will not be able to strive towards that common good. We need to recognise that things do not operate linearly in neat binary choices in order to begin to see our participation in, and effect on, the system. Building community – humanising ourselves – is the first step towards interdependent growth and the full potential of our society. Community is an emergent property of the system. It requires participation and empathy. It has to be carefully planted in each of us and diligently cared for in order to grow. It is futile to try to achieve it by imposing a centralised, static, top-down path.

The projects illustrated here demonstrate innovative ways of involving the various players (the public, private and social sectors) and redefining their roles and levels of inclusion. To evaluate urban interventions at any scale it is important to assess factors such as their sustainability (environmental, social and economic) – for example, whether they are self-sustaining or dependent on external endowments in

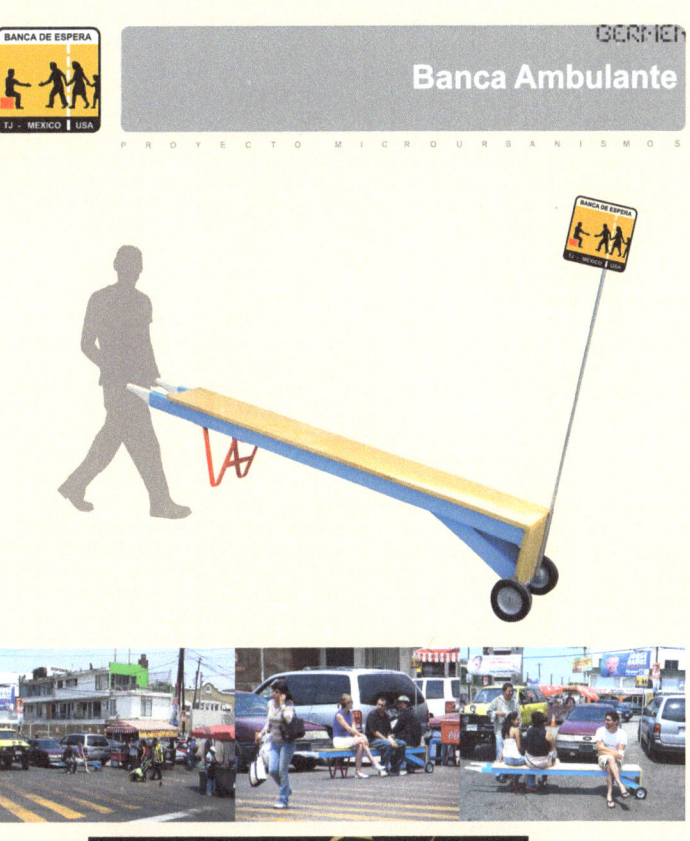

A refurbished factory complex that houses theatres, gymnasiums, a swimming pool, library, leisure areas, restaurants, galleries, workshops and other services, it offers sports, cultural, health and environment education programmes, as well as special programmes for children and senior citizens.

Lina Bo Bardi, SESC Pompéia, São Paulo, 1986
right: The SESC Pompéia proves that a social enterprise can be economically sustainable through excellent facilities and content.

Pedro Reyes, Leverage, 2006
opposite: In this variation on a see-saw there is a clear asymmetric relationship; one person equals in power a group of nine others. However, the single player needs the group to wield his or her influence. At first this seems a materialisation of the hierarchies and power inequities found in almost all human organisations. The 'oppressor' against the 'oppressed'. Another interpretation could shift problems into opportunities – a potential 'social leverage', or the power of an individual to transform his or her group. If you change your own habits you are multiplying your efforts by one. If you manage to introduce a change within a group, the effect is multiplied by 10, by 100, by 1,000.

  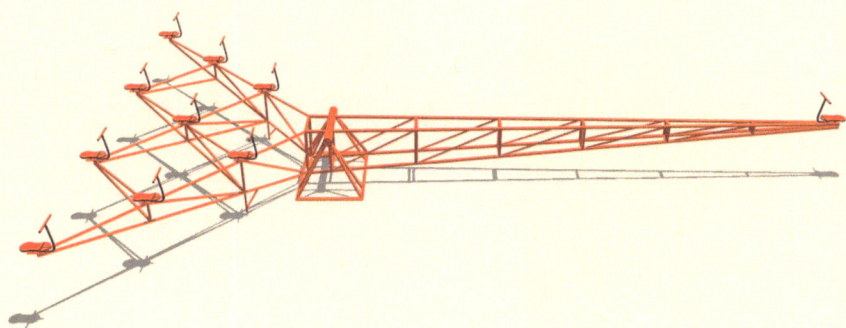

the long run – and their understanding of local culture. Also important is their agency (top-down or bottom-up, centrally planned versus organisational or community-based), the degree of participation of the community and resulting ownership of the project by the respective communities, as well as replicability and scalability potential, and sense of entrepreneurship. Do these projects generate value and exchange for it? This way we can measure how successful they are in creating a new balance in society.

Lina Bo Bardi's large-scale intervention, the SESC Pompéia community, cultural and sports centre (1977–86) in São Paulo, is a good example of a private institution created by a non-profit organisation formed by the city's business owners. A refurbished factory complex that houses theatres, gymnasiums, a swimming pool, library, leisure areas, restaurants, galleries, workshops and other services, it offers sports, cultural, health and environment education programmes, as well as special programmes for children and senior citizens. There are now more than 30 SESC centres in the state of São Paulo, and each is responsible, through user fees, for its own management and upkeep, though the unique political and economic conditions at the time of the founding of the SESC render it almost impossible to replicate today.

However, current conditions in Latin America also present great opportunities for the development of new tools for architects and artists to participate in the building and organising of communities while designing the built environment. Recent projects have included microscale interventions of a bottom-up nature – from the temporary transformation of private property into public spaces, to an adaptation of a children's playground attraction that reveals the leverage we have as individuals. Here, the architects (or their collectives) become the leaders, enrolling the people, local governments and institutions to create stronger communities.

There is an old Chinese proverb: 'If we continue the way we are going, we might get where we are headed.' As Latin America celebrates the bicentennial of the beginning of its quest for independence, it is presented with a true opportunity for transformation: to own its struggle and to grow from it, to become the first true civilisation of the world – civilised by its people and not its governments. But this change has to begin with each and every one of us. ⌂

Notes
1. Matt Ridley, *The Rational Optimist: How Prosperity Evolves*, HarperCollins (New York), 2010.
2. Hernando de Soto, *The Other Path: The Invisible Revolution in the Third World*, HarperCollins (New York), 1989, and *The Mystery of Capital: Why Capitalism Triumphs in the West and Fails Everywhere Else*, Basic Books (New York), 2000.
3. Keith Raniere, *Oportunidades de Negocio*, Conocimiento, Coordinación de Ciencia y Tecnología de Nuevo León (Monterrey), No 108, September 2010, p 85.
4. Alain Finkielkraut, *In the Name of Humanity: Reflections on the Twentieth Century*, Columbia University Press (New York), 2000.
5. Enrique Martin-Moreno, 'It Takes Three: The "People," Businessmen, and Government Officials', *Harvard Design Magazine*, No 28, Spring/Summer 2008, p 41.
6. See www.inlakech.org.mx.
7. Michael Gecan, *Going Public: An Organizer's Guide to Citizen Action*, Anchor Books (New York), 2004.

Text © 2011 John Wiley & Sons Ltd. Images: p 128 images by Alejandra Carlock and Arturo Alanis; p 129 © Image by Mariana Musi; p 130 © Louise Marie Cardoso Ganz; p 131(t) © Giacomo Castagnola; p 131(b) © Raúl Cárdenas Osuna; p 132 © SESC Sao Paulo, photo Nilton Silva; p 133 © Courtesy of Yvon Lambert Gallery

Mariana Leguía

UNIVERSITIES
THE CASES OF BUENOS AIRES,

Stepping into the vacuum left by state and public services, architecture departments in universities have become key players in the development of their regions. As guest-editor of this issue, **Mariana Leguía** explains how this has led to a new teaching and research model, where universities act as mediators between government, private investors, NGOs and local communities. She looks at the activities of institutions in Argentina, Peru, Mexico and Brazil that are proactive in this field.

Javier Fernández Castro, Villa 31/Barrio 31 Carlos Mugica, Buenos Aires, 2002–
above: Work on the existing infrastructure identified a plaza as the main entrance to the neighbourhood from the bus terminal. The proposed lateral esplanade contemplates the regeneration of the existing rail tracks. The main services for the neighbourhood were thus distributed throughout the plaza, taking advantage of the space underneath the elevated road.

(Y)ncluye (Maya Ballén and Mariana Leguía), New Methodologies in Ica, Peru, 2004
opposite: Perspective of the community centre.

AS MEDIATORS
LIMA, MEXICO AND SÃO PAULO

Latin America's major cities have grown dramatically since 1950[1] when upon arrival, rural–urban migrants were faced with innumerable barriers preventing them from entering into formal employment.[2] This is reflected in the growth of Latin America's shadow economy, increasing from 30 per cent to 40 per cent of the overall economy between 1990 and 2003 alone.[3] This growth has weakened Latin American governments who are faced with increasing infrastructural costs with a smaller proportion of official income from which to draw taxes.

The resulting inability of some Latin American nation-states to provide basic services and housing for all its citizens, along with perceived corruption, means many communities have little faith in government institutions (as discussed in the previous article, see pp 128–33). In the absence of the state, communities rely on themselves for many basic services,[4] leading to the replacement of public services with private services.[5]

Privately operated informal 'public' transport, private police or neighbourhood security are common in Latin America, as well as what De Soto calls 'extralegal' agreements, where informal property titles are recognised within communities, but not within official government registries.

Exploding urban populations in Latin America have led to multipolar cities and fractal segregation, increasing both densification and urban sprawl. While extremely challenging, these factors have created the role for universities to become key players in the development of the region, allowing for a reinterpretation of pedagogy where universities act as mediators between government, private investors, NGOs and local communities.

Responding to the challenge, many universities have been developing new methodologies to work within these informal areas of the city.

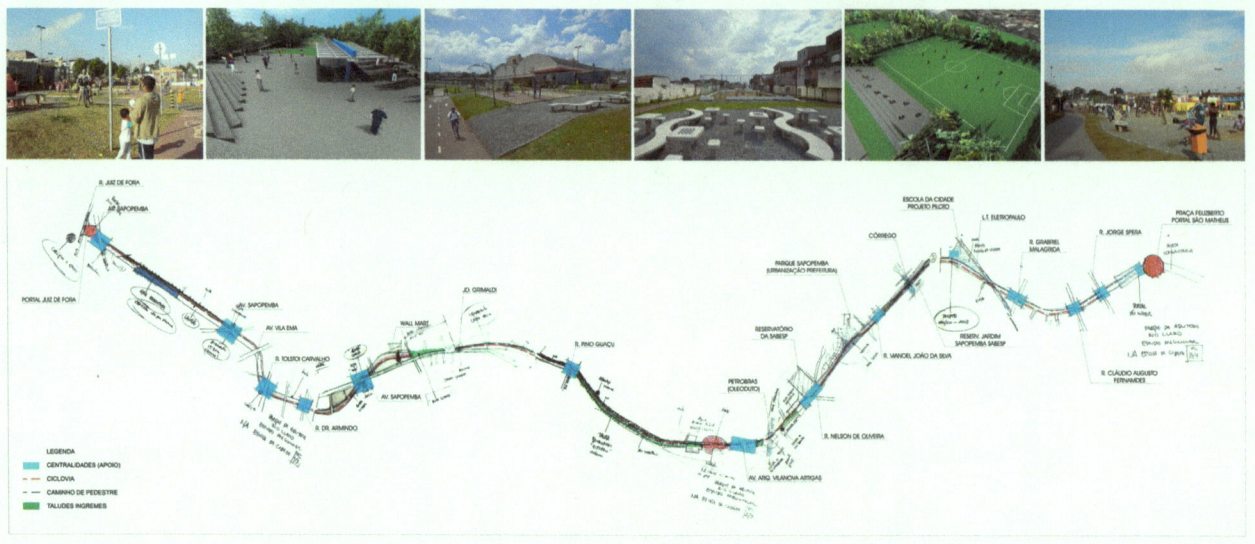

NUCLEUS APPLICATION
AEC - ASSOCIATION ESCOLA DA CIDADE

METHODOLOGY

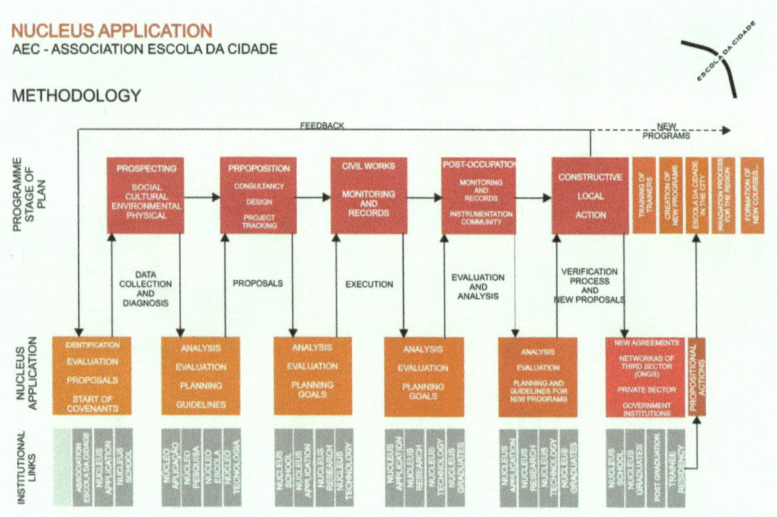

The use of communication-type games and easily approachable visual imagery are just two of the tools common in this new decision-making process where architects encourage the participation of citizens in design. Integrating the users within the process is not a novelty. The innovation consists in articulating possible worlds and social relations that are materialised in a project, through its fabrication and its performance over time. The main difference between past examples of socially engaged practices and the ones being used today is that now it is not about grand projects and utopias, but about modelling possible worlds and the small-scale utopias of everyday life. These quotidian spaces are not codified through built form, but within the pure state of usage and the relations carried within the idea of the project.[6]

Many projects exemplify the mediation of universities and NGOs in Latin America. The five brief case studies included here cover Buenos Aires, São Paulo, Lima and Mexico. All illustrate universities where faculty members and students work together as practitioners, developing alternative methods for community engagement in excluded sectors of their cities, and have in common the following concepts and approaches:

- taking into account local and existent users and involving them in the decision-making process;
- consideration of the informal urban fabric along with its respective social and spatial networks;
- development of new methodologies for communication and interaction to obtain an understanding of the community's perception and subjective experience of place, and more accurate spatial information; and
- a focus on public space; strong independent communities consolidate when they are represented as a common entity within their public realm.

Asociacao Escola da Cidade (School of the City Association), Audutora Rio Claro (Park of Integration), São Paulo
In 1996, a group of liberal professionals from the areas of architectural research and multidisciplinary teaching decided to create an architectural programme with a new pedagogical and administrative structure that could also meet the Brazilian

Asociacao Escola da Cidade (School of the City Association), Audutora Rio Claro (Park of Integration), São Paulo, 2002
opposite top and centre: The architectural, urban and landscape aspects of the Audutora Rio Claro, or Park of Integration, were structured by way of activity nodes, pedestrian passages, cycle routes, the planting of trees and greenery, public squares, and facilities for sports and leisure activities for different social groups. The total area is approximately 224,000 square metres (2.41 million square feet) and the park is now used by 320,000 people daily.

Flavio Janches/Blinder Janches & Co, Intervention strategy for Villa Tranquila, Buenos Aires, 2008–
opposite bottom: The ideas for this project evolved from weekly meetings between students and faculty members, municipality representatives and the local community. The design of the public spaces is configured through a modular kit of parts that can be adapted in terms of dimensions and materials as well as the activities within the existent conditions of each case scenario.

below: Proposals defined through the meetings and discussions included small parks, an amphitheatre for music and theatre, play areas, sports areas, daycare centres, education centres and libraries.

bottom: A Dutch foundation with representation in Buenos Aires gives funding for the construction of playgrounds for children living in marginal areas. The opening of the first of such 'playspaces' in Villa Tranquila shows strong interaction between community and place, identifying the space as a part of daily life, as if it had always been there.

national requirements. The objective of Asociacao Escola de Cidade, or School of the City, was to give rise to a new generation of architects and city planners with a commitment towards the improvement of their society and city. The school operates with various funding generated through private and public grants, and payments for specific projects it is commissioned to undertake. NGOs, foundations, governments and associations all provide work in critical areas of the city and across the country, and the pupils learn from real projects while receiving a free education in return for their service to the community.[7]

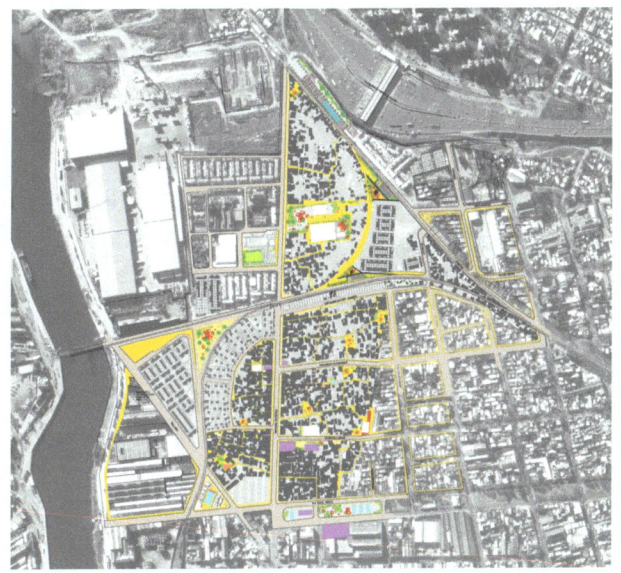

In December of 2001, the School of the City was invited by the government of the state of São Paulo to participate in a programme of workshops for the improvement of areas of the city where violence was particularly widespread. The allocated site was a 7.5-kilometre (4.6-mile) strip (varying in width), a remnant of urban growth, in the Sapopemba district, an unattractive, neglected and unused space home to drug use and serious crime. As this linear space cuts through diverse urbanised areas with differing physical and social characteristics, a consultation process with the local communities of each sector was required to unveil the activities, desires and needs of each. The proposal for the Park of Integration was thus organised as a sequence of spaces for different uses (for example, sports facilities, community centres and children's playgrounds) in relation to the surrounding zoning and neighbourhood, acting as an organiser for different types of event. The participation process was important in order to integrate the community, involving them from the inception of the project, and making them the most important element for the definition, assembly and direction of the park.

The aim of the project was both to promote community participation through an inclusive programme and to generate self-sustained use of the park. At the same time it is an exemplar of academic and practical work in which architects and students acted as mediators between government agencies and the local communities for the democratisation and redistribution of leisure areas and facilities in the city, converting an urban void, or margin, into an active area of integration.

> The site's location in the centre of the city next to two of the wealthiest neighbourhoods, Recoleta and Barrio Norte, makes Barrio 31 Carlos Mugica one of the most emblematic informal areas in Buenos Aires.

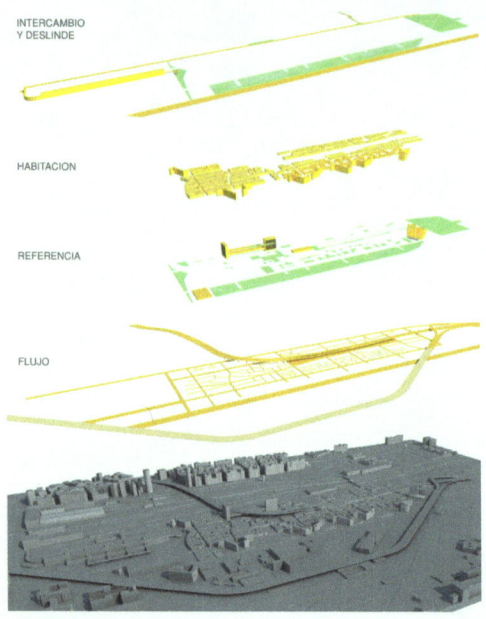

Flavio Janches/Blinder Janches & Co, Intervention strategy for Villa Tranquila, Buenos Aires

Flavio Janches and his office, Blinder Janches & Co architects, have been working in the *villas miserias* (shantytowns) of Argentina since 2000 along with students from the faculty of architecture and urbanism at the University of Buenos Aires where Janches currently teaches.[8]

The project team has been focusing on supporting the networks and interactions found within these local informal neighbourhoods by reinforcing the role of public spaces as areas for education and social gathering. Its latest work (ongoing since 2008), located in the Villa Tranquila settlement next to the river on the southern edge of Buenos Aires, summarises its activities and interests.

The methodology consisted of studying and mapping the site, and conducting interviews and workshops with the community at different stages of the project. The workshops revealed the community networks operating informally within the *villa*, which were otherwise not formally recorded by the municipality. Instead of approaching the site as a tabula rasa, analysis and urban regeneration instead took into account the 'self-generating capacity of these areas, which could create the potential for their reinsertion within the formal city'.[9] To do so, it was first necessary to locate the places and programmes at the edge of the slum that could break the barrier between the formal city and the non-formal city. At a smaller scale, it was important to look at ways to distribute, throughout the neighbourhood, programmes that could break the barriers between existing internal fragmentations. In addition, a network of very small public spaces was developed for small groups or families to help them build their own community.

The proposal consolidated the site's pre-existing networks and activities, and is described by the architect as 'a materialisation of the values of the community, representing the reality of its experience'. Even during the construction, it was important to involve the local residents to actually build the projects that resulted from the workshops. This has helped in developing relationships between the community and the architects, builders or local institutions funding the projects throughout the ongoing process, and also ensured that the community is committed to the long-term maintenance of their improved neighbourhood.

Javier Fernández Castro, Villa 31/Barrio 31 Carlos Mugica, Buenos Aires

Villa 31, now called Barrio 31 Carlos Mugica,[10] began as an urban research project in 2002, and continues its development today as a built project thanks to the collective work of students from the architecture department (Facultad de Arquitectura, Diseño y Urbanismo, Universidad de Buenos Aires – FADU) at the University of Buenos Aires, and faculty members led by professor of architecture and urbanism Javier Fernández Castro.

The site's location in the centre of the city next to two of the wealthiest neighbourhoods, Recoleta and Barrio Norte, makes Barrio 31 Carlos Mugica one of the most emblematic informal areas in Buenos Aires. It covers 39 hectares (96.3 acres) and houses 35,000 people (11,000 families). Working with the community for eight years, surviving only on scholarships and private sponsorship,[11] FADU successfully lobbied the state to turn this theoretical project into a reality. In 2010, the project was officially adopted by the government and renamed 'Plan de urbanización de las villas 31 y 31 bis' by the Comisión de Vivienda, the government agency that deals with housing issues.

Prior to Fernández Castro's initiative, the city had planned to demolish the *villa*. Following the Favela-Barrio project, the team's approach was to identify how existing social and spatial capital could be maintained or repaired. This approach represented considerable savings in government spending on the regeneration of the area. As in the other case studies illustrated here, part of the methodology was constant and regular contact with the local people to understand the dynamics of the site.[12]

The team's work resulted in the renovation of 60 per cent of the area's existing homes, and 40 per cent new homes. It also provided an opportunity for the integration of other services and infrastructures within the formal and informal areas of the city.

Javier Fernández Castro, Villa 31/Barrio 31 Carlos Mugica, Buenos Aires, 2002–
opposite: The proposal included three intervention scales: the macroscale, integrating the neighbourhood with the immediate context and city, adding a new programme and housing along the border; the intermediary scale, working within the different parts of the neighbourhood to make the area more permeable; and the microscale, finding the right location to open up new functions through punctual interventions.

below: Throughout the consultation process, the usual tools for urban analysis were complemented by a series of workshops created to explore the collective subjectivity of the community. Students were able to interpret the demands of locals and project this into an integrated urban regeneration masterplan.

Working with the community for eight years, surviving only on scholarships and private sponsorship, FADU successfully lobbied the state to turn this theoretical project into a reality.

Maya Ballén, Mariana Leguía and Claudia Amico, Architecture and Participation Workshop, Chincha, Peru, 2007
below: Interventions included a new playground for children and the reconfiguration of an old public toilet building located on a key site (at the entrance) into a welcoming living mural and bus stop.

opposite top: Local participation in the main square.

(Y)ncluye (Maya Ballén and Mariana Leguía), Community Centre, Pisco, Peru, 2004
bottom: The role of the architect was to act as a mediator and to create structures of interaction to extract relevant information in order to develop the right programmatic set of tools for the project. In this way, the project was able to generate meaning within the community.

Espacio Expresión, 'Cómo transformar la ciudad?' (How to transform the city?), Lima, 2009
opposite bottom: The aim of the 'Cómo transformar la ciudad?' international event organised by Espacio Expresión in August 2009 was to generate proposals for the urban development of Pisco, to attract private-sector financing for a strategic programme for the site.

(Y)ncluye, New Methodologies in Ica, Peru

In 2004, faculty members of the Catholic University of Peru and architects Mariana Leguía and Maya Ballén of (Y)ncluye[13] were commissioned to design a local community centre in Pisco, a city 200 kilometres (124.2 miles) south of Lima. The site was located in a self-built neighbourhood, next to an area planned for a 2,000-square-metre (21,527-square-foot) public park and a new public school. At the time, only some of the surrounding plots were delineated with walls, but more than 60 per cent of the area was still vacant.

The architects' main aim was to turn the site into a theatre for community activities, exploring with the locals new ways of designing using participatory methods. Together with students they worked on site, looking at how they could facilitate the local people in making important decisions about the project's design.

The participatory process involved four clear stages. The first was the recollection of the site's existing spatial data and precedents. The second was the generation of new information through questionnaires for adults and exercises for local children in which they were asked, among other things, to make drawings (mental maps) of the area. These exercises were developed in conjunction with a sociologist and a psychologist who helped in extracting conclusions from the material. The third stage included a number of workshops to define the programmatic conditions and to define what a 'community centre' was for the residents. This exercise was repeated several times via various encounters.

Lastly, the group developed a game in which players were asked to place blocks representing the programme within a grid structure. In this way, the community was able to participate in, and help design, even the final stage of the project, in which the arrangement of the building and the programmatic conditions in relation to the public space at the site were conveyed.

Unfortunately, the 2007 Peru earthquake, with Pisco as its epicentre, devastated the region and led to the cancellation of the project's funding. Since then, the relief effort has highlighted a further need for universities and young practices to work with the community, rethinking conventional approaches in a city that needed to be rebuilt.

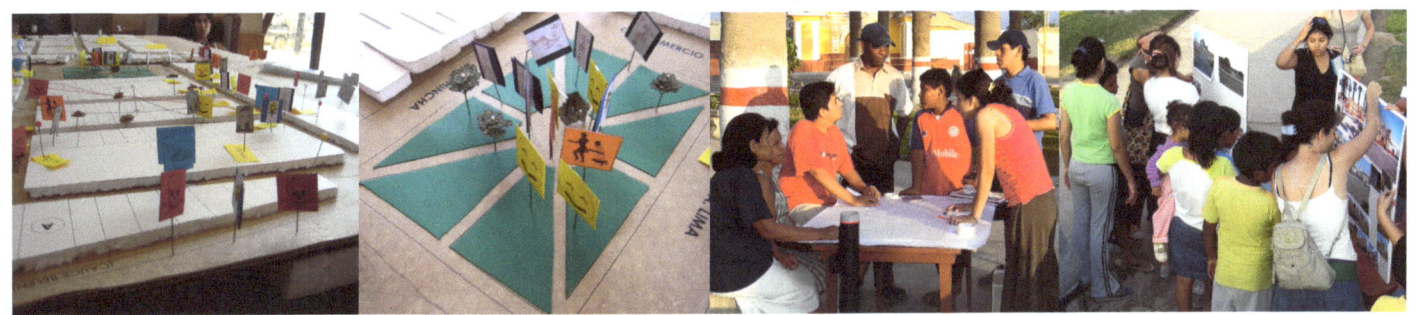

In response to this new challenge, in February 2008 (Y)ncluye, together with architect Claudia Amico, developed a summer course at the Catholic University for international and local students entitled Architecture and Participation, aimed at engaging students in a participatory design process with the community of Chincha, an area next to Pisco, which was also severely affected by the earthquake. After a series of workshops and analysis of the area, the students were asked to come up with new strategies of communication in order to establish not only the aims and desires of the community, but also new ways of recording the peoples' 'imaginaries'[14] of the place. With a small budget donated by an NGO, the group developed three minor interventions which it was hoped would have a major positive impact on the area, consolidating certain of the town's programmes at the urban scale – for example, a corner that was informally used as a bus stop and a garden was transformed into a children's playground.[15]

Claudia Amico continues to work with students in developing participatory methodologies to engage with the Pisco community through her NGO, Espacio Expresion.[16]

Arturo Ortiz Struck, Chimalhuacán Community Project, Mexico

Since 2005, architect Arturo Ortiz Struck has been working in the informal settlements within the municipality of Chimalhuacán, a suburb of Mexico City. During this time he has developed several projects in conjunction with the voluntary social service programme of various Mexican universities, and in particular with the faculty of architecture and urbanism at the Ibero-American University where he currently teaches.

One of his most recent projects consisted of a series of workshops with residents of Chimalhuacán to develop individual housing projects. He describes this ongoing experience with families in irregular settlements as 'working with the possibility of developing an architectural project defined by the feelings and imaginaries of each family'.[17]

In this way, the architects involved explain to residents the best way to take advantage of the available technical resources. On realising that the houses designed by the residents were too hot, poorly ventilated and expensive to construct, Ortiz Struck

The architects' main aim was to turn the site into a theatre for community activities, exploring with the locals new ways of designing using participatory methods. Together with students they worked on site, looking at how they could facilitate the local people in making important decisions about the project's design.

ETAPA 1

ETAPA 3

ETAPA 2

ETAPA 4

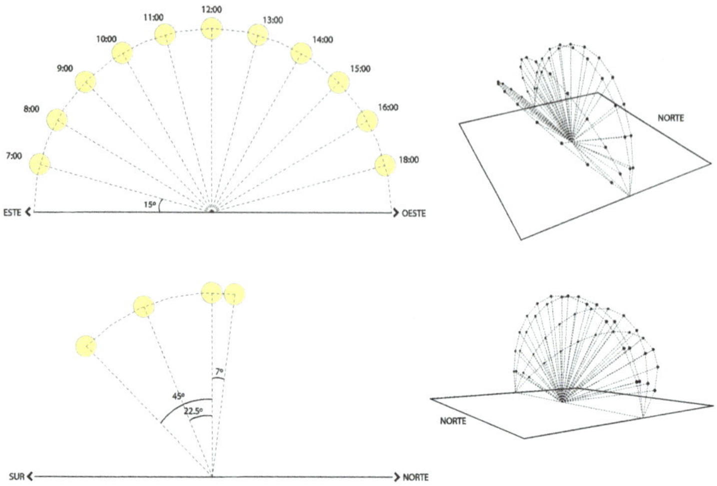

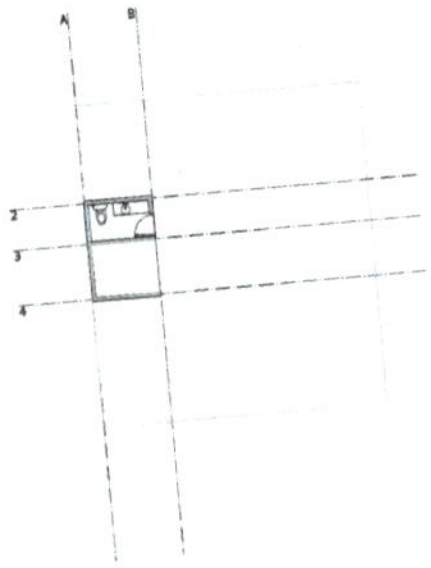

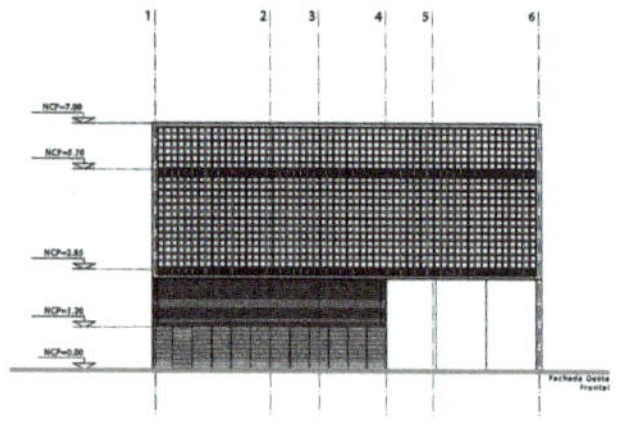

The importance of each project was in the process of designing together; the key was to design the tools to facilitate participation towards a common goal.

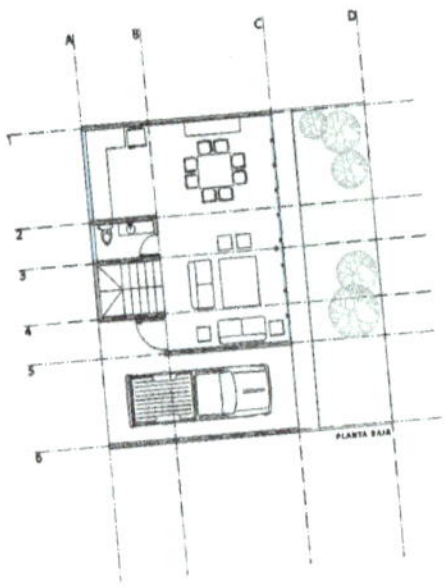

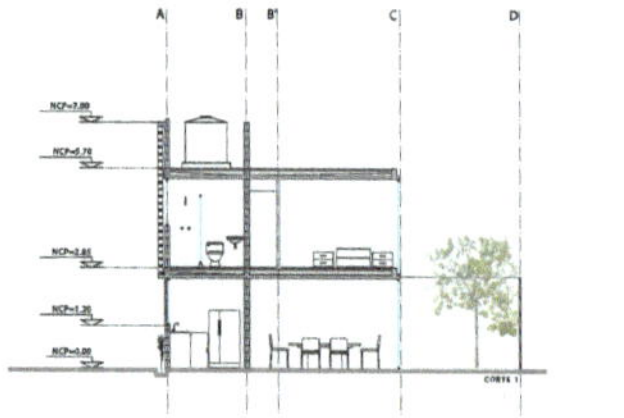

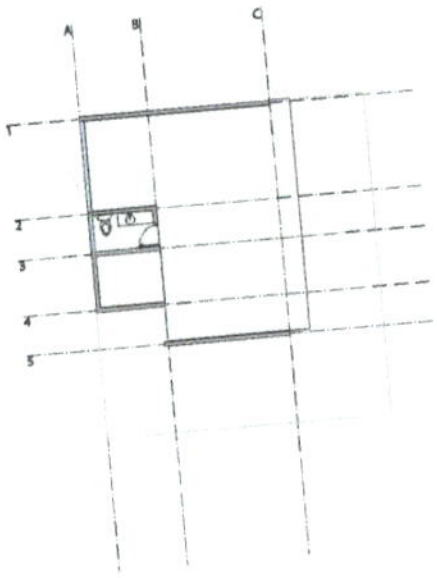

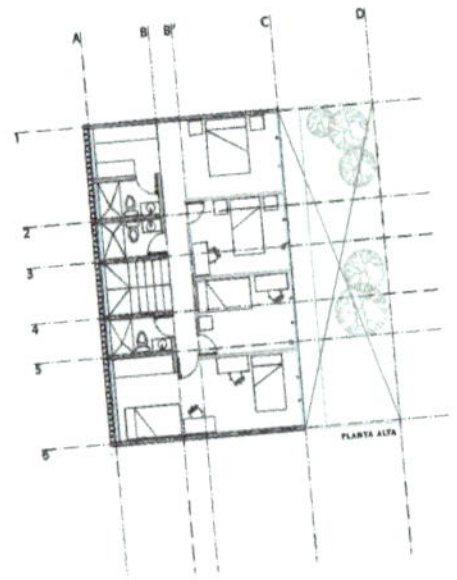

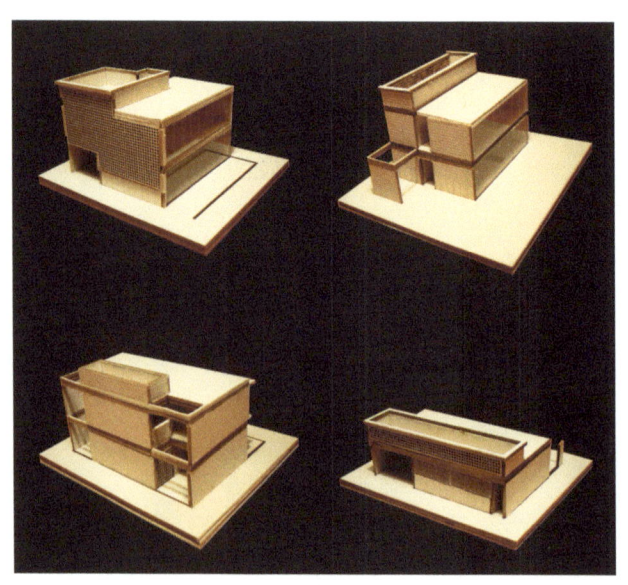

Arturo Ortiz Struck, Chimalhuacán Community Project, Mexico, 2005–
opposite, top and left: The methodology for this project created a set of tools to develop interaction and communication between the architect and the future owners of the houses. The parameters of the workshop focused on issues including lighting, ventilation, access, relation to the street and the sustainable use of resources such as water, construction materials and electricity.

opposite, centre and bottom: Different models and plans for the housing.

initiated a new project with them to facilitate better living conditions through the use of natural lighting and ventilation, and through rethinking the structural elements. For example, the perimeter wall is typically the first thing residents build. With this knowledge, a central strategy for the architect was to define this as a 'service wall' – effectively defining the organisation of the house for future development by placing services for the bathroom and kitchen along the outside wall.

The importance of each project was in the process of designing together; the key was to design the tools to facilitate participation towards a common goal. Thus a crucial role for the architect and his team was to prompt families in Chimalhuacán to ensure their imagination is included in, and will construct, the language transmitted by the built fabric. He continues to work in the area, in his words 'working at the point of origin of aesthetics: building thoughts that come from feelings'.[18]

Conclusion

The case studies here have demonstrated various methodologies towards a common goal of linking architectural practice with pedagogy. In this context, architects play new roles as mediators, facilitators and enablers, working to understand the community and its interaction with the city as integral parts of the design process.

In this sense, the role of pedagogy in Latin America is twofold. Firstly, it serves to guide students towards ethically and socially responsive practice. Secondly, it provides a mediator between national and international institutions and local communities, offering the possibility of establishing new models to support the natural diversity of the informal sector, and to search for alternative methodologies in response to some of the most serious problems facing Latin America today. Common in their approach is the recording and interpreting of collective imaginaries as part of resolving issues of housing, public buildings or the public realm. Implicit in this new approach is the personal encounter between the user and the architect, who designs a project based on the subjective pluralities offered through a diverse reading of dissimilar experiences pointing towards a common end: the imagined city, constructed from the imaginaries of its residents. ⌁

Notes

1. 'The combined population of today's four mega-cities (Mexico City, São Paulo, Buenos Aires, and Rio de Janeiro) increased from around 13 million in 1950 to around 60 million in 1990.' See Alan Gilbert, *The Mega-City in Latin America*, United Nations University Press (New York), 1996.
2. See Hernando de Soto, *The Mystery of Capital*, Basic Books (New York), 2000, p 17.
3. 'Rising Informality: Reversing the Tide', World Bank, August 2005. See http://rru.worldbank.org/PublicPolicyJournal.
4. In *The Mystery of Capital*, De Soto states that people in informal settlements are 'spontaneously organizing themselves into separate, extralegal groups until government can provide'. De Soto, op cit, p 73. In an interview, some of which is included on pages 64–7 of this issue, he expands further on this, stating: 'At the time, the context was solidarity. I mean seeing these people get organised. One guy helps the other guy do his wall, and the other guy helps him pour his roof, all of that is wonderful, but it's expensive.'
5. C Basombrío, *Inseguridad ciudadana y delito común*, Lima Instituto defensa Legal (Peru), 2003.
6. Nicholas Bourriaud, *Relational Aesthetics*, Adriana Noble (Buenos Aires), 2006. Referenced in Maya Ballén, *To Make Space, Leaving Space*, Universidad Ricardo Palma (Lima), July 2007.
7. All information, figures and quotes in this text on the Asociacao Escola de Cidade are from the author's conversations with Ciro Pirondi and the text provided by him, entitled: 'A experiencia da Escola de cidade na cidade de Sao Paulo', 2009.
8. The project connected local students with international students from TU Delft in the Netherlands, and later with Max Rohm and John Beardsley in a studio hosted by Harvard University.
9. All information, figures and quotes in this text on the Villa Tranquila project are from the author's conversations with Janches Flavio and the text provided by him, entitled: 'How to intervene in peripheral conditions?', 23 June 2009.
10. Carlos Mugica was a priest who worked and was murdered in the area in the 1970s. The locals wanted to name the neighbourhood after him.
11. The proposal centred on replicating the experience of the Favela-Barrio programme in Brazil (a government programme that started in 1993 in Rio de Janeiro, aiming to improve informal areas with the participation of multidisciplinary teams and local communities) within the *villas* of Buenos Aires. It won first prize at the Ibero-American Architecture Biennale in Chile in 2002.
12. All information, figures and quotes in this text on Barrio 31 Carlos Mugica are from the author's interview with Javier Fernández Castro in June 2010, and the text provided by him, entitled: 'Barrio 31 Carlos Mugica'.
13. Founded in 2002, the Peru-based group (Y)incluye (wwww.yncluye.com) consists of architects Mariana Leguía, Nelson Munares and Maya Ballén.
14. The term 'imaginaries', when referring to the urban realm, involves a feeling of attachment to, or rejection of, the representation of a place, acquired over time due to certain events or ways in which it is or can be used, not necessarily related to the function that it was designed for.
15. A collective group of artists called Brigada Muralista assisted with this project: see http://brigadamuralista.blogspot.com/.
16. www.espacioexpresion.org/.
17. Arturo Ortiz Struck, fragment of lecture at the Blok Conference, Belgrade, Serbia, 2010.
18. All information, figures and quotes in this text on the Mexico community projects are from the author's correspondence and interview with Arturo Ortiz Struck in Mexico City in July 2010.

Text © 2011 John Wiley & Sons Ltd. Images: pp 134 © Javier Fernandez Castro; pp 135, 140, 141(t) © Maya Ballen, Mariana Leguia; p 136(t&c) © Ciro Pirondi; pp 136(b), 137 © Flavio Janches; pp 138-9 © Javier Fernandez Castro; p 141(b) Claudia Amico; pp 142-3 © Arturo Ortiz Struck

COUNTERPOINT

Daniela Fabricius

LOOKING BEYOND INFORMALITY

The great mass of built urban space produced in the last decades – whether in the form of slums or real-estate development – has presented architects with a new set of questions concerning their role in shaping the city. A recent *New York Times* article claims that 'architects aren't ready for an urbanized planet'.[1] The article shows particular concern for the estimated one billion slum dwellers in the world today, pointing out that only 5 per cent of the building work under way in the world's expanding cities is actually planned.

It is all too easy to be optimistic about the economic and social future of Latin America. **Daniela Fabricius**, the author of *100% Favela: The Informal Geographies of Rio de Janeiro* (forthcoming), calls into question architects working within the realpolitik of a globalised, post-nationalist world. Could an all too ready acceptance of existing conditions and the adoption of informality leave inhabitants short-changed? For to live informally is also to live precariously – no substitute for secure and prosperous living.

Perhaps more than ever, the relevance of architecture has been placed under scrutiny.

This was not always the case. In the postwar decades international Modernism changed the nature of cities around the world. Few regions embraced and defined the optimism of this era like Latin America. The exemplary projects of the period defined what it meant to be a modern state and culture. But more significantly, they also demonstrated that a multiplicity of Modernisms could challenge Eurocentric notions of progress. These national Modernisms were no longer derived from the architecture of the northern hemisphere, but from a complex set of regional conditions. The Modernist architecture of Latin America was among the most progressive and original in the world.

By the 1960s Latin American cities paid dearly for the price of utopia, often quite literally in the form of foreign debt. What followed was a decidedly post-utopian and postmodern era. During this period Latin American cities saw the effects of rapid urbanisation, dictatorship, violence, political instability and neglect, which have only recently subsided. The relative improvement of urban conditions and the attainability of goals on a small scale have since given rise to a new, albeit cautious, optimism. The consensus today is that utopian schemes are no longer possible, and that we should work within the realpolitik of a globalised, post-nationalist world.

Whose Optimism?

The new optimism around Latin America does not take place only within architectural circles. Economists have noted that the curbing of inflation, the reduction of national debts and political stability have made much of Latin America an 'investor-friendly' zone. Some of this has been the result of years of globalisation. In the 1990s a controversial series of macroeconomic policies known as the Washington Consensus were implemented in Latin America. Measures included the privatisation of public utilities,

Unplanned occupation of the Billings Reservoir area, which supplies water to the city of São Paulo.

trade liberalisation and deregulation. These and similar market-based policies became the object of criticism of the anti-globalisation and popular leftist movements in Latin America. Critics argued that the liberalisation of these economies made them more vulnerable to global instabilities, and indeed several countries, like Ecuador and Argentina, experienced major crises. In recent years, however, there has been a trend towards stability and steady growth. Economists claim that these years have been Latin America's strongest since the 1960s.[2]

One of the most prominent examples has been Brazil, which has been identified as one of the global BRICs (Brazil, Russia, India and China), a term referring to growing economies that are on the way to becoming global leaders.[3] Brazil has been especially visible as the country prepares for the World Cup in 2014, and the Olympic and Paralympic Games in 2016. Brazil's economy has been strong, but wealth is not the biggest concern for most Brazilians – distribution of wealth is.

The same problem can be extended to much of the region. Historically, per capita wealth in Latin America has remained relatively low even in prosperous times. The region has been and remains one of the most economically divided parts of the world. It is also diverse, and includes smaller and less powerful countries that are frequently overlooked because they have not fully embraced globalisation. As investor interest grows, so does the danger that the region will once again become vulnerable to speculation and too rapid growth.

I ask 'whose optimism' because it is all too easy to conflate two forms of optimism – that surrounding economic performance and that surrounding social progress. While the two can be mutually beneficial they are more often at odds. Latin America today is characterised by an unlikely combination of nationalist leftist governments and economies open to privatisation and foreign investment, both of which seem to inspire optimism. This creates conflict in some places, and confusion in others. How do we separate optimism from opportunism? Shouldn't political and social stability be an end in itself, and not at the service of economic attractiveness?

Informality Embraced

One source of optimism for architects lies in informal communities. Once viewed as the scourge of Latin American cities, these neighbourhoods are now seen as viable components of post-utopian planning. Many of the new projects in these neighbourhoods are now compatible with investor dollars and government interests.[4] This was not always the case. In the 1960s, Latin American architects who were active in communities of the urban poor were usually so without official support. During this period their European colleagues also took an interest in the unplanned architecture found in urban slums around the world. Informality was seen as a way to move beyond the exhaustion and failures of the modern movement, and a way to critique the ideology of state-controlled planning.[5] The rhetoric of informality – flexibility, spontaneity, desire, choice – was used to design utopian spaces in cities like London and Amsterdam. Today this counter-Modernist approach to design has returned as a set of strategies applied in low-income districts. More and more, in Latin America especially, informality is no longer viewed as a problem to be solved through design so much as a condition that offers its own set of solutions. And indeed, after decades of razing and destroying communities to make way for Modernist housing, or of simply neglecting informal areas, the practice of investing in these communities has become mainstream.

Architects were not the only ones who discovered informality. The term 'informal' entered public vocabulary in the early 1970s largely through the work of economist Keith Hart. Hart derived the concept while doing field research in Ghana, where he observed that contrary to unemployment statistics most Ghanians had work, only it was not officially documented.[6] The term quickly came to be used to designate all unregulated activity of the global poor. After a series of global crises in the 1970s that led to a retreat from planned economies, the notion of the informal economy was embraced as a solution to developing the so-called third

world. An undocumented worker, once called 'unemployed', then 10 years later 'illegally employed', had by the 1980s become an 'entrepreneur'. Rather than resisting informality, this new approach allowed it to become a defensible and self-sustaining concept.

It seems that informality is no longer an exceptional or radical condition in cities – in fact, it is arguably the defining quality of many major metropolises today. Furthermore, the defence of informality has strayed far from the activists of the 1960s who protected slums from the bulldozers of state planners and developers. Today, the tolerance of informality is becoming an object of consensus.

What does this mean for architects? Those architects who chose to work with, and not against, informal architecture were the first to consider the desires and choice of the urban poor in designing their environments. However, 50 years later this notion, like large-scale planning before it, can be looked at less idealistically. To be sure, architects are in a difficult spot. Those who are committed to the improvement of the lives of the urban poor have little choice but to work within the informal paradigm, and there is no doubt that the projects of upgrading informal communities are almost always immediately beneficial to residents. These projects, and the dedicated work of their architects, deserve the recognition they have received. But just as architects were once critical of the Modernist paradigm that had been handed to them, should there not be a similar consideration of the consequences of informality?

The Aporia of the Informal

In recent years the public image of informal urbanism has received a much-needed makeover, especially in Latin America. Infrastructural improvements and public art projects have helped to ease the stigma or even total blindness towards these urban areas and their residents. But in this acceptance of informality it is all too easy to forget that to live informally is to live precariously. Informality does not represent a solution or an end, but a new set of conditions and challenges. This is especially evident when it comes to employment. The 'wageless life' of an informal worker has no more solved previous problems of unemployment than slums have 'solved' the question of housing. The International Labour Organization (ILO) all but supported informal employment as a solution to unemployment in the 1970s. But it has since changed its position. According to the ILO, the informal economy has grown beyond the expectations of economists,[7] and cannot provide the protection and security of formal employment or 'decent' work conditions.[8]

opposite left: Concrete house in the Rocinha favela, Rio de Janeiro.

opposite right: Favelas alongside the highway in São Paulo.

below: A commuter train passes by the Favela Do Moinho in São Paulo. The favela, which residents claim is home to 700 families, is tucked away between a highway and railway line and includes a former factory building that is occupied by squatters.

The same questions can be applied at the level of housing. Have we also put too much faith in informality? Both at the level of the individual home and of the community the disadvantages of informal life are clear. Admittedly the situation in Latin America is better now than it has been – for example, today the majority of residents in the favelas in large cities in Brazil have adequate infrastructural services, which was not the case only 30 years ago. But communities still suffer from drug and police violence, from being located in places that are difficult to commute from, from poor health and educational facilities, and from a social stigma. Studies have also documented the environmental and health impact when communities spread into natural areas and urban water reservoirs, when there is flooding or inadequate sewage, and the toxic exposure of living close to industrial areas not otherwise considered fit for human habitation.

Informality is perhaps one of the most visible aspects of today's 'risk society' as identified by Ulrich Beck.[9] According to Beck, modernisation has both produced risk (in areas like national security, health and the environment) and invented measures for managing it. In a 'world risk society' informal populations have been made the most vulnerable and yet they receive the least amount of protection. In a society that is based on the self as the primary agent it is the poor who have the least amount of agency.

One could argue that alternative structures of support for informal residents do exist. National and foreign NGOs make informal life manageable. However, they provide to urban residents only what should be theirs by right as citizens, but in the form of charity. This is reminiscent of the situation of stateless people that Hannah Arendt once described as the 'aporia of human rights'.[10] According to Arendt, rights are neither natural nor inalienable, but are dependent on participation in a sovereign political organisation. People without rights are those who have lost their distinctive political qualities and have become 'human beings and nothing else'.[11] NGOs compensate for the needs of informal populations by recognising their humanity, but this cannot compensate for political participation.

Residents of informal communities defend their neighbourhoods and the right to live in them. The houses are their property and their investment and should not be taken away; they have built the communities themselves, often against great odds. It is true that the forms of solidarity found in informal neighbourhoods are rarely present in masterplanned housing projects. But must this solidarity come at such a high price? Have we placed too great a burden on the communities themselves?

Micro-Macro

The problems associated with large-scale urban planning have also created new interest in the small-scale project. Recent urban interventions in Latin America and elsewhere have favoured the approach of 'urban acupuncture'.[12] The notion of acupuncture suggests an alternative to the invasive 'urban surgery' made famous by Le Corbusier. Instead of viewing the urban body as composed of parts or organs, urban acupuncture treats it as a continuous nervous system that need only be manipulated locally in order to 'release energy' that has global effects. This approach has been most famously theorised by former Curitiba mayor Jaime Lerner.[13] Curitiba became a model city in the 1960s due to the success of its light bus-based transportation network. This system, however, was not a small, localised intervention but a highly planned infrastructure for controlled yet flexible growth as part of the city's 1965 Master Plan. The success of the system can more accurately be attributed to the consideration of both the macro and the micro scale. Lerner's more recent initiative-based programmes target environmental and social problems through citizen participation. Encouraging urban residents to recycle garbage or tend trees planted by the city does not ask them to depend on their own resources or the market, but to actively participate in the improvement of the city as a whole. The implementation of these micro-structural programmes is only possible through a planned and centralised urban government initiative.[14]

Micro-urban interventions and similar approaches like micro-financing[15] search for alternatives to large-scale, centralised planning, and are based on the belief that self-organising processes will be sparked by minimal, local interventions. The micro-

below: Aerial view of the Heliopolis favela in São Paulo. Heliopolis is the largest favela in São Paulo and is home to more than 125,000 residents.

opposite: Police patrol the Alemão favela complex in Rio de Janeiro after its occupation by the military.

intervention, however, is a gamble. There is no guarantee that it will have more than a minimal effect, and serve in the end as only a symbolic substitution for real investment in poor areas. Where the micro-intervention is perhaps most effective is when it is combined with an organised macro-scale plan.

Large-scale, centralised planning or urban surgery is certainly not over in Latin America. In Brazil, Rio de Janeiro is preparing for the 2016 Olympics by proposing major architectural and infrastructural investments with an estimated budget of $14.4 billion. While the planning committee promises that the project will have benefits for all citizens, including residents in favelas, these benefits are indirect and cannot be guaranteed. One wonders why this type of large-scale planning and investment takes place for an event like the Olympics, and not for the everyday lives of residents. Why, when it comes to the question of the urban poor, is the emphasis on the micro, and when it comes to the global financial elite and tourism, is it on the macro?

Beyond Informality

For architects working in informal communities, Latin America does indeed offer a unique set of conditions. In most regions in the world, urban slums resemble those found in Latin America decades ago, with houses built from wood, mud or corrugated metal, problems with disease, and lack of basic infrastructures. By contrast, the favelas in Brazil and many other countries have changed dramatically, with improved access to utilities and multistorey concrete buildings that often resemble ordinary working-class neighbourhoods. Life in these communities is viable and often thriving, especially when the problem of drug-related violence can be controlled. We can celebrate the resilience and power of these communities, and support the investments residents have made in building their environment against many odds. However, there is only so much that an individual resident can do. Many favela residents invest in the inside of their houses, leaving the outside unfinished; this is symbolic of the limited reach and resources of residents in shaping their communities. Construction is slow, difficult and costly to residents. Public spaces and streets become congested as residents focus only on expanding their own property. Beyond their own house or perhaps a small business, residents have little power to shape their communities as a whole, or to provide much-needed services like transportation, education and health care.

The most successful projects in informal communities – like the much-acclaimed interventions in Medellín, Colombia – seem to be the ones that help to integrate these neighbourhoods into the city and provide residents with services comparable to those in the 'formal' city. In other words, these interventions do not insist on preserving informality, but work towards regularising and formalising these neighbourhoods. Holding on to the belief that favelas succeed because of their singular quality – namely their informality – reinforces their segregation and the belief that these are 'other' spaces.

Informality presents a dilemma because it suggests both creative and resourceful solutions, and a loss of security and protection. It is too easy to forget that informality is a substitution for secure and prosperous living and working conditions, disempowering those who could potentially levy unemployment or lack of housing for a political voice. We have now recognised informal populations, which was a crucial step following the violence against these residents in Latin America in the 1960s and 1970s. And indeed that moment did seem like one of hope and optimism. How can architects now look beyond informality to address the new challenges that arose from it?

Latent Utopias

In conclusion I would like to comment once more on the question of utopia. How post-utopian is Latin America really? Some have called favelas 'partial utopias'.[16] Leftist politics in Latin America following the Cold War have been described as a 'utopia unarmed'.[17] I would argue that utopian thought still drives architecture in Latin America, whether it is the utopia of a 'radical pragmatism', of Rio de Janeiro as an Olympic city, or the utopia of community. The ongoing effort to distance ourselves from the Modernist past has made us blind to what persists from that era – and what has been too quickly dismissed. New projects in Latin America are no less fraught with idealism and ideology than their Modernist predecessors were. However, they also open the path for new possibilities. Perhaps the important question is not so much whether these projects are utopian, but rather what vision of utopia they are proposing. We should not be afraid of utopian thought that goes beyond the status quo – beyond the demands of the market and social pragmatism – towards a more expanded role for architects in an urbanised world. ⌁

Notes

1. Amelia Gentleman, 'Architects Aren't Ready for an Urbanized Planet', Letter From India, *The New York Times*, 20 August 2007.
2. 'The five years to 2008 were Latin America's best since the 1960s, with economic growth averaging 5.5% a year and inflation generally in single digits.' Michael Reid, 'A Special Report on Latin America', *The Economist*, 9 September 2001; see www.economist.com/node/16964114. Last accessed 3 January 2011.
3. Jim O'Neil, *Building Better Global Economic BRICs*, Global Economics Paper No 66, Goldman Sachs Economic Research Group, 2001. That enthusiasm around Brazil has been especially palpable can be attributed in no small part to its relatively neutral diplomatic position in relationship to Europe and the US (especially when compared to Russia and China).
4. In Brazil especially, the favelas have had an ambiguous status, both representing the vitality of the country – its source of 'hope' and energy – and its shortcomings. Publicity for the Olympic Games is already revealing this familiar pattern.
5. Even Le Corbusier, who is better known for his critiques of the urban slum, praised Rio's favelas as early as 1929. An informal aesthetic was later developed by Team X members like the Smithsons and Aldo van Eyck in the 1960s, while in the 1970s architects took an interest in squatters, whether they be in London or in Lima.
6. Keith Hart, 'Informal Income Opportunities and Urban Employment in Ghana', *Journal of Modern African Studies*, Vol 11, No 1, March 1973, pp 62–8.
7. Informal labour currently makes up 58 per cent of employment in Latin America, where it also accounts for over 80 per cent of new jobs. International Labour Organization, *Decent Work and the Informal Economy*, International Labour Conference, 90th Session, International Labour Office (Geneva), 2002.
8. The insecurities faced by informal workers include a lack of legal protection or ability to enforce contracts, difficulty organising for representation, irregular and often low incomes, dependence on informal institutions for credit or training, limited access to public benefits, having to pay bribes and difficulties with public authorities. *Decent Work and the Informal Economy*, op cit.
9. Ulrich Beck, *Risk Society: Towards a New Modernity*, Sage Publications (London), 1992.
10. Hannah Arendt, *The Origins of Totalitarianism*, Harcourt, Brace, Jovanovich (New York), 1973, pp 290–302.
11. Ibid, p 302.
12. Jaime Lerner, *Acupunctura Urbana*, Editora Record (Rio de Janeiro), 2003.
13. Ibid.
14. It is also useful to remember that Curitiba is a moderately sized city with a population of just under 2 million.
15. Micro-finance is a system of loans made to the poor in order to support entrepreneurial activities. This practice has received mixed reviews. While it does provide convenient access to funds and often immediate relief from poverty, there are problems like predatory interest rates, debt burdens and funds being used for needs like food or health care rather than income-producing activities. Furthermore, micro-loans once again place the burden on the poor to generate income, rather than encourage medium and large-scale businesses that could provide wages and greater security. In Nicaragua there has been an enormous backlash against micro-lenders: the 'No Pago' (No Pay) movement, accusing lenders of usury, has organised violent protests outside micro-lending offices and encourages followers to refuse repayment.
16. See Jean-François Lejeune, 'Dreams of Order: Utopia, Cruelty, and Modernity', *Cruelty and Utopia: Cities and Landscapes of Latin America*, Princeton Architectural Press (New York), 2005, p 48.
17. Jorge Castañeda, *Utopia Unarmed: the Latin American Left After the Cold War*, Random House (New York), 1993.

Text © 2011 John Wiley & Sons Ltd. Images: p 144 © Daniela Fabricius; pp 145, 146(r) © Nelson Kon; p 146(l) © Andres Cypriano; pp 147-8 © Noah Addis/Corbis; p 149 © Joedson Alves/dpa/Corbis

CONTRIBUTORS

Alejandro Aravena graduated from the Catholic University of Chile, where he is currently Elemental-Copec Professor. He established Alejandro Aravena Architects in 1994. He was a visiting professor at Harvard Graduate School of Design (GSD) from 2000 to 2005. He is a member of the Pritzker Prize jury and has been named International Fellow of the Royal Institute of British Architects (RIBA). Professional work includes educational facilities, institutional, corporate and public buildings, museums and housing. Awards include the Silver Lion at the XI Venice Biennale, the Marcus Prize 2010, the Avonni Prize for Innovator of the Year and the Erich Schelling Architecture Medal 2006 (Germany). His work has been widely published and exhibited in lectures and exhibitions in more than 30 countries. Since 2006 he has been an executive director of Elemental SA, a for-profit company with a social conscience that works on infrastructure, transportation, public space and housing projects in partnership with the Catholic University and the Chilean oil company COPEC.

Ricky Burdett is a professor of urban studies and of political science at the London School of Economics (LSE) and a director of the LSE Cities and the Urban Age programme. He is also a global distinguished professor at the Institute of Public Knowledge at New York University. He is chief adviser on architecture and urbanism for the London 2012 Olympics and the Olympic Park Legacy Company, and was architectural adviser to the mayor of London from 2001 to 2006. He has curated numerous exhibitions including 'Global Cities' at Tate Modern (2007), was director of the 2006 Architecture Biennale in Venice and chairman of the jury for the 2007 Mies van der Rohe Prize. He is architectural adviser to the City of Genoa and a member of the Milan Expo 2015 steering committee. He is a council member of the Royal College of Art and sits on the mayor of London's Promote London Board.

Fernanda Canales graduated from the Ibero-American University in Mexico City (1997), where she went on to become a professor of design and urbanism, and has an MA from the Universitat Politècnica de Catalunya (UPC) in Barcelona (2001). She is currently completing a PhD at the Escuela Técnica Superior de Arquitectura de Madrid. Her independent practice of architecture and research is based in Mexico City. Her office is currently engaged in both public and private projects, for which she has won several competitions, including the new CEDIM Campus in Monterrey as well as the competition for a theatre complex in Guadalajara. Her work has been shown internationally, including at the 2004 Rotterdam Biennale, 2005 Bienal de Arquitectura de São Paulo and the 2006 Venice Biennale. In 2010 she received an Honorific Distinction as best young architect from the Colegio de Arquitectos de México.

Lorenzo Castro holds a degree in architecture from the Javeriana University in Bogotá (1988). Between 1998 and 2001, during the mayoralty of Enrique Peñalosa, he was the director of the city's Taller Profesional del Espacio Público (Professional Studio of Public Space). Through Bogotá's Spatial Plan (2000), he proposed a strategy for public plazas, a plan for pedestrian avenues, and gave definition to the TransMilenio bus rapid transit (BRT) project, as well as tracing the city's network of cycle routes, and participating as a member of its Committee for District Parks. Since 1990 he has lectured at various universities within Colombia including Javeriana, the National University of Colombia, Jorge Tadeo Lozano and Pontificia Bolivariana, and currently lectures at the University of the Andes. He has also been a guest lecturer for landscape and architecture master's students within the National University of Cuenca, Ecuador. He has taken part in a number of international conferences and events in Mexico, the US, Bolivia, Venezuela, the Dutch Antilles, Puerto Rico, Germany, Spain and the UK. He has twice been awarded the National Karl Brunner Prize, and the Pan-American Prize for Architecture (both 2004 and 2010).

Teddy Cruz was born in Guatemala City. He obtained a master's in design studies from Harvard University in 1997 and established his research-based architecture practice in San Diego, California, in 2000. He has been recognised internationally for his urban research on the Tijuana–San Diego border, received the prestigious Rome Prize in Architecture, and in 2005 was the first recipient of the James Stirling Memorial Lecture on the City Prize. His work has been profiled in publications including the *New York Times*, *Domus* and *Harvard Design Magazine*. In 2008 he represented the US at the Venice Architecture Biennale, and this year his work was included in MoMA's 'Small Scale, Big Change' exhibition. He is currently a professor in public culture and urbanism in the Visual Arts Department at the University of California, San Diego, where he co-founded the Center for Urban Ecologies (CUE).

Derek Dellekamp founded **Dellekamp Arquitectos** in 1999, where he continues to be the creative mind behind each of the office's projects. He also co-founded MXDF, a Mexico City-based urban research workshop, in 2004. From 2004 to 2005 he lectured as an adjunct professor in Mexican universities, and is currently a visiting professor at the Rice School of Architecture. Dellekamp Arquitectos is dedicated to the development and supervision of architectural projects regardless of scale or programme type with a rigorous research methodology. It aims to find unique solutions to the specific conditions of each project in order to maximise its intended budget, image, use, context and spirit. The coordination and collaboration with various disciplines such as engineering, graphic design, industrial design, environmental engineering and landscape architecture makes up a great part of its activities. The practice is also involved in ongoing architectural research and is constantly a part of the academic and teaching realms, as well as research studies, lectures, publications, biennales and exhibitions.

Alejandro Echeverri has been a professor and was the director of the Study Group in Architecture at the Universidad Pontificia Bolivariana of Medellín (2002–3), and was an invited professor of urbanism at the ETSAB, Barcelona, from 1999 to 2000. His work received the National Architectural Design Award, given by the Colombian Architectural Association, in 1996, and he won the National Urban Planning Award given by the Colombian Architectural Association in 2008, the Urban Design Award from the Pan American Biennale, Quito, in 2008, and the Curry Stone Prize 2009. He was general manager of the Empresa de Desarrollo Urbano (EDU), of the municipality of Medellín from 2004 to 2005, and the director of urban projects for the municipality of Medellín from 2005 to 2008. In addition to his private practice, he is also a director of urbamMedellín, the University of EAFIT urban research centre.

Daniela Fabricius researches and writes on issues relating to the contemporary city, and is the editor and author of the book *100% Favela* (Actar, forthcoming), which focuses on the favelas of Brazil and their urban context. She holds a BA in visual art and comparative literature from Brown University in Providence, Rhode Island, and an MArch from Columbia University, and has taught at the Pratt Institute and the University of Pennsylvania. She is currently a PhD candidate at Princeton University's School of Architecture.

Created in 1999 by fellow students (Fernando Forte, Lourenço Gimenes and Rodrigo Marcondes Ferraz) from the faculty of architecture and urbanism at the University of São Paulo, **Forte, Gimenes & Marcondes Ferraz (FGMF)** produces contemporary architecture without any restraints regarding the use of material and building techniques, seeking to explore the connection between architecture, environment and humankind. No matter what the project, it prioritises the interdependence between the built object, its environment and the end user.

EquipoArquitectura is a team founded in 2003 by the Chileans **Fernando García-Huidobro** and **Nicolás Tugas**, and Peruvian **Diego Torres Torriti**, all of them architects from the Pontificia Universidad Católica de Chile. García-Huidobro and Torres Torriti are also part of the Elemental team, a do-tank devoted to developing projects of social interest and public impact in Chile and, more recently, abroad. Tugas currently works at CCRS Arquitectes in Barcelona, which focuses on different scales of urbanism.

Jorge Mario Jáuregui is an architect-urbanist based in Rio de Janeiro. He graduated from the National University of Rosário, Argentina, and from the Federal University of Rio de Janeiro. He has been researching and working with the sociospatial division between Rio's favelas and the rest of the city since the 1990s. He is also coordinator of the Architectural and Urban Studies Center of Rio de Janeiro, associate researcher at the Laboratory of Morphology SICyT-FADU/UBA Buenos Aires, and a member of the Art and Psychoanalysis Cartel of the psychoanalytic *Letra Freudiana* Institution in Rio de Janeiro. He is responsible for more than 20 projects of the Favela-Barrio (Slum-to-Neighbourhood) programme implemented by the Rio city government beginning in the 1990s. Since 2007 he has been working on two large-scale urban redevelopment projects in the communities of Complexo do Alemão and Complexo de Manguinhos for President Lula's PAC (Growth Acceleration Programme), which were opened in 2010. Current projects under development include site works related to the 2014 World Cup and 2016 Olympic Games. He was the recipient of the Sixth Veronica Rudge Green Prize in Urban Design, from Harvard GSD, in 2000.

Adam Kaasa is the communications and outreach manager for LSE Cities. He is also a PhD candidate at the LSE Cities programme, focusing on ideas about architecture and urbanism in relation to political authority, media and circulation. He is the London coordinator for the NYLON seminars and conferences, a transatlantic intellectual working group between universities in and around London and New York, and teaches in the sociology department at the LSE.

Sharif S Kahatt is an architect and urban designer, founder of K+M Arquitectura y Urbanismo and professor in the Faculty of Architecture at the Catholic University of Peru. A graduate from Ricardo Palma University in Lima, he holds a Master of Architecture in Urban Design from Harvard GSD. He has taught studios and courses, published articles, given lectures and worked on projects in Peru, Spain, Mexico and the US. He is currently finishing his doctoral dissertation at the ETSAB, Barcelona, and works in Lima.

Angus Laurie co-founded LLAMA Urban Design in July 2007. He is based in Lima and his current project in the north of Peru aims to make communities more sustainable through densifying town centres to support amenities such as schools and hospitals, by improving connections between disparate communities, and by diversifying the economy to help the towns move away from their dependence on mining. He is a professor of urban design in the Faculty of Architecture of the Catholic University of Peru. Before this, he worked in London on a number of major urban projects including the Covent Garden masterplan with Kohn Pederson Fox, co-authored the Public Realm Strategy for Greater London, and provided advice for CABE's upcoming public realm guidance as well as for the London Olympics project High Street 2012 while working with Alan Baxter and Associates.

Gary Leggett is a designer currently based in New Haven, Connecticut. He received his BA in architecture from Princeton University and a master's in urban planning from the Harvard GSD. In 2008 he received the Druker Traveling Fellowship and travelled extensively in the Amazon, documenting his travels through film and photography. He is a former researcher of the Jan Van Eyck Academy in Maastricht, the Netherlands.

Enrique Martin-Moreno is an architect and planner, and principal of Martin-Moreno architects. His professional practice focuses on expanding the tools of architecture to participate in the different urban dynamics at play. He co-curated the 'Urban Voids' exhibition at the Museum of Mexico City, and was curator of the Mexican Pavilion at the Lisbon Architecture Triennale in 2007. He also participated in the 2006 Venice Architecture Biennale, and the 2005 Rotterdam International Biennale of Architecture. Since 2003 he has been a faculty member at the Ibero-American University of Mexico City where he teaches urban studies and architectural design. He has also led research-based architecture studios at the Southern California Institute of Architecture (Sci_Arc) and the Arizona State University (ASU). He received his professional degree in architecture from the Ibero-American University in 1999, and a master's in architecture from Harvard GSD in 2002.

Fernando de Mello Franco obtained his PhD from the Faculty of Architecture and Urbanism at the University of São Paulo. He is principal at MMBB Arquitetos and a professor at São Judas Tadeu University, and was previously a visiting professor at Harvard GSD. His Watery Voids (2007) project received the Best Entry Award at the 3rd International Architecture Biennale Rotterdam (IABR). He is currently a co-curator of the 5th IABR (2012).

Adriana Navarro-Sertich is a graduate student in architecture at the University of California, Berkeley, where she is also pursuing a master's degree in city and regional planning. Born and raised in Colombia, she received a BS Arch (Honours) from the University of Virginia in 2004. As a 2010 John K Branner Fellow, she has been travelling the world, focusing her research on sociocultural aspects of design, and specifically analysing the relationship between architecture, planning and informality.

Enrique Peñalosa has lectured internationally in numerous environmental, governmental, urban design and policy and university forums, and has advised governments in Asia, Africa, Australia, Latin America and the US. His vision and proposals have significantly influenced policies in numerous cities throughout the world. He is currently president of the board of the Institute for Transportation and Development Policy (ITDP) of New York. He is a consultant on urban vision, strategy and policy. As mayor of Bogotá, he profoundly transformed the city, turning it from one with neither bearings, self-esteem or hope into an international example for improvements in quality of life, mobility and equity in developing world cities. He created the TransMilenio bus-based transit system; a network of bicycle paths; slum improvement projects; a land bank to provide low-income housing with quality urbanism; greenways and pedestrian promenades for low-income neighborhoods; radical improvements to the city centre; daily car-use restrictions during peak hours and an annual Car Free Day; formidable libraries and parks; and dozens of high-quality public schools, nurseries and community centres. He holds a BA in economics and history from Duke University, a master's degree in government from the National School of Adminstration (IIAP) in Paris, and a DESS in public administration from the University of Paris II.

Patricio del Real is a PhD candidate in architectural history and theory at Columbia University's Graduate School of Architecture, Planning and Preservation (GSAPP). His current research focuses on the construction of a Latin American imaginary through modern architecture during the early years of the Cold War. His second area of research engages contemporary vernacular practices, focusing on Havana, where he has also participated in the construction of informal structures. He has taught architecture since 1991 in the US and Latin America. He was previously the director of the Clemson University Architecture Center in Barcelona.

Saskia Sassen is the Robert S Lynd Professor of Sociology and co-chair of the Committee on Global Thought, Columbia University. Her most recent books include *Territory, Authority, Rights: From Medieval to Global Assemblages* (Princeton University Press, 2008) and *A Sociology of Globalization* (Norton, 2007). For UNESCO, she set up a five-year project on sustainable human settlement based on a network of researchers and activists in over 30 countries; now published as one of the volumes of the *Encyclopedia of Life Support Systems* (EOLSS) (www.eolss.net). She has written for the *Guardian*, *Financial Times*, *New York Times*, *Le Monde Diplomatique*, *International Herald Tribune* and *Newsweek International*. She contributes regularly to OpenDemocracy.net and Huffington.com.

Hernando de Soto is currently president of the Institute for Liberty and Democracy, an internationally recognised think tank headquartered in Lima, which is committed to creating legal systems to help the poor access property and business rights. Named as one of the leading innovators in the world by *Time* and *Forbes* magazines, more than 20,000 readers of *Prospect* and *Foreign Policy* ranked him as one of the world's top 13 'public intellectuals'. He has served as president of the executive committee of the Copper Exporting Countries Organization, as CEO of Universal Engineering Corporation, as a principal of the Swiss Bank Corporation Consultant Group and as a governor of Peru's Central Reserve Bank. He has advised heads of state in several countries on property and business reform programmes, and is the author of *The Other Path* (1986), and his seminal work, *The Mystery of Capital* (Basic Books, 2000).

Supersudaca is a network of architects formed in 2001. Its nodes are based in Argentina, Belgium, Chile, Curaçao, the Netherlands, Peru and Uruguay. Supersudaca's profile is increasingly diverse in subjects affecting the environment. Caribbean tourism, China's influence, direct action in public space and collective housing are some of its recurrent themes explored from Tokyo to Talca, from Cancún to Cambodia. It was recognised with the best entry award at the 2nd International Biennale of Architecture Rotterdam (2005), the best research project at the Fourth Ibero-American Biennale (2004) and 'among the 20 architects that will change the future' by *Icon* magazine (2009). In the design realm, Supersudaca has obtained first prize in the international competition for the experimental social housing project in Ceuta, Spain (2006) and the Museum of Modern Art of Medellín (2010).

Patricia Romero-Lankao is a social scientist at the National Center for Atmospheric Research in the US. She has developed a considerable body of work on urbanisation and the environment, and in particular on how urban development impacts our climate and water; what societal factors explain cities' resilience to heat waves, atmospheric pollution, floods and sea-level rise; and more specifically on how particular cities manage and can better meet the challenges of reducing emissions while improving resilience to environmental impacts. She is one of the coordinating convening authors of the Nobel Prize-winning Intergovernmental Panel on Climate Change's 'Fourth Assessment Report'.

ABOUT ARCHITECTURAL DESIGN

INDIVIDUAL BACKLIST ISSUES OF △D ARE AVAILABLE FOR PURCHASE AT £22.99 / US$45
TO ORDER AND SUBSCRIBE SEE BELOW

What is Architectural Design?

Founded in 1930, *Architectural Design* (△D) is an influential and prestigious publication. It combines the currency and topicality of a newsstand journal with the rigour and production qualities of a book. With an almost unrivalled reputation worldwide, it is consistently at the forefront of cultural thought and design.

Each title of △D is edited by an invited guest-editor, who is an international expert in the field. Renowned for being at the leading edge of design and new technologies, △D also covers themes as diverse as: architectural history, the environment, interior design, landscape architecture and urban design.

Provocative and inspirational, △D inspires theoretical, creative and technological advances. It questions the outcome of technical innovations as well as the far-reaching social, cultural and environmental challenges that present themselves today.

For further information on △D, subscriptions and purchasing single issues see: www.architectural-design-magazine.com

How to Subscribe

With 6 issues a year, you can subscribe to △D (either print or online), or buy titles individually.

Subscribe today to receive 6 issues delivered direct to your door!

INSTITUTIONAL SUBSCRIPTION
£230 / US$431 combined print & online

INSTITUTIONAL SUBSCRIPTION
£200 / US$375 print or online

INDIVIDUAL RATE SUBSCRIPTION
£120 / US$189 print only

STUDENT RATE SUBSCRIPTION
£75 / US$117 print only

To subscribe:
Tel: +44 (0) 843 828
Email: cs-journals@wiley.com

Volume 80 No 1
ISBN 978 0470 743195

Volume 80 No 2
ISBN 978 0470 717141

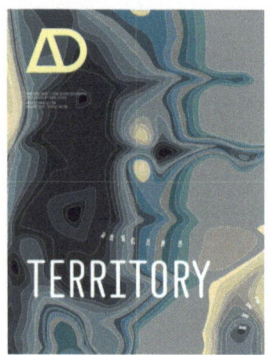

Volume 80 No 3
ISBN 978 0470 721650

Volume 80 No 4
ISBN 978 0470 742273

Volume 80 No 5
ISBN 978 0470 744987

Volume 80 No 6
ISBN 978 0470 746622

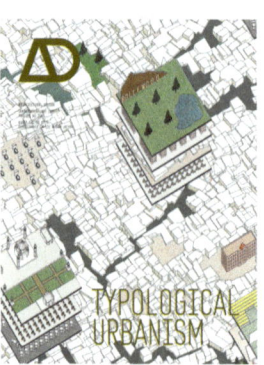

Volume 81 No 1
ISBN 978 0470 747209

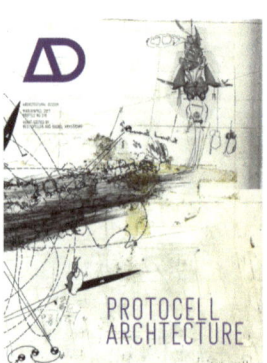

Volume 81 No 2
ISBN 978 0470 748282

www.ingramcontent.com/pod-product-compliance
Lightning Source LLC
LaVergne TN
LVHW070825250326
834741LV00034B/204